QUALITATIVE METHODS AND ANALYSIS IN ORGANIZATIONAL RESEARCH

D0220453

QUALITATIVE METHODS AND ANALYSIS IN ORGANIZATIONAL RESEARCH

A Practical Guide

edited by
Gillian Symon and Catherine Cassell

SAGE Publications
London • Thousand Oaks • New Delhi

Editorial selection and Chapter 1 © Gillian Symon
and Catherine Cassell 1998
Chapter 2 © Gill Musson 1998
Chapter 3 © Phil Johnson 1998
Chapter 4 © Elizabeth Chell 1998
Chapter 5 © Jo Silvester 1998
Chapter 6 © Gillian Symon 1998
Chapter 7 © Nigel King 1998
Chapter 8 © Yiannis Gabriel 1998
Chapter 9 © Dalvir Samra-Fredericks 1998
Chapter 10 © David Stiles 1998
Chapter 11 © Chris Clegg and Susan Walsh 1998
Chapter 12 © Joe Nason and David Golding 1998

First published 1998

SAGE Publications Ltd
6 Bonhill Street
London EC2A 4PU

SAGE Publications Inc
2455 Teller Road
Thousand Oaks, California 91320

SAGE Publications India Pvt Ltd
32, M-Block Market
Greater Kailash – I
New Delhi 110 048

British Library Cataloguing in Publication data

A catalogue record for this book is
available from the British Library

ISBN 0 7619 5350 7
ISBN 0 7619 5351 5 (pbk)

Library of Congress catalog record available

Typeset by Photoprint, Torquay, Devon
Printed in Great Britain by Biddles Ltd, Guildford, Surrey

This book is dedicated to the memory of
Stephanie Anne Cassell (1939–1997) and
Norman Cassell (1935–1998)

Contents

Notes on Contributors

Catherine Cassell works at the University of Sheffield where she is a Project Manager in the Institute of Work Psychology and a Lecturer in HRM/Organization Behaviour in the University's Management School. Previously she was a Research Fellow and Senior Lecturer at Sheffield Business School, part of Sheffield Hallam University. She has a wide range of research interests and has published in the areas of technology and organizational change; managing diversity and gender at work; business ethics; and research methodology. Current research projects focus on European HRM policies in the transport industry; benchmarking and change management in SMEs; and performance evaluation and control systems in manufacturing companies. She retains a keen interest in issues of research methodology and has worked with Gillian Symon for a number of years in this area. She is Co-Editor with Gillian Symon of *Qualitative Methods in Organizational Research: A Practical Guide* (Sage, 1994).

Elizabeth Chell is the holder of the Alcan Chair of Management at the University of Newcastle upon Tyne, UK, where she is also Director of the Centre for the Study of Entrepreneurship. Professor Chell has published principally in the fields of organizational behaviour and management. Her current research interests include gender and business performance, entrepreneurial behaviour and personality, management competence and small firm performance in food processing and the hospitality industries. Professor Chell is a member of the RSA, the BPS and the BAM. She is also a member of the executive of the European Council for Small Business.

Chris Clegg is Professor of Organizational Psychology and a Fellow of the British Psychological Society. He works at the Institute of Work Psychology at the University of Sheffield. Professor Clegg's research interests include: work organization and job design, allocation of system functions, socio-technical design, the development and use of information technology, cognition in organizations, organizational change and action research. He has collaborated with a number of organizations. His current work is concerned with studying the development, implementation, use and evaluation of new technologies and new working practices. Part of this involves developing and testing new methods for improving innovations in these areas and for incorporating explicit consideration of human and organizational issues. Professor Clegg has published widely in his field, and has held research grants with a number of UK and European funding bodies.

Yiannis Gabriel is a Senior Lecturer in Organizational Studies at the School of Management, University of Bath. His main research interests are in organizational and psychoanalytic theories, consumer studies, and organizational symbolism and culture. He is currently involved in a study of organizational stories and fantasies as unmanaged elements in organizations. Dr Gabriel is author of *Freud and Society* and *Working Lives in Catering* (both Routledge), and co-author of *Organizing and Organizations*, *The Unmanageable Consumer: Contemporary Consumption and its Fragmentation*, and *Experiencing Organizations* (all Sage). Other publications include recent articles on computer folklore, organizational nostalgia, chaos and complexity in organizations, fantasies of organizational members about their leaders, and research methodology using stories and narratives. He is Joint Editor of *Management Learning*.

David Golding is a Senior Research Fellow in the School of Management, University of Hull. He has 20 years of industrial experience in both small and large organizations, in both the public and the private sector, and in both the UK and the USA; and 15 years of research experience (in projects funded by government, ESRC, CAPITB and local authority). He has contributed to a number of books and published widely in management and sociology journals.

Phil Johnson is Principal Lecturer in Organization Behaviour and Research Methodology in the School of Business and Management, Sheffield Hallam University. He has undertaken research and published in the areas of behavioural aspects of accounting, methodology, management control and business ethics. However, one of his main interests remains research methodology with specific reference to epistemological issues.

Nigel King is Senior Lecturer in Psychology in the Department of Behavioural Sciences, University of Huddersfield. He has a long-standing interest in the use of qualitative methods in applied research, especially in health care organizations. Other interests include organizational change, creativity, Jungian psychology, and paranormal beliefs and phenomena. He is co-author with Neil Anderson of *Innovation and Change in Organizations* (Routledge, 1995).

Gill Musson graduated in communication studies, a multi-disciplinary degree, at the then Sheffield City Polytechnic, and went on to complete a PhD in occupational psychology at the University of Sheffield. She is currently a Senior Lecturer in Strategy and Organizational Behaviour at Sheffield Business School, part of Sheffield Hallam University. She has published in the areas of managing change in clinical and manufacturing contexts; the role of language in reflecting and structuring realities; and the dynamics of translating evidence-based medicine into practice. Her current research interests, based on qualitative methodologies, continue to include the dynamics involved in changing clinical behaviour, the nature of language use in constructing versions of reality, and the characteristics of organizational learning in manufacturing environments.

Joe Nason is a Senior Lecturer in the Hull Business School at the University of Lincolnshire and Humberside. Prior to becoming a lecturer he worked for over 23 years in a number of organizations within both the for-profit and not-for-profit sectors.

Dalvir Samra-Fredericks is a Lecturer in the Strategic Management Group at Aston Business School, Aston University. Her overall research interest is in real time manager interactions. In particular, she has focused on the talk of senior managers and directors in the boardroom and through audio and video recordings seeks to understand the nature of strategy development. The stance adopted is that the resources for *doing* strategy, for the simultaneous enactment of role-identities and for revealing the 'reflexivity of action and structure' are all available and amenable to analysis if talk-in-interaction is captured *as it happens*. She seeks to explore what constitutes 'competence' (for example, in the boardroom) whilst attempting to preserve the dynamic complexity of human interaction when face-meets-face in organizations.

Jo Silvester graduated in psychology from the University of York, thereafter completing a PhD at the University of Leeds and an MSc in occupational psychology at Birkbeck College, University of London. She worked as a Consultant Occupational Psychologist for a number of years before returning to academia and is presently Lecturer in Organizational Psychology at City University. Her research interests include decision processes and impression management in the selection interview, attributional models of sales and customer care situations and unfair discrimination in the workplace. She has also used attributional coding to analyse organizational culture.

David Stiles worked as a marketer, economist and strategic planner for two UK building societies and the Welsh Development Agency, before joining Cardiff Business School in 1990. He is now Lecturer in Strategy and Marketing, teaching strategic management at both postgraduate and undergraduate levels. His current research focuses on the development of organizational strategies for higher education, the police, financial services, art and small business organizations in the UK and North America. He is also publishing on Sino-Western joint ventures in the People's Republic of China. In terms of qualitative research, David is particularly interested in the application of pictorial techniques in focus groups and face-to-face interviews.

Gillian Symon is a Lecturer and Researcher in the Department of Organizational Psychology, Birkbeck College, University of London. She has conducted and published research concerning a variety of issues around the design and implementation of new technology in organizations. Recently she has focused on detailed investigations of the work of systems analysts and designers in context. She is also interested in discovering and developing alternative research methods and techniques and has collaborated with Catherine Cassell over many years in furthering debate about research methodology in organizational psychology, including the joint editorship of *Qualitative Methods in Organizational Research: A Practical Guide* (Sage, 1994).

Susan Walsh is a Senior Lecturer in Clinical Psychology at the Department of Psychology, University of Sheffield, and a Consultant Clinical Psychologist working for Psychological Health Sheffield. Dr Walsh's current research focuses on the ways in which psychotherapeutic knowledge can inform organizational change and the exploration of organizational vicious circles.

Acknowledgements

We would like to thank our work colleagues at the Department of Organizational Psychology, Birkbeck College; the Change Management Research Centre, Sheffield Hallam University; and the Institute of Work Psychology, University of Sheffield, for their ongoing discussions with us about research methodology. In particular Chris Clegg, Joanne Duberley, Phil Johnson, Brian Parkinson and Susan Walsh have always been interested in exchanging thoughts. Last but not least we'd like to thank Brian and Bob for listening to our ideas, picking us up from the station, taping 'Coronation Street' and 'ER' when required, and looking after the boys.

Gillian Symon and Catherine Cassell

1 Reflections on the Use of Qualitative Methods

Gillian Symon and Catherine Cassell

This is the second book we have edited focusing on qualitative methods in organizational research. In the first volume (Cassell and Symon, 1994) we argued that the wide range of qualitative methods used in organizational research was not well documented. We suggested that there was a need both to highlight the existence of such methods and to describe in detail how they can be used in practice. This second volume shares and extends those concerns. Thus this current book adds to a burgeoning literature (e.g. Banister et al., 1994; Richardson, 1996) representing an increasing interest in research methodologies and techniques which differ from the (commonly) accepted natural science model. Here the focus is on organizational research and practice (complementing our previous volume) and the detailed description and examination of alternative data analysis techniques. In this introductory chapter we provide some background to the continuing debates in the area of research methodology and our approach to editing this second volume.

Paradigms and methods

The last few years have seen an explosion of interest in qualitative methods, particularly within our own disciplinary base of psychology (e.g. Bannister et al., 1994; Miles and Huberman, 1994; Richardson, 1996; Smith et al., 1995a). A number of commentators have proffered explanations for this phenomenon. Henwood and Nicolson (1995) suggest that, although the methodological repertoire of psychology has generally included qualitative methods, these have tended to be seen as appropriate for the pilot phase of a project or as an adjunct to other research designs. Yet as stand-alone techniques there are clear areas of contribution which are now being recognized. Henwood and Pidgeon (1995: 116) argue that there are two particular issues within psychology that enhanced use of the 'qualitative paradigm', as they call it, can address. Firstly, they suggest that an overemphasis on theory testing, as is typically the case within traditional approaches to psychology, can produce a worrying underemphasis on the systematic generation of new theory. Such generation of theory, traditionally 'grounded' in data, is a key principle of qualitative research. The use of qualitative methods can therefore counteract the perceived current imbalance between theory testing and theory generation. Secondly, they suggest that qualitative approaches, with their emphasis on exploring the research participants' own situated experiences, offset the critique of much psychological research that the richness and significance of individual experience is neglected in favour of overarching reductionist explanations.

So one argument put forward is that qualitative methods can make a valuable contribution to the research process. However, the dominance of the positivist paradigm within psychology is also now being challenged more fundamentally (e.g. Parker, 1989; Potter and Wetherell, 1987; Smith et al., 1995b). Feminist research perspectives, for example, have: highlighted the power asymmetry between the researcher and the researched; critiqued the view of the apolitical, value-free researcher; and emphasized that men and women may have different experiences that cannot be reduced to a generalizable 'human' perspective (Griffin, 1995; Mies, 1983; Stanley and Wise, 1983). As Griffin states:

> This has led many feminists working in psychology to adopt non-positivist approaches to the research process, and particularly to the increasing popularity of work employing qualitative methods of data collection and/or analysis (e.g. Wilkinson, 1986). Debate continues as to whether feminist-standpoint research (FSR) is inherently non-positivist and qualitative (Bowles and Klein, 1983), but the link between FSR and qualitative methods remains strong in social psychology. (1995: 120)

A further critique of the classical natural science methodology, upon which the positivism of social science is based (Henwood, 1996), stems from the postmodernist perspective within the social sciences. Positivism is grounded in the assumption that it is possible to accumulate sense data that allow us to neutrally apprehend an external and independently existing social/natural reality. Therefore it is possible to separate the knower (subject) from the known (object), through the deployment of a theory-neutral observational language. It is precisely the possibility of such a subject–object dualism that postmodernist epistemologies and ontologies question. Slife and Williams (1995) suggest that whereas traditional epistemologies, upon which the scientific method is based, consider social processes (e.g. intergroup rivalry) to be developed from measurable individual principles (e.g. so-called cognitive processes like judgement and decision-making), many postmodern approaches consider that individual principles derive from social processes. The focus of analysis then becomes those social processes, e.g. communicative acts such as language. Because meaning is seen as coming from discourse (rather than an objective reality), knowledge is viewed as an ongoing process of creation, rather than something deduced from absolute laws and principles. Postmodernist approaches lend themselves to methodologies and research techniques that allow us to discern how definitions of truth and reality are continually being revised through the richness of context. For many postmodernists (e.g. Potter and Wetherell, 1987) this translates into research methods which focus on talk and text as sources of 'data'. (However, see Kilduff and Mehra, 1997 for a discussion of post-modernist eclectism in method use.) The research act itself is seen as socially constructed and key concerns are the issues of inter-subjectivity and reflexivity:

> Instead of trying to erase all personal traces of the researcher from the work so as to provide the reader with an illusion of unmediated access to the subject, postmodernists seek to demystify the technology of mediation by explicitly detailing the involvement of the researcher. (Kilduff and Mehra, 1997: 464)

In describing these current debates within social science research, it becomes apparent that the distinction between qualitative and quantitative techniques is only a small part of a far wider debate about epistemology and ontology. In practice, the focus on the qualitative/quantitative debate is almost a red herring. Of more significance are the conventions by which we describe and accept knowledge as warranted (epistemology) and our stance on the nature of social reality (ontology): is there an objective reality? Can reality exist independently of the processes of knowing? This broadening of the debate leads into discussions on the nature of conflicting paradigms within social research and issues of paradigm (in)commensurability. Guba and Lincoln define a paradigm as:

> a set of *basic beliefs* (or metaphysics) that deals with ultimates or first principles. It represents a worldview that defines, for its holder, the nature of the 'world', the individual's place in it, and the range of possible relationships to that world and its parts, as, for example cosmologies and theologies do. The beliefs are basic in the sense that they must be accepted simply on faith (however well-argued); there is no way to establish their ultimate truthfulness. (1994: 107, italics authors' own)

Of particular significance in the context of this volume is the extent to which a particular technique (e.g. interviewing, observation, surveys) can be utilized within a number of different paradigms. For some of the contributors to this book, there is an explicit marriage of technique to a particular paradigm. For other contributors the issue is more pragmatic – about selecting the right technique, bearing in mind the strengths and weaknesses of the variety of techniques available for the research questions to be addressed. In this latter case, paradigmatic considerations are simply not an issue. These two approaches illustrate the distinction made by Bryman (1988) between 'epistemological' and 'technical' justifications for using qualitative methods. In the first case, qualitative methods may be used because they are regarded as more in tune with the researcher's paradigmatic commitments, and in the second, they are regarded as more 'useful' for the problem at hand – and thus can be used within a number of different (even conflicting) paradigms. Henwood argues that:

> The technical version coexists most readily within a positivist framework, and thus it is rather less agnostic on the question of epistemology . . . Researchers who adopt a more . . . interpretative, constructionist (or deconstructionist) stance have

a clear affinity for qualitative research . . . plus a strong conviction that choice of method is liberated and informed by the position one takes within the epistemological debate. (1996: 29)

In this context it is worth noting that one of the outcomes of a positivist framework is protection from epistemic self-reflection (Johnson, 1995). Such a process does not arise as an issue within a research framework predicated on the existence of an objective truth.

We recognize that the kind of eclectic approach taken in this book with regard to contributors' underlying epistemological positions could create problems for some readers. In a review of our last book, Dachler (1997) suggested that, as a result of the contributors taking different epistemological and ontological stances, an inconsistency was created that served to counteract the stated aim of the book, that of raising the profile of qualitative methods. The underlying message seems to be that 'true' qualitative methods only draw on a subjectivist ontology and a constructivist (or possibly interpretivist) epistemology. However, our task here is to present practical demonstrations of the range of (researcher-defined) qualitative techniques available. In doing this, we need to recognize the many ways in which organizational researchers are using qualitative techniques within a range of philosophical frameworks. In common with many other commentators (e.g. Reed, 1992; Smith et al., 1995b), we believe that 'it is important at this stage for many different voices to be heard' (1995b: 3), and to aim for an inclusive discipline:

> no method grants privileged access to truth . . . and all research approaches are embodied in cultural practice that postmodernists seek to make explicit. (Kilduff and Mehra, 1997)

In other words, it is our aim not to privilege a particular account, but to open the field to alternatives. In this volume, some contributors lean towards a neo-positivist framework which, whilst acknowledging the significance of actors' subjectivity in their construction of meaningful action, considers that it is possible to neutrally elucidate the dimensions of these cultural processes. Alternatively, other contributors, while also emphasizing the significance of actors' subjectivity, do not claim privileged access to an actor's social constructions and would problematize this aspect of the relationship between the researcher and the researched, questioning how one can ever experience the experience of another 'neutrally'. Given these varying approaches, contributors are, in a sense, providing their own interpretations of 'qualitative methods', each of which is influenced by different views of ontology, epistemology and the significance of *verstehen* in action.

Practical demonstrations of methods

Our aim in both this book and the previous volume is to provide detailed descriptions of qualitative methods which can furnish both researchers and practitioners with a reference point for how the method has been used previously in organizational research, together with recommendations for how it can be applied, and indications of potential problems.

The discussion of the appropriateness of a 'cookbook' or 'recipe' approach to describing methods – in which ways of conducting research are seen to be reduced to a series of prescribed sequential stages (Dey, 1993) – has some bearing on this goal. Dey suggests that recipe knowledge has been devalued in our society, particularly in academic circles. Perhaps the notion of making complex debates accessible creates problems for some? However, as Dey argues, recipes, by indicating which ingredients to use, and what procedures to follow, can provide an important *foundation*. Clearly, learning the recipe is not the same as learning a particular skill, but it can be a useful guide. Taking making pastry as an analogy, initially one may need to measure out specific quantities and follow procedures specified in a written account; however, when one becomes more skilled at the feel of the dough, the recipe appears less significant. Essentially, we see the chapters in this book as guides to particular methods rather than rule books – guides which allow the interested to get some footing in the area. We are not suggesting that research has to be conducted on the basis of explicitly formulated rules. Or that different researchers following these rules will get the same results. Or even that rules need to be applied with consistency necessarily. Indeed the contributors themselves are clear that their accounts, while detailed and accessible, are not the 'one best way' but more a sharing of experiences.

Overall, the contributors have tried to provide suggestions about how to use the methods in practical terms whilst avoiding a deterministic or prescriptive tone. This aim we feel is achieved by the provision of detailed accounts of how the contributors have actually *used* the methods in their own work.

Qualitative data analysis

In our first volume all the chapters concerned qualitative techniques of data collection with some description of how the data collected were analysed. In this volume, however, there are a number of chapters specifically focusing on techniques of data analysis. This is a deliberate choice. Despite the increased popularity and use of qualitative methods there is relatively less information available about how to conduct qualitative data analysis – although there are some notable exceptions (Dey, 1993; Miles and Huberman, 1994; Silverman, 1993; Strauss and Corbin, 1990).

In qualitative research, of course, the distinction between data collection and data analysis may not be clear-cut. In practice, for example, as a series of interviews progresses, the researcher will often be creating, testing and modifying analytic categories as an iterative process, such that data analysis may be considered 'an organic whole that begins in the data-gathering stage and does not end until the writing is complete' (Potter, 1996: 120).

Despite this potential false dichotomy, we felt it was important to focus on the analysis process in some detail, as it is our experience that researchers often find it difficult to access material that distinguishes different types of data analysis, and, significantly, links them to their differing epistemological and ontological bases. Without the tools for incisive and insightful data analysis and interpretation, the amount of data generated through the use of qualitative methods can seem overwhelming and the analysis process itself confused and confusing. Insightful analysis is really at the heart of success-ful qualitative investigations. As Wolcott suggests: 'the real mystique of qualitative inquiry lies in the process of *using* data rather than in the processes of *gathering* data' (1990: 1, italics author's own). He continues that:

> With experience, most researchers become less compulsive about collecting data and more proficient at using the data they collect, but the problem of transforming unruly experience into an authoritative, written account never totally disappears. (1990: 10)

Perhaps it is the difficulty of accessing accounts of data analysis that has led some authors to be concerned with the quality of research conclusions that have emerged from studies using qualitative techniques. Silverman (1993) outlines his 'discomfort' with a large proportion of the qualitative research to be found in leading academic journals. He lists a number of related tendencies which give rise to this concern, for example, 'the use of data-extracts which support the researcher's argument, without any proof that contrary evidence has been reviewed' (1993: ix). In this volume some of the contributors outline precisely such processes of reviewing and debating negative instances in a manner which strengthens their 'truth claims', e.g. Johnson (analytic induction) and Silvester (attributional coding).

A key question here concerns the criteria against which the findings of qualitative research are evaluated. The traditional criteria on which research is evaluated stem from a positivist paradigm where tests of the reliability and validity of the data are seen as integral to the 'rigorous' conduct of research. Some qualitative researchers seek to apply these criteria to their own work using a variety of techniques, such as inter-rater reliability (King, 1994).

However, assessing the output from qualitative techniques on the criteria generated to assess quantitative techniques creates problems for other qualitative researchers. Again the role of epistemological and ontological assumptions is significant. From alternative perspectives such criteria are unobtainable and not necessarily desirable, as research outcomes are viewed as the result of the interaction between the respondent and the researcher. It is argued within these paradigms that analysis is an interpretive process which precludes the very idea of a 'scientific objectivity' as implied by reliability and validity.

However, most qualitative researchers do wish to justify their inter-pretations of their data in some way. Consequently, authors have generated lists of alternative criteria suited to assessing the 'rigour' of qualitative research. The best known of these are Guba and Lincoln's (1989) 'authenti-city' criteria. These authenticity criteria are explicitly formulated to reflect the concerns of alternative paradigms:

1 resonance (the extent to which the research process reflects the under-lying paradigm);
2 rhetoric (the strength of the presenting argument);
3 empowerment (the extent to which the findings enable readers to take action);
4 applicability (the extent to which readers can apply the findings to their own contexts).

Consequently, these could be considered appropriate criteria against which to assess the chapters that follow. In addition, some contributors outline criteria by which, in their judgement, high quality research using their particular technique can be assessed.

Conclusion

The chapters that follow reveal the diversity of qualitative methods available and some of the subtle distinctions between them. We hope they will provide a stimulus to readers to consider alternative approaches to inves-tigating their chosen research area. As in the previous volume, each chapter takes a particular method as its theme. The authors outline the method and how it has been used in organizational research in the past. They then provide an example of using the method from their own work and conclude with an evaluation of its strengths and weaknesses. We recognize that this structure can in practice create an artificial distinction between the method and the research context. However, it is our intention to provide clear accounts of the methods which would then encourage others to consider how such methods may benefit their work in other contexts.

The chapters cover a wide range of different types of organizations and sectors. In each chapter the authors outline the reasons why they chose to use a particular research method for the research issue they were facing. Consequently, the contributions also highlight the range of work issues and environments in which qualitative methods can allow an alternative per-spective and produce useful and informative insights.

For us, the chapters in this book represent another 'snapshot' of the variety of qualitative techniques currently being used in organizational research. A diverse range of conceptualizations of qualitative methods exists and our aim is to reflect some of these in a manner that will be both accessible and useful to researchers and practitioners – encouraging alternative perspectives to be advanced, debated and put into practice.

Notes

We would like to thank Phil Johnson and Brian Parkinson for their constructive feedback on an earlier version of this chapter.

References

Banister, P., Burman, E., Parker, I., Taylor, M. and Tindall, C. (1994) *Qualitative Methods in Psychology: A Research Guide*. Buckingham: Open University Press.

Bowles, G. and Klein, R.D. (eds) (1983) *Theories of Women's Studies*. London: Routledge and Kegan Paul.

Bryman, A. (1988) *Quantity and Quality in Social Research*. London: Unwin Hyman.

Cassell, C. and Symon, G. (1994) *Qualitative Methods in Organizational Research: A Practical Guide*. London: Sage.

Dachler, P.D. (1997) 'Does the distinction between qualitative and quantitative methods make sense?', Review of C. Cassell and G. Symon (eds) *Qualitative Methods in Organizational Research* in *Organisation Studies*, 18 (4): 709–24.

Dey, I. (1993) *Qualitative Data Analysis: A User-Friendly Guide for Social Scientists*. London: Routledge.

Griffin, C. (1995) 'Feminism, social psychology and qualitative research', *The Psychologist: Bulletin of the British Psychological Society*, 8 (3): 119–21.

Guba, E. and Lincoln, Y. (1989) *Fourth Generation Evaluation*. Newbury Park, CA: Sage.

Guba, E. and Lincoln, Y. (1994) 'Competing paradigms in qualitative research', in N. Denzin and Y. Lincoln (eds), *Handbook of Qualitative Research*. Newbury Park, CA: Sage.

Henwood, K. (1996) 'Qualitative inquiry: perspectives, methods and psychology', in J. Richardson (ed.), *Handbook of Qualitative Research Methods for Psychology and the Social Sciences*. Leicester: BPS Books.

Henwood, K. and Nicolson, P. (1995) 'Qualitative research', *The Psychologist: Bulletin of the British Psychological Society*, 8 (3): 109–10.

Henwood, K. and Pidgeon, N. (1995) 'Grounded theory and psychological research', *The Psychologist: Bulletin of the British Psychological Society*, 8 (3) 115–18.

Johnson, P.D. (1995) 'Towards an epistemology for radical accounting . . . beyond objectivism and relativism', *Critical Perspectives on Accounting*, 6: 485–509.

Kilduff, M. and Mehra, A. (1997) 'Postmodernism and organizational research', *Academy of Management Review*, 22: 453–81.

King, N. (1994) 'The qualitative research interview', in C. Cassell and G. Symon (eds), *Qualitative Methods in Organizational Research: A Practical Guide*. London: Sage.

Mies, M. (1983) 'Towards a methodology for feminist research', in G. Bowles and R.D. Klein (eds), *Theories of Women's Studies*. London: Routledge and Kegan Paul.

Miles, M. and Huberman, M. (1994) *Qualitative Data Analysis*, 2nd edn. Thousand Oaks, CA: Sage.

Parker, I. (1989) *The Crisis in Modern Social Psychology – And How to End it*. London: Routledge.

Potter, J. (1996) *An Analysis of Thinking and Research about Qualitative Methods*. Mahwah, NJ: LEA.

Potter, J. and Wetherell, M. (1987) *Discourse and Social Psychology*. London: Sage.

Reed, M. (1992) 'Introduction', in M. Reed and M. Hughes (eds), *Rethinking Organization: New Directions in Organization Theory and Analysis*. London: Sage.

Richardson, J. (ed.) (1996) *Handbook of Qualitative Research Methods for Psychology and the Social Sciences*. Leicester: BPS Books.

Silverman, D. (1993) *Interpreting Qualitative Data: Methods for Analysing Talk, Text and Interaction*. London: Sage.

Slife, B.D. and Williams, R.N. (1995) *What's Behind the Research? Hidden Assumptions in the Behavioral Sciences*. Thousand Oaks, CA: Sage.

Smith, J., Harré, R. and Van Langenhove, L. (eds) (1995a) *Rethinking Methods in Psychology*. London: Sage.

Smith, J., Harré, R. and Van Langenhove, L. (eds) (1995b) *Rethinking Psychology*. London: Sage.

Stanley, L. and Wise, S. (1983) *Breaking Out: Feminist Consciousness and Feminist Research*. London: Routledge and Kegan Paul

Strauss, A.L. and Corbin, J. (1990) *Basics of Qualitative Research: Grounded Theory Procedures and Techniques*. Newbury Park, CA: Sage

Wilkinson, S. (ed.) (1986) *Feminist Social Psychology: Developing Theory and Practice*. Milton Keynes: Open University Press.

Wolcott, H.F. (1990) *Writing up Qualitative Research*. London: Sage.

2   Life Histories

Gill Musson

This chapter gives some background to the development of the life history technique, followed by an analysis of its relevance to organizational research, and some empirical examples of its application in case studies drawn from doctoral research. The chapter concludes by evaluating the usefulness of the approach and summarizing the circumstances in which it might best be used. Further discussion of life history methodology can be found in Johnson's discussion of analytic induction in Chapter 3.

The life history approach

Life history methodology focuses on the ways in which individuals account for and theorize about their actions in the social world over time. The subjective interpretation of the situation in which people find themselves, past or present, is its cornerstone. It is predicated on the fundamental assumption that 'if men [*sic*] define those situations as real, they are real in their consequences' (Thomas, 1966: 300). As such the method prioritizes individual explanations and interpretations of actions and events, viewing them as lenses through which to access the meaning which human beings attribute to their experience. Life history methodology, then, is firmly rooted in an interpretive framework and specifically in the symbolic interactionist paradigm which views human beings as living in a world of 'meaningful objects – not in an environment of stimuli or self-constituted entities. This world is socially produced in that the meanings are fabricated through the process of social interaction' (Blumer, 1969: 540; see Hammersley, 1989 for a detailed exposition of symbolic interactionism). Thus, through the processes of symbolic interaction different groups come to create and maintain different worlds. But these worlds are not presumed to be static. Rather, they are fluid and dynamic, colliding and overlapping, continually being created and re-created, changing as the objects which compose them are changed in meaning. Thus, the reflexivity of human beings is central to this perspective and it is this process of reflexivity, how human beings theorize and explain their past, present and future, which the life history methodology seeks to capture.

Background to the method

Life history methodology has a long history. It was the central approach used by sociologists in the US in the 1920s and 1930s (now known as the Chicago School: see for example Bogardus, 1926; Znaniecki, 1934) and its use also gathered momentum in Europe during that period. It was also the approach advocated by social psychologists such as Allport who used the method from the 1940s until his death in the late 1960s. However, since then it has been used infrequently. This reflects the general eclipsing of qualitative methodologies by the quantitative approaches which characterized social science research during the mid part of this century. The revival of interest in qualitative techniques during the 1960s, particularly in sociology (cf. Blumer, 1969), was not taken up by organizational researchers until relatively recently, and some disciplines applied to management science, such as psychology, still show a reluctance to use such techniques if journal publications are anything to go by. But even with this renewed interest in qualitative techniques, life history as a methodology has not been used overtly by organizational and management researchers. Often, however, there is an implicit use of the method in organizational analysis although it is commonly unacknowledged and undiscussed.

The method gives researchers a tool with which to access the sense of reality that people have about their own world, and attempts to give 'voice' to that reality. It provides a fundamental source of knowledge about how people experience and make sense of themselves and their environments, thus allowing the actors to speak for themselves. In some circumstances the voices may then be interpreted, but the process of interpretation will always attempt to reflect the actors' perspective, rather than simply that of the researcher. This is not to say that the approach accepts the account of the individual as some kind of unproblematic version of an objective 'truth'. Rather, the method is predicated on the assumption that 'all perspectives dangle from some person's problematic. Views, truths and conceptions of the real can never be wholly ripped away from the people who experience them' (Plummer, 1983: 57). But neither does the method seek to deny that people exist within particular structural and institutional constraints. Instead, it specifically locates itself in the nexus between deterministic structures and individual agency, between those factors which might be described as relatively objective, and the subjective interpretation of the individual (Casey, 1993; Elder, 1981). It recognizes the dialectical relationship between these two processes: that human beings, through their actions, impose themselves on and create their worlds, but they do so in a world which presents itself as already constituted through a network of typifications. These typifications – for example, group norms, group meanings, group language – express the systematic and coherent 'rationality' or 'grammar' of the context, and thus reflect, and in turn constitute, the culture or system of shared meaning in which the individual is located. The approach recognizes that individuals are situated within specific historical networks of human relationships, and that meanings are generated and decisions taken with reference to that particular living tradition. In sum, the approach views 'the individual, embedded in a network of relationships and statuses, as the irreducible unit of analysis' (Mathews, 1977: 37).

From this point of view it is a mistake to view life histories as totally individualistic. Of course they reflect the experiences of the individual through a given period of time, but because lives move resolutely through history and structure they can also provide an understanding which extends beyond the individual and into the wider context of organizations, institutions, cultures and societies. As Thompson (in Bertaux, 1981) points out, a life history cannot be told without constant reference to historical change, social or organizational. In a period when constant change is perceived as the norm and much organizational and management research is devoted to trying to understand it, life histories can provide a useful window through which to widen our understanding of the change process within organizations. The method can avoid the common research error which Becker (1966: xiii) noted three decades ago but which still holds true today: that process is an 'overworked notion' in research, in that researchers often talk a lot about ongoing processes whilst using methods which prevent them from uncovering the very processes which they seek to identify.

The life history method also recognizes the collusion of the researcher in the research process. It does not presume that the researcher is some impartial, value-free entity, who unproblematically engages in the research process to produce objective accounts of a reified truth. Rather, the approach recognizes that the researcher also brings implicit and explicit theories to the research situation, and the task of the researcher includes surfacing these in the struggle for balance between theory in the researcher's head and theory employed by the people in the research situation. The first task of the researcher, therefore, must be to produce her own life history, recognizing the fundamental tenet spelt out by Casey that 'I give myself shape ultimately from the point of view of the community [or communities] to which I belong' (1993: 166).

The explicating of the researcher's basic assumptions and theoretical frameworks is a central aspect of the validity of the method. In addition, validity is achieved through the congruence of research explanations with the meanings with which members construct their realities and accomplish their everyday activities. Part of the methodological rigour, then, entails allowing the explanations of the researcher to be subjected to the scrutiny of organizational members to see whether these accounts resonate with and inform the members' own understandings of their subjective experiences. Even though the concepts and categories used in this process might be allowed to emerge from the data (see Glaser and Strauss, 1967 for a full discussion of grounded theory, or Henwood and Pigeon, 1992 for a condensed version), they must best interpret the particular material by retaining the meaning of the actors involved. In this sense, the concepts and constructs developed in a particular life history will be context specific. How then do we judge the descriptive adequacy of the material? How do we know what material is relevant, and when enough relevant material has been gathered? Jones (1983), drawing on work by Dollard (1938), suggests that the following five related criteria can be applied to answering such questions, and will ensure that the methodology is used appropriately.

First, the person must be viewed as a member of a cultural milieu, which will determine the stocks of knowledge, including the particular kind of 'common sense' (Gramsci, 1980), to which the individual has access. Second, the research process must acknowledge that significant others such as family, peers and leaders will play a central role in the socialization process of the individual. Third, the meaning systems, or particular taken-for-granted assumptions, rules, codes or standards, routinely invoked to accomplish everyday activities, must be specified within the research. Fourth, the research should illustrate how definitions of reality change over time by describing the processual nature of the individual's experience. And finally, the actions of the individual should be continually associated with the social context. Implicit in this last point is the understanding that just as the typifications used by the individual can change over time, so can those that define the social context. By keeping these criteria in mind, the researcher will ensure that the dynamics of the situation are adequately accounted for during the research process, and thus that the focus is maintained on the relationship between social reality and subjective meaning.

Application of the method in organizational analysis

Of course, the relevance of a particular method depends primarily on the research questions being asked. But any organizational researcher seeking to understand, in depth, how organizations function and the ways in which individuals make sense of and act upon their organizational worlds, can benefit from using the life history method. The central argument in support of this claim is that organizations are not reified entities which exist outside of the people who populate them (Morgan, 1986). Rather, people create organizational worlds just as they create the other worlds which they inhabit. Of course, some people can be more influential than others in this creation: powerful leaders, for example, can play a central role in defining organizational meanings and realities.

Some of the specific benefits of applying the method are as follows. First, understanding how organizations function involves understanding the ambiguities, uncertainties and problematics which individuals experience and resolve on a daily basis. Allowing people to explain for themselves the experience of contradictions and confusions, moments of indecision and turning points, can illustrate graphically how organizational socialization processes are accomplished, for example, and consequently illuminate our understanding of how individuals and organizations function, more than methods which reduce experience to abstracted definitions and moribund descriptions. In this case the focus of the research would be specific lives, as they have been construed and developed, within the organization.

Second, the technique allows the researcher access to the network of typifications, or interpretive schemes, which individuals *bring* to their roles in particular organizations. Much research is devoted to understanding how people make sense of their organizational worlds but few techniques explicitly acknowledge that individuals come to organizational life with an already constructed set of assumptions, norms and values which will influence the way organizational events are construed and interpreted. Yet understanding how people make sense of their roles, specific organizational events and the accomplishment of everyday practices is intricately linked to the subjective experiences of the individual in other social contexts. This may be particularly relevant if the research question involves understanding the motivations and influences which powerful organizational leaders, or specific groups, bring to bear on organizations (see for example Bloor and Dawson, 1994). The method can expose the manner in which entrepreneurs or founders come to hold their particular beliefs and versions of rationality, and how they impose these definitions on others. Since such factors are increasingly seen as the prime functions of leaders in organizations (Bate, 1994; Schein, 1985), the method may be particularly relevant here. In such instances, the method might focus on the development of one particular life history, rather than a collection of organizational life histories.

The organizational literature is replete with studies of organizational culture but very few studies actually give specific advice about how to conduct a cultural analysis which captures the complexity and dynamism of cultural processes. Life history methodology can provide this. As Jones points out, 'the world of formal organisation can be viewed as a network of typifications, as a particular form of language that has been produced historically through the rational and expressive acts of its population' (1983: 154). This organizational language, or grammar of action, provides the basic rules for organizational activity. In this sense, this grammar of action *is* the organizational culture. Understanding how this language is constituted, through gathering organizational life history data, can give students an analytic handle on the cultural composition of organizations. This under-standing should include the recognition that organizational languages or grammars are constituted in three main ways (Jones, 1983), each of which is central to the way organizational lives develop.

First, organizations, like individuals, do not exist in a vacuum. The constitutive rules or grammars of action of an organization reflect a rationality embodied in the wider environment(s) of which the organization is a part. This is similar to what Pettigrew (1987) describes as the outer context of the organization. Organizations are part of a wider milieu which will influence the constitutive rules of organizational action. These rules are embodied in the language of the organization, and are reproduced through it. For example, the language of health care organizations in the UK now includes an economic discourse, which was introduced externally, but which now influences and informs the activity of all health care organizations.

Second, organizational languages are constituted collectively, and represent and reproduce a collective memory of events (see Middleton and Edwards, 1991 for a detailed exposition on memory as a socially constituted activity). These collective memories, which provide recipes for action, are expressed through all aspects of the organization, including repertoires of myths and stories, but also the more concrete organizational forms of structure, technology, systems and procedures. Third, the constitution of an organizational grammar of action is an ongoing process. Changes in that grammar, which arise from and through the interplay and tension of shared and competing interpretations of organizational members, are reflected and reproduced by changes in the organizational language. For example, the introduction of economic rules and discourses in the UK health care environment could not be accommodated within the existing meaning structures of some health care organizations (see Musson and Cohen, 1996), and therefore the organizational grammar of these organizations changed to accommodate these new meanings. These changes were reflected in the language, which in turn served to cement these new meaning structures and provide new recipes for action. Similar processes, such as changes in control systems or the redefinition of success, can be tracked through changes in organizational language, which in turn can be traced through the life histories of organizational members.

Understanding the constitution of organizational languages, and the concomitant recipes for action, can help organizational researchers to understand how these networks of typifications condition the experience of organizational members. Life histories provide a method for doing this, but they also allow us to follow the dialectical process by which these typifications are simultaneously changed through members' interpretations and actions.

Data collection and analysis

As will be evident by now, the life history technique takes talk as data, as the disclosing tablet which reveals how people are constituted by, and in turn serve to constitute, organizational realities (Forester, 1992). Although talk can take many forms, for example in written texts such as organizational reports, correspondence or diaries of organizational members, it is primarily through semi-structured or unstructured interviewing that life history data are commonly collected (see King, 1994 for a detailed discussion of interview techniques).

Asking people to talk about their life histories in order to unearth their understandings entails listening to their stories. People do not tend to express their experiences, or describe their sense making processes, in terms of succinct, abstract generalizations. Such generalizations and inferences at once remove the richness that a story preserves. Researchers need to understand that people construct narrative accounts as part of the sense making process, and as a way of preserving and communicating information, and that they do this through the telling of stories (see Gabriel, Chapter 8 in this volume). For example, Baumeister and Newman (1994) note the frustration that resulted from asking successful businessmen to furnish the abstract principles underlying their success, rather than being prepared to listen to their stories of successful ventures. It is the researcher's task to draw from life history narratives the principles on which the stories are founded, not the task of the storyteller. In this sense, the researcher must be content to listen to and record stories which allow the individual to make sense of her or his experience. However, simply in terms of time constraints, it would be nonsense to suggest that researchers simply go into organizations and ask people to tell them whatever story pops into their head at that particular time. Obviously, the research question, and the specific phenomena which are of interest, will help the researcher to structure the facilitation of the storytelling process by asking appropriate questions (see for example Casey, 1993).

In the research described in the next section, I directed the storytelling process to a large extent by asking individuals to tell me about when and how their understanding of the purpose of the organization shifted. However, I accepted as central to them the story which they gave me in response to this question. These stories differed from focusing on the history of an individual's marital difficulties, to telling me a story about an individual patient and the way she was treated by the GPs in the practice. Both these stories gave me data about the culture of the organization and the way in which organizational members made sense of the past and the present. Likewise, I asked people to tell me about their lives in previous organizations and how they had experienced these; what they had found rewarding, constraining or difficult to make sense of, and how this differed in their current organization. Again, the open ended structure of the narratives allowed people to introduce subjects of major importance to them.

In addition, depending on the nature of the research question, it is possible to ask people to construct time lines which detail the significant events which they construe to be important in their own or the organization's history (see Plummer, 1983 and Isabella, 1990). But again the researcher must be content to listen to the stories which people give around these events, rather than simply asking the individual for the inferences which they have drawn from them. A further source of data in life history methodology can be obtained by collecting documentary evidence about the individual or the organization (see Forster, 1994 for details of this method). Such data can illuminate the stories that people tell, providing additional perspectives on the holistic context in which sense making takes place. For example, documentary data may give the researcher a glimpse of the way that the problem or issue was construed at the time it was experienced. Of course, this could be a formal or official view, as in a company report for example, but this does not invalidate it as data since all views, formal or informal, official or unofficial, tell us something about the ways in which people experience and act upon particular phenomena.

Having obtained the data, the researcher is left with two analytical problems. The first involves what to do with the mass of data. The second involves the fundamental problematic around surfacing taken-for-granted assumptions. Basic assumptions are notoriously inaccessible in that they exist at a level whereby people are commonly unable to articulate them, even though their behaviour is in accordance with the rules which they embody (Garfinkel, 1967; Schein, 1985). Jones (1983) suggests that researchers can deal with both these problems through a process of setting up a series of oppositions, at the same time as developing concepts which best 'fit' the data by exposing the themes and orientations, whilst preserving the internal logic of the material. The process involves setting up oppositions: first, within members' accounts; second, between members' accounts; and third, between members' accounts and the researcher's constructions of the situation. During this iterative process, the researcher will be developing constructs and concepts which expose and describe the theoretical frameworks of individuals, at the same time as subjecting these to the theoretical orientation developed by the researcher. The object is to retain the integrity of the data whilst seeking to confront its internal logic and thus explain the relationship to taken-for-granted assumptions. The researcher should involve members as much as possible in this process by taking the ensuing theoretical explanations back to them for comment. The carrying out of this complex process is best illustrated through the description of empirical work contained in the next section.

Some empirical examples

The examples referred to in this section are taken from doctoral work on how general medical practitioners (GPs) in the UK have experienced and understood the 1990 health care reforms which have impacted on their daily practice (Musson, 1994). In sum, the reforms have, for the first time in the history of the NHS, linked *directly* the clinical activity of GPs, and the ability to document that activity, to the financial reward which they receive. This has served to change significantly the way GPs organize and deliver their service. The research sought to understand how these changes were construed and accommodated by the GPs, and the effects on their service orientation and professional identity.

It would be tempting at this point to indicate that life history methodology was a well thought out, predetermined method at the start of the doctoral research, but this would not reflect the truth of the situation. It is much more the case that during the in-depth research with six general practices carried out over two years it became more and more apparent that the life histories of key actors were significant in the way the changes were construed, understood and experienced, and that allowing people to tell something of their life histories illuminated the sense making process. The original planned methodology involved using a variety of techniques including participant observation, semi-structured interviews, group discussions and analysis of documentation. This was eventually supplemented with informal interview data which focused specifically on collecting individual life histories. As Plummer (1996: 54) notes, this reflects a 'less formal life history strategy' of triangulated data collection, mixing participant observation, formal and informal interview data and field notes, rather than the more traditional method of encouraging people to write their own life history, or to record specific life history interviews over a period of time. Although it might be useful for the reader to be told here exactly how to do a life history interview, the method does not readily lend itself to such prescriptions. It is more a question of the interviewer taking the role of a 'non-directive, phenomenologically aware counsellor' (1996: 53), trying to 'grasp the native's point of view, his [*sic*] relation to life, to realise his vision of the world' (Malinowski, 1922: 25). So the researcher must prepare to be as flexible and fluid as the situation demands, allowing the lead to be taken by the storyteller, rather than trying to impose some rigid predetermined framework on to the interview situation.

What follows are some extracts where life history data were able to enhance the understandings surfaced by the other methods. These extracts will also be used to describe the oppositional process outlined in the previous section. The extracts are necessarily short, but hopefully comprehensive enough to demonstrate how the methodology is useful in organizational analysis. They include actual quotes from the research data wherever possible.

Example 1: oppositions within members' accounts

In this three doctor practice Dr A was the senior partner and had practised single handed for many years before being joined by the other two doctors relatively recently. The practice was managed and run by him, organized like clockwork, with efficient, comprehensive systems and detailed procedures in place to support every activity. All of these systems had been devised by Dr A who had commented in a life history interview that 'I would have preferred to be an accountant but my family pressurized me into medicine.' He saw no connection between this thwarted desire and the way he ran the practice, and of course, there is no way of knowing in a concrete sense how these views originated. Nevertheless, he felt that 'all businesses should be organized like this whether they sell cars or offer a medical service.' But what is perhaps of more interest here is that the information systems manager, recently employed as a result of the information requirements of the NHS reforms, viewed the practice as having 'too much emphasis on systems and information management'. When I asked her what she, as information systems manager, meant by this statement, she replied 'because it has no soul', and proceeded to tell me a story about the previous practice which she had worked in, which 'had a much greater emphasis on individual patient care, although it was very badly organized but it provided a better service for patients'. Her story illustrated that she was making sense of her past and present experiences by setting up an opposition between care tailored to individual patient needs and delivered by 'really caring doctors', and the more population oriented care delivered by 'this system'. Analysis of her account revealed two basic assumptions: first, that patients experienced better care in the previous practice despite the disorganization; and second, that there was something about systematized care delivery that precluded an individual patient orientation.

Both of these assumptions could be challenged to a large extent by the data on disease management and referrals gathered from both these practices as part of the research (Musson, 1994), although quality of care is notoriously difficult to measure in any meaningful way. But this would be to miss the point. What the analysis revealed was the political antagonism which this woman held about the new information requirements in general practice activity, and the ambiguity and contradictions which this invoked because these new information requirements were the source of her employment. This opposition was further exacerbated because she was very ambitious and 'keen to succeed', but she was doing so in an area of activity which challenged the political ideas that she had long held about good delivery of care. Moreover, her life history revealed that she had come from a background where 'women don't have proper careers' and that 'doing this job causes me lots of problems at home'. Still, she viewed the job as 'my chance to make my mark'. In sum, Dr A's life history helped to reveal how the norms, values and practices prevalent in the organization of the practice had come about, and the information systems manager's life stories illustrated the oppositions, contradictions and ambiguities she faced in making sense of her daily activity.

Example 2: oppositions between members' accounts

The following data are drawn from research in another practice which took part in the project. The practice had very recently employed a practice manager as a response to the new legislation, despite being very strongly opposed to the principles and practices of the reforms. At the time of the research the practice manager was experiencing some difficulties in 'fitting into the practice – I'm like a square peg in a round hole.' The scale of these difficulties can be demonstrated through describing a relatively minor, but significant, incident about whether her office door should be left open or closed. From her arrival, the practice manager had left the door between her office and the reception area, which housed the rest of the office staff, open throughout the day. The reception staff, for whom she was responsible, interpreted this action as 'spying on us', and resented what they perceived as her interference in the way they carried out their work. She, on the other hand, felt that she was 'only doing my job by making sure everything's running smoothly and that I'm available if needed – I see that as my responsibility.' At first glance these can seem like very superficial disagreements, easily explained as interpersonal difficulties. But they actually embodied the different, and competing, assumptions deeply held by the various members of the practice, and which made up the network of typifications which served to structure their realities. Some of these typifications are discussed below.

Prior to the arrival of the practice manager, this three doctor, seven staff practice had prided itself on its very flat structure and its 'caring family' ethos. This family structure reflected the desire held by all the doctors, but particularly Dr B, to create a caring, cohesive, collective loyalty within, and to, the practice, which 'also includes the patients – we wouldn't have a practice without the patients.' This family orientation was reflected in the stories which staff told about the practice's past. For example, 'Dr B has been like a father to me' was how one receptionist described her relationship with the founder, whilst another told stories about 'all the support I received from here when I was going through my divorce – support that you'd expect from your family.'

The structure worked in the sense that relations based on the personal rather than the hierarchical evolved, together with the view that nobody was much higher or much lower in importance than anybody else. This was uncommon in general practice and these relations were manifested and reinforced in a variety of ways. For example, the use of first name terms for doctors, staff and patients conveyed friendship, and therefore reinforced the notion of relationships of equality. Similarly, many practice discussions were organized around issues unconnected with the usual functions of general practice. One such discussion took place about the political implications of the Gulf War, for example, reflecting the commonly shared political views held in the practice, and reinforcing the notion of the practice as a liberal, egalitarian organization. However, in reality the doctors held the locus of control, and an unspoken rule had evolved over many years which embodied the implicit knowledge that the doctors' views and therefore their authority were never really to be questioned. This contradiction was managed through a high level of trust and mutual respect which existed in the 'family' prior to the new legislation and the employment of the practice manager.

This family orientation and related structure were accompanied by a high value on clinical expertise and autonomy, but a very low value on management principles and techniques. The latter were seen as secular activities, potentially damaging to the sacred clinical orientation of the practice (Laughlin, 1991). Despite this, the doctors hired a management consultant to control and direct the appointment of a practice manager in response to the new reforms, again reflecting the value placed on expertise. The person appointed came from a highly bureaucratic background with a lot of experience in the wider NHS system. She was charged with implementing the reforms, which required the reorganization of much practice activity, but she was largely denied the power to do so, and struggles over the modification of organizational realities and practices ensued. These struggles became evident in organizational language. For example, 'she even talks differently to us – I know that she's got to look at the financial side but that's the only language she knows' was a typical comment found in stories about her effect on the practice. This reference illustrates how the economic discourse, the language of patients as profit and loss, began to surface in daily discussions about service provision. Similarly, the following example shows how this discourse served to restructure the realities of other members of the practice.

Prior to the practice manager's appointment, tetanus injections had been administered on a ten yearly basis on the grounds that 'ten years is a clinically justifiable time gap.' This had always been done on an *ad hoc* basis, whenever a patient's clinical profile suggested that it was necessary. The practice had not purchased the injections directly because 'there was no clinical advantage in buying it ourselves and we didn't want to be involved in anything purely for financial gain.' This quote refers to the financial saving which the practice could have made through direct purchase, because wholesale costs were significantly lower than the retail price which the practice could reclaim. After much debate, the practice manager did persuade the practice to purchase the vaccinations wholesale on the assumption that there would be no direct effect on the clinical decision to offer or administer the vaccination. However, shortly after the practice began purchasing the vaccine, the practice manager persuaded the doctors and nurses to adopt a system whereby a patient's tetanus status was checked as a matter of routine, and an injection offered on a five yearly basis for which the practice received a significant financial benefit under the new legislation. One of the nurses explained the rationale behind this change of heart as follows: 'when the PM pointed out just how much tetanus did earn I was converted – well people still die of tetanus anyway, not many but they do, and this way we might eradicate it . . . I said it was immoral at first, we'd always opted for the ten year rather than the five year gap, and we shouldn't do it, but . . . it's still not quite a money spinner but . . .' This quote was typical of many which illustrated the internal rationalization processes evident in coming to terms with oppositions created by clinical changes that were essentially economically driven.

The appointment of the practice manager not only surfaced the contradictions which had previously been covertly managed within the practice, issues around locus of control for example, but also highlighted the contradictions inherent in the relationship between the recent reforms and the service philosophy integral to the practice. The incident around the open office door encapsulated the way these new oppositions became manifest in daily activity, as the practice manager came to symbolize the hostile environment that she had been recruited to buffer.

Example 3: oppositions between members' accounts and the researcher's construction of events

This section continues with the data described in the previous section to illustrate how the researcher can confront the accounts of organizational members with other theoretical interpretations. Of course, I have been doing this to some extent throughout the previous two examples, since it is impossible for researchers to report data objectively: description and analysis are intricately entwined. However, this section reports on my practical involvement in confronting the members' explanations of events, and the basic assumptions and oppositions which they contained. It is difficult to be succinct about this part of the process within the confines of this chapter, partly because it is very complex, but also because in this instance it was a very emotional experience for everybody involved (see Musson, 1994 for a detailed account).

By the end of the practice manager's first year, conflict, which was normally suppressed in the practice, had begun to bubble to the surface in a way which nobody knew how to handle, and the organization was in crisis. In an attempt to resolve rapidly deteriorating relationships, the doctors called an evening meeting between themselves and the practice manager, to which the researcher was invited, 'to talk honestly to each other'. The meeting took place in a very emotionally charged atmosphere and the talk centred very much on disagreements about specific and relatively minor issues, and after three hours little progress had been made. Listening to this conversation, and in the light of the interview data already gathered, the following four interrelated factors seemed central to me about how the situation had developed thus far. These factors formed my theoretical construction of the situation.

First, the practice manager had been appointed to deal with the reforms which the doctors, and the rest of the practice, would have very much preferred to ignore. In this sense her marginalization began even before she started working in the practice. Second, her appointment not only symbolized the encroachment of these reforms, but also ruptured the highly valued flat 'family' structure. Third, the practice manager had a world view, a fundamental value system, and norms about appropriate ways of organizing which were very different from those of the doctors. For example, her long experience in hierarchical organizations, whose norms she had internalized, were in direct opposition to those of the doctors. In addition, her political views on issues such as unemployment, for example, which she described as 'coming from years of experience of living amongst people who sponge off the system', were different from the beliefs held by other people in the practice. And finally, the power differential, although unacknowledged and submerged, prevented her from 'succeeding in my terms in putting things right round here'. Although she struggled to enforce the norms which fitted her particular version of reality, she did not have the power to do so to any large extent, but she did have sufficient power to become an extremely disruptive force even though this was not her intent. The resulting struggles were focused around minor issues, such as the open door, but they were actually manifestations of these much deeper oppositions and differences.

At this point I was invited to give my view of the situation and offered a diagnosis which included these theoretical interpretations. I was surprised that none of the actors had considered these possible interpretations because they seemed obvious to me. But I recognized that they were, at least in part, a product of being relatively detached from the situation and having access to data denied to others (life history data for example), and the time to ponder over it. My feelings about the response to my interpretation were at once positive and negative. My explanation was described as 'very valuable – it's shed some light on the problem' and its validity did seem to be accepted by all the actors who 'had not thought of it like that before even though it makes such sense to me now'. From this perspective I felt that some measure of enlightenment had been achieved through confronting the oppositions held between the key players. However, the meeting finally ended after four hours on a dismal note, because as Dr B said at the time, 'I don't see what we can do to resolve the situation because we're coming from such different ideas.' Indeed, the situation was never amicably resolved, but space precludes any further discussion here.

These empirical examples have demonstrated how life history methodology and data can deepen the understanding of how people construct their organizational realities against the backdrop of external structures and institutions. The data illustrate that meaning is situated. People make sense of their experiences through the interaction of their 'psychological tool kit' (Werstch, 1991b: 94), the contents of which are often used with little or no reflection, and the context in which sense making takes place (see Bakhtin, 1981 for a theoretical discussion of how the contents of the tool kit originate and are modified). Life history methodology gives the researcher a tool with which to access the contents of the individual's 'tool kit', and a lens through which to analyse the way the tool kit mediates the sense making process.

Evaluating the method

Life history methodology is best used in circumstances where the researcher seeks to understand the complex processes which people use in making sense of their organizational realities. Research questions which might be answered using this approach include: how does socialization takes place in organizations? How are organizational careers created and understood? How do certain managerial styles come to be accepted as 'natural'? How do particular 'grammars of action' develop in organizations? What is the role of particular individuals and groups in creating and maintaining those 'grammars of action'? What influence do leaders and founders have on how organizations develop and change? In addition, the method can be used to give voice to otherwise unheard accounts. Much organizational research often takes a managerial focus, as if this is the only version of organizational reality, but organizations are made up of many diverse groups of people, the voices of which are rarely heard in research (Casey, 1993). In short, research projects which start from the premise that organizational realities are not concrete, reified entities, but are constructed in and through the individuals and groups which populate them, can benefit from using this technique.

The method can be used either in conjunction with other methods, or as a technique on its own. However, my own preference is for using a variety of methods together so that they complement each other, providing, at least potentially, a more fertile data set. For example, participant observation (see Waddington, 1994) can be combined with life history data to provide a richer, more holistic picture than perhaps either method could furnish on its own (see Musson, 1994). As Denzin (1978: 252) points out, the more objective stance of participant observation or survey techniques can be balanced with 'the internal, covert and reflective elements of social behaviour and experience' accessed through interpretive techniques. Similarly, discourse analysis can be applied to data generated through life history methodology to strengthen the analysis (see Marshall, 1994 for details of discourse analysis as a method).

The major problem of using the method is that it is immensely time consuming for both the researcher and the actors involved. Gathering and analysing life history data commonly involve the researcher in many hours of data collection, and analysis can be an uncertain process requiring a high tolerance of ambiguity over considerable periods of time. Although the resulting accounts might read as if the data collection and analysis were planned, linear and unproblematic, this does not reflect my experience. A further issue involves writing up qualitative research in general, and life history data in particular. Plummer (1983) offers some useful guidelines to writing life histories which enable students to break the process up into the three components of purpose, intrusion and mechanics. Following these helps the researcher to be clear about: the purpose of the writing, that is who you are writing for and what you hope to achieve; how much you allow yourself to intrude upon the gathered materials through editing or inter-pretation; and how you actually write the life history, which will clearly depend upon the earlier decisions of purpose and intrusion. However, students of organizations are rarely given any advice or tuition in the *art* of writing, and if they are it is usually in the objective scientific tradition, impersonal and distanced from the subject. This is precisely *not* what is required for the writing of life histories, for as Plummer notes, 'It is to the tools of the novelist, the poet and the artist that the social scientist should perhaps turn in the qualitative humanistic tradition' (1983: 106). These are the tools which can best reflect the richness of qualitative texts, but unfortunately they are also those which are not readily accepted in many traditional, scholarly publications. Similarly, they tend to lead to much lengthier articles than the norms of scientific journals allow. Both these factors can mean that publication can be difficult to achieve. Other problems associated with this kind of research include the emotional repercussions which can result (see Musson, 1994: Chapters 7 and 8), and reporting data which compromise neither the richness of the stories nor the actors' anonymity. These are factors which the life history researcher must be prepared to face.

To conclude, the researcher engaged in life history research should understand what she or he is bringing to the research process – the norms, values and basic assumptions which make up his or her own network of typifications and constructions. These will influence how she views her own reality and that of others in the research process. Indeed, the very choice of method reflects this, for as Rosen notes, 'the selection of a research topic and a corresponding method . . . are indicative of that which the researcher believes is important to see in the world and to know' (1991: 21).

References

Bakhtin, M.M. (1981) *The Dialogic Imagination*, ed. M. Holquist, trans. M. Holquist and C. Emerson. Austin, TX: University of Texas Press.

Bate, P. (1994) *Strategies for Cultural Change*. Oxford: Butterworth-Heinemann.

Baumeister, R.E. and Newman, L.S. (1994) 'How stories make sense of personal experiences and motives that shape autobiographical narratives', *Personality and Socio-Psychology Bulletin*, 20 (6): 676–90.

Becker, H.S. (1966) 'Introduction to *The Jack Roller* by Clifford Shaw (Chicago: University of Chicago Press)', in H.S. Becker, *Sociological Work* (1971). London: Allen Lane.

Bertaux, D. (1981) *Biography and Society*. Chicago: University of Chicago Press.

Bloor, G. and Dawson, P. (1994) 'Understanding professional culture in organizational context', *Organization Studies*, 15 (2): 275–95.

Blumer, H. (1969) *Symbolic Interactionism*. Englewood Cliffs, NJ: Prentice-Hall.

Bogardus, E.S. (1926) *The New Social Research*. Los Angeles: Press of Jesse Ray Miller.

Casey, K. (1993) *I Answer with My Life: Life Histories of Women Teachers Working for Social Change*. London: Routledge.

Denzin, N.K. (1978) *The Research Act*, 2nd edn. Chicago: Aldine.

Dollard, J. (1938) 'The life history in community studies', *American Sociological Review*, 3: 724–37.

Elder, G. (1981) 'History and life course', in D. Bertaux (ed.), *Biography and Society*. Chicago: University of Chicago Press.

Forester, J. (1992) 'Fieldwork in a Habermasian way', in M. Alvesson and H. Willmott (eds), *Critical Management Studies*. London: Sage.

Forster, N. (1994) 'The analysis of company documentation', in C. Cassell and G. Symon (eds), *Qualitative Methods in Organizational Research: A Practical Guide*. London: Sage.

Garfinkel, H. (1967) *Studies in Ethnomethodology*. Englewood Cliffs, NJ: Prentice-Hall.

Glaser, B.G. and Strauss, A.L. (1967) *The Discovery of Grounded Theory: Strategies for Qualitative Research*. New York: Aldine.

Gramsci, A. (1980) *Selections from the Prison Notebooks of Antonio Gramsci*, ed. and trans. Q. Hoare and G.N. Smith. New York: International.

Hammersley, M. (1989) *The Dilemma of Qualitative Method: Herbert Blumer and the Chicago Tradition*. London: Routledge.

Henwood, K.L. and Pidgeon, N.C. (1992) 'Qualitative research and psychological theorizing', *British Journal of Psychology*, 83: 97–111.

Isabella, L.A. (1990) 'Evolving interpretations as a change unfolds: how managers construe key organizational events', *Academy of Management Journal*, 33 (1): 7–41.

Jones, G.R. (1983) 'Life history methodology', in G. Morgan (ed.), *Beyond Method: Strategies for Social Research*. Beverley Hills, CA: Sage.

King, N. (1994) 'The qualitative research interview', in C. Cassell and G. Symon (eds), *Qualitative Methods in Organizational Research: A Practical Guide*. London: Sage.

Laughlin, R.C. (1991) 'Environmental disturbances and organizational transitions and transformations: some alternative models', *Organization Studies*, 12 (2): 209–32.

Malinowski, B. (1922) *Argonauts of the Western Pacific*. London: Routledge & Kegan Paul.

Marshall, H. (1994) 'Discourse analysis in an occupational context', in C. Cassell and G. Symon (eds), *Qualitative Methods in Organizational Research: A Practical Guide*. London: Sage.

Mathews, F. (1977) *Quest for an American Sociology: Robert E. Park and the Chicago School*. Montreal: McGill–Queens University Press.

Middleton, D. and Edwards, D. (eds) (1991) *Collective Remembering*. London: Sage.

Morgan, G. (1986) *Images of Organization*. Beverley Hills, CA: Sage.

Musson, G. (1994) 'Organizational responses to an environmental disturbance: case studies of change in general medical practice'. PhD Thesis, University of Sheffield.

Musson, G. and Cohen, L. (1996) 'The enterprise discourse: an empirical analysis of its effects', paper presented to the 6th Annual Communication and Culture Conference, Beijing, August 1996.

Pettigrew, A.M. (1987) 'Context and action in the transformation of the firm', *Journal of Management Studies*, 24 (6): 649–70.

Plummer, K. (1983) *Documents of Life: An Introduction to the Problems and Literature of the Humanistic Method*. London: Allen & Unwin.

Plummer, K. (1996) 'Life story research', in J.A. Smith, R. Harré and L. Van Langenhove (eds), *Rethinking Methods in Psychology*. London: Sage.

Rosen, M. (1991) 'Coming to terms with the field: understanding and doing organizational ethnography', *Journal of Management Studies*, 28 (1): 1–24.

Schein, E.H. (1985) *Organizational Culture and Leadership*. London: Jossey-Bass.

Thomas, W.I. (1966) in M. Janowitz (ed.), *Organisation and Social Personality: Selected Papers*. Chicago: University of Chicago Press.

Waddington, D. (1994) 'Participant observation', in C. Cassell and G. Symon (eds), *Qualitative Methods in Organizational Research: A Practical Guide*. London: Sage.

Werstch, J.V. (1991b) *Voices of the Mind: A Sociocultural Approach to Mind*. Hemel Hempstead: Harvester Wheatsheaf.

Znaniecki, F. (1934) *The Method of Sociology*. New York: Farrar & Rhinehart.

3 Analytic Induction

Phil Johnson

Usually analytic induction (AI) is defined as involving the intensive examination of a strategically selected number of cases so as to empirically establish the causes of a specific phenomenon. Intrinsic to the approach is 'the "public" readjustment of definitions, concepts, and hypotheses' (Manning, 1982: 283). However despite several notable exceptions (e.g. Lindesmith, 1947; Cressey, 1953; Becker, 1973; Bloor, 1976), there seem to be few published examples of research, particularly organizational research, that use AI. Moreover, even in 'qualitative' methodology books, AI often appears to be ignored (e.g. Banister et al., 1994; Glesne and Peshkin, 1992) or limited to a short outline (e.g. Silverman, 1993). Perhaps this situation is all the more surprising given the claim that, when suitably refined, AI 'seems a plausible reconstruction of the logic of theoretical science' (Hammersley and Atkinson, 1995: 236).

Given this situation, the aims of this chapter are to outline the rationale and procedures of AI through a brief discussion of its epistemological commitments, a review of its historical development and an illustration of its empirical application in an accountancy/industrial-relations context. The chapter will then conclude with a discussion of some of the problems implicit in AI.

The epistemological commitments of AI

The term 'induction' refers to the processes by which observers reflect upon their experience of social phenomena and then attempt to formulate explanations that may be used to form an abstract rule, or guiding principle, which can be extrapolated to explain and predict new or similar experiences (Kolb et al., 1979). Hence AI is a set of methodological procedures which attempt to systematically generate theory grounded in observation of the empirical world. As such it sharply contrasts with deductive procedures in which a conceptual and theoretical structure is constructed prior to observation and then is ostensibly tested through confrontation with the 'facts' of a cognitively accessible empirical world (see Wallace, 1971: 16–25).

Although debate between rival proponents of induction and deduction is complex (see e.g., Lessnoff, 1974), the justification for induction in the social sciences usually revolves around two related claims. Firstly, it is argued that in contrast to the speculative and *a priori* nature of deductively tested theory, explanations of social phenomena which are inductively grounded in systematic empirical research are more likely to fit the data because theory building and data collection are closely interlinked (Wiseman, 1978) and therefore are more plausible and accessible (Glaser and Strauss, 1967). Secondly, there is the argument that deduction's etic analyses, in which an *a priori* external frame of reference is imposed upon the behaviour of social phenomena in order to explain them, are inappropriate where the phenomena in question have subjective capabilities (see Shotter, 1975; Giddens, 1976; Gill and Johnson, 1997). It follows that social science research must entail emic analyses where explanations of human action are generated inductively from an *a posteriori* understanding of the interpretations deployed (i.e. cultures) by the actors who are being studied.

Hammersley and Atkinson (1995) argue that ethnographic fieldwork shares these inductive commitments. However, ethnographers' explanations of observed behaviour often remain at the level of *a posteriori* 'thick description' (Geertz, 1973; Denzin, 1978) of actors' interpretive procedures which goes beyond the 'reporting of an act (thin description) but describes the intentions, motives, meanings, contexts, situations, and circumstances of action' (1978: 39). In this, theorization is limited to providing a conceptual framework for understanding actors' cultures. While the theoretical aims of AI include such descriptive frameworks, AI avoids what Loftland (1970) has called 'analytic interruptus' by also trying to explain and predict through positing causal models. The ontological and epistemological ambiguities this creates will be returned to later.

The development of AI

In his discussion of the procedures for generating categories from sociological data, Znaniecki (1934) coined the term 'analytic induction'. Although he claimed that AI was the 'true' method of the natural sciences and ought to be that of the social sciences, Znaniecki did not provide accessible examples of its methodological procedures. It is in Cressey's (1953: 16) work that such a formulation might be found. Basically Cressey suggests the following stages:

1   A rough definition of the phenomenon to be explained is formulated.
2   A hypothetical explanation of the phenomenon is developed.
3   One case is examined with the objective of determining whether or not the hypothesis fits the observed facts.
4   If the hypothesis does not fit the facts, either the hypothesis is reformulated, or the phenomenon to be explained is redefined so that the case is excluded.

5   The procedure of examining cases, and excluding any negative cases by hypothesis reformulation or phenomenon redefinition, is continued until a universal relationship that fits the observed facts is established.

6   Cases outside the area circumscribed by the definition are examined to determine whether or not the final hypothesis applies to them. Conditions which are always present when the phenomenon is present should not be present when the phenomenon is absent.

Denzin (1978: 192), who largely follows Cressey, suggests that AI allows 'fact', observation, concept, proposition and theory to be closely articulated. Where Denzin does not seem to follow Cressey is with regard to stage 6, and indeed Cressey himself does not seem to have fully appreciated the practical implications of this stage in his own research (see Robinson, 1951). This has led Hammersley (1989: 169) to observe that this last step is not a standard feature of AI, a matter which creates certain problems that need to be resolved.

Nevertheless Cressey's approach appears to fit Mitchell's demand for the exhaustive 'strategic' selection of cases through the articulation of a formal model that forces the researcher to 'formulate and state his [sic] theories in such a way so as to indicate crucial tests of the theory and permit the explicit search for negative cases' (1983: 197). This is because AI enables theory development to occur through two processes: firstly the hypothesis itself may be modified, and/or secondly the phenomenon of interest may be redefined. With either process the range of application of the hypothesis is limited to exclude, or extended to embrace, new observations. The result should be a causally homogeneous category with no negative cases (Kidder, 1981). For Fielding and Fielding the result of this procedure is that 'statistical tests are actually unnecessary' (1986: 89). In this manner, a grounded theory is inductively generated out of data which are applicable to a number of cases and it constitutes a generalization.

How cases are chosen depends upon what Glaser and Strauss call 'theoretical sampling' (1967: 184). In this, having developed a theory to explain observations of a particular case of the phenomenon, a researcher can decide on theoretical grounds to choose to examine new cases that will provide good contrasts and comparisons and thereby confront the emergent theory with the patterning of social events under different circumstances.

This approach to AI has been heavily criticized by Robinson (1951). In his critique of Znaniecki (1934) and Cressey (1950; 1953), Robinson (1951: 200) argues that in their version of AI the procedures used are inadequate because they result in the articulation of only 'the necessary, and not the sufficient conditions for the phenomenon to be explained'. This is because their approach fails to analyse situations in which the phenomenon does not occur. Thus Robinson argues that AI in this form only studies cases where the phenomenon to be explained occurs: so as to identify sufficient conditions, cases have to be studied where the conditions specified by the hypothesis hold so as to elucidate whether or not the phenomenon occurs there. It is to deal with this problem that Bloor (1976; 1978) develops a set of procedures for AI that allows for the differentiation of necessary and sufficient conditions.

With regard to both Lindesmith (1947) and Cressey (1950), Bloor argues that the problem with both studies was 'that the researchers were unable to distinguish between the necessary and sufficient causes of addiction or embezzlement . . . [since] they lacked control groups in which necessary but

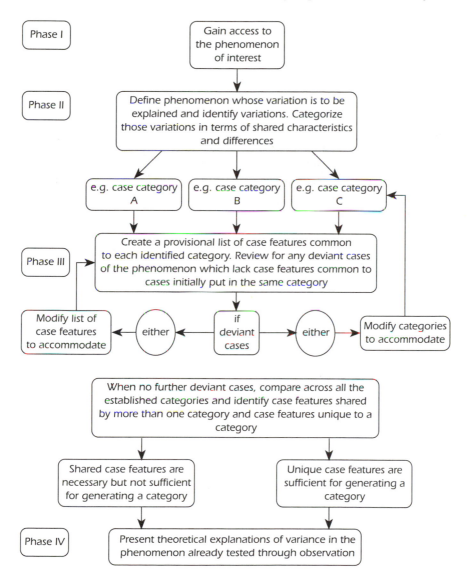

Figure 3.1 **Adaptation of Bloor's approach to analytic induction (Gill and Johnson, 1997: 123; adapted from Bloor, 1976; 1978)**

not sufficient cases could be located' (1978: 547). Bloor avoids this problem by developing an approach which categorizes, in terms of similarity and difference, variations in the phenomenon to be explained so that 'cases in other categories could stand as a control group for those cases in the category I was analysing' (1978: 547). Bloor's approach may be seen to entail four basic steps and is summarized by Figure 3.1.

I shall now illustrate the application of Bloor's model by reviewing how it was used to describe and explain how senior shop stewards interpret disclosed accounting information in collective bargaining.

The empirical application of AI

The background to the research

Unfortunately space precludes a full elaboration of the theoretical and empirical background of this research which was undertaken in the late 1980s; therefore I shall limit myself to a brief overview. It arose out of a dissatisfaction with the conventional portrayal of accounting as an activity which unproblematically serves the public interest, which provides users with unbiased information and which occupies a privileged position divorced from any sectional interest (see Johnson, 1995). Moreover, it was also evident that accounting was gaining prominence, in the eyes of many institutional audiences, as a warranted means of regulating many aspects of our lives (Knights and Willmott, 1993). One context in which there was much debate about the role and use of accounting information was its disclosure by management to employee representatives during collective bargaining. However this debate was largely couched in a modernist orientation which assumed that accounting data neutrally arbitrated the financial reality confronting participants. Furthermore, this debate was characterized by a deterministic perspective that ignored recipients' (i.e. senior shop stewards') interpretation of this information. How those knowledgeable actors interpreted, acted upon and thereby mediated disclosed accounting information (DAI) remained uninvestigated.

Therefore the empirical focus of this research was to examine the significance of DAI in senior shop stewards' constructions of organizational reality and tentatively delineate the factors that engendered these propensities through the generation of grounded theory. Obviously there were different possible ways of pursuing these objectives. One could have been to observe and analyse actual collective bargaining processes in their everyday social contexts. However, getting access to such events appeared unlikely. Therefore a more viable strategy was pursued which entailed following Bloor's approach to AI and applying it to life histories collected by interviewing a sample of individual senior shop stewards. Below I shall give an account of this research, with each phase in data collection and analysis corresponding to those illustrated in Figure 3.1.

Phase I: gaining access

My first attempt at gaining access to a sample of senior shop stewards entailed a formal approach to a local official of a major trade union during which I expressed a desire to interview members about how 'useful' they found DAI. Initially this gatekeeper appeared sympathetic, but it soon became evident that his help would entail intolerable constraints. Essentially he wanted to 'vet' what I was going to ask 'his lads' and in particular he wished to 'have a look at my questionnaire' whose contents would have to be sanctioned by the 'district committee' before its distribution. He claimed that if he approved it, there would be 'no problem' and that he could easily 'sort out some helpful stewards'. It was just after this point that I made my excuses and left, deciding that this avenue would not provide the quality of access that I needed.

Upon reflection I felt even if his sponsorship had materialized, there was the danger that I would become associated with the particular organizational cabal with which he was associated – processes which would influence informants' responses in any future interaction (see Trice, 1956). I also suspected that his sponsorship would entail his control over the form of access (i.e. a sanctioned questionnaire pro forma) and over whom I was allowed access to. This may have meant the selection of shop stewards who displayed 'appropriate' attitudes and behaviours with the partial exclusion of those who were perceived as 'deviant' (Berreman, 1962).

Instead initial contact with a selection of informants was facilitated by a friend I knew from my prior membership of a major blue-collar trade union. In many respects he was my equivalent of Whyte's (1955) 'Doc' since he acted as an intermediary and informal sponsor by mobilizing an extant social network through introducing me to senior shop stewards and vouchsafing for me. In this he unwittingly presented these potential informants with a rather vague description of my intentions because I had described the research as being concerned with 'plant-level industrial relations and how things had changed over the past few years'. I had decided upon this ethically dubious ploy for several reasons.

My prior failure to get access may have been due to the nature of my research interests. Perhaps DAI was more controversial than I thought. However I still had to provide a plausible account of myself which would ensure access, avoid exposing my substantive concerns, and yet leave scope to manipulate interviews around to those concerns without violating any established psychological contract. Through this ploy I thought I might convince informants that I was not personally threatening since I would appear to be not directly concerned with them as individuals. For Douglas such a tactic might ease access by convincing informants that the researcher is 'not really studying them . . . he [sic] tries to show them that he is really studying something else, with which they are . . . involved' (1976: 170). Moreover I was concerned that prior disclosure of my research focus might influence how informants reacted to my questions – even limiting their responses to a 'front work' (Goffman, 1969) of stock answers. Meanwhile I was also aware that sponsors can have a significant influence upon the conduct and outcomes of field research, by consciously or inadvertently directing the researcher into extant culturally and physically bounded webs of social relationship (Berreman, 1962; Hansen, 1977). The catch-22 is that sponsors are also usually essential in enabling access in the first place. By keeping my research interests hidden I hoped to avoid some of these problems and at the same time, once in a senior shop steward network, unilaterally cultivate a further network of informants that would meet the demands of AI.

Although informants' initial compliance had been appropriated by the intercession of my sponsor, I was concerned to resolve any persisting anxieties. So an important element in my impression management was to make informants feel comfortable and gain their trust by interviewing them on their own 'turf' (Lyman and Scott, 1970) as well as engaging in initial 'interaction rituals' (Goffman, 1972) so as to establish feelings of 'mutuality' (Beynon, 1983) – that we had something in common in terms of interest and experience. Through these interaction rituals rapport was usually established and gradually I eased conversation around to their roles as senior shop stewards. Through the felicity of my sponsor, informants had an initial idea of what I wanted to talk about. I tended to reinforce this impression by stating my interest in their experiences as senior shop stewards and how their roles might have recently changed. Basically, I was using Douglas's 'principle of indirection' (1983: 137) to encourage their self-disclosure and then subtly manipulate dialogue towards my main focus – DAI.

Phase II: defining the phenomenon and identifying variations

As the term implies, processes of AI focus upon the analysis and interpretation of data. Except for induction, AI does not specify how data should be collected. In principle it can therefore be used to analyse data that derive from any method of collecting data that has been applied in an inductive fashion, such as life histories, participant observation, repertory grids etc. In the research reported here data were collected through life history interviews. This was because life history research is regarded as having a primary concern with the 'phenomenal role of lived experience, with the ways in which individuals interpret their own lives and the world around them' (Plummer, 1983: 167). This allows access to how individuals 'create and portray' (Jones, 1983: 147) their social worlds. Significantly life history interviews are taken to avoid the problems that beset the 'brisk' interview (Bulmer, 1975) in which respondents are impelled, by the structured prompts of the interviewer, to make statements which, although fitting into the researcher's conceptual and theoretical pro forma, give little opportunity for the respondents to articulate the ways in which they conceptualize and understand their own worlds.

Although life histories can be used to 'provoke, suggest and anticipate later theorizations' (Plummer, 1983: 124), a research strategy guided by AI procedurally formalizes this process and explicitly introduces theoretical concerns during fieldwork. But because AI entails sampling according to emergent theoretical criteria so as to enable comparison, inevitably some of the depth traditional in life histories is traded off. Essentially, these overt theoretical objectives militated against the orthodox use of life histories, as exemplified by Shaw (1966) and Bogdan (1974), in which the outcome is in the form of comprehensive biographies of single subjects. Thus I used life history interviews to generate and document informants' accounts of their lived-in organizational realities with an emergent focus upon how they perceived DAI in collective bargaining.

Where it was practical I had decided to interview each informant at least twice. The first round of interviews was aimed at gaining their confidence and eliciting descriptive data that could be used to generate dimensions of similarity and difference across the whole cohort (see Spradley, 1979) regarding their perceptions of, and orientations towards, DAI. By guiding the interview around pertinent issues through the use of various prompts and questions, the nature of which was contingent upon the 'state of play' in our interaction, I elicited and documented their perspectives. These processes necessitated some degree of skill and intuition on my part, especially in regard to when to remain silent or to follow up some comment immediately, or how to phrase mutually intelligible prompts which allowed informants' elaboration upon a significant issue without inadvertently fixing the terms in which they spoke, or the perspectives which they articulated. In some of the earlier interviews I suspect that I made blunders, but through reflection upon these mistakes I was able to learn how to unobtrusively guide informants to the issues of greatest interest to me at this particular stage of fieldwork.

As I proceeded in this fallible manner, I regularly reviewed my field notes and compared informants' accounts so as to identify the similarities and differences in their accounting orientations out of which I would establish an initial taxonomy of categories. Although this remained my main focus at this stage, I also attempted to identify possible relationships between these emergent orientations and other phenomena identifiable in their accounts. These phenomena could constitute possible case features and thereby represent future areas of exploration in subsequent interviews. In sum I was at this stage following a process similar to what Glaser and Strauss call the 'constant comparative method', in that the researcher

> starts thinking in terms of the full range of types of the category, its dimensions, the conditions under which it is pronounced or minimized, its major consequences, its relation to other categories, and its other properties. (1967: 106)

After 13 life history interviews, each of around three hours duration, I began to perceive that I had constructed an initial taxonomy of 'observer-identified' (Loftland, 1971) categories and their conceptual properties while staying within the limits of the data (Glaser, 1978). This had entailed comparing informants' accounts so as to identify similarities and differences, thereby constructing the uniformities underlying and defining the emergent categories. I then conducted a further three interviews so as to check the exhaustiveness of this taxonomy. Since no new accounting orientations or categorical properties emerged, I had to assume that I had reached the point which Glaser and Strauss call 'theoretical saturation' where 'no additional data are being found whereby the sociologist can develop properties of the category' (1967: 61).

Thus by the end of phase II of AI it was possible to differentiate three types of accounting orientation articulated by senior shop stewards. These I called the 'financial realist' (six informants), the 'financial sceptic' (eight informants) and the 'financial cynic' (two informants). This last category was initially undifferentiated from the emergent 'realist' orientation. However as I accumulated more primary data, it became evident that there were deviant cases within the 'realist' category which were reassigned to constitute the 'cynic' category.

Initially I had begun this differentiation through my attention being drawn to how informants perceived DAI either as providing an objective/veracious representation of organizational affairs, or as providing a fallacious and managerially contrived construction. These apparent differences in informants' life histories led to the initial construction of the 'realist' and 'sceptic' categories. However the data also suggested variability in the 'realist' category around how they made sense of social relationships in their work organizations. With regard to this characteristic, two of these shop stewards were closer to 'sceptics' – something which combined with a veracious view of DAI to produce an accounting orientation which was differentiable from both 'sceptics' and 'realists'. Thus the whole cohort were further differentiated according to their interpretations of intra-organizational relationships, i.e. those informants who perceived there to be a conflict of interest between their constituents and management as opposed to those who perceived that there was no difference of interest between their constituents and management. This process of comparison enabled the subsequent differentiation and articulation of the 'cynic' category.

Unfortunately space prevents a fuller presentation of the primary data which illustrate the properties of each category. Instead I will present them in summary form in Figure 3.2, with typical quotes to illustrate aspects of the dimensions which constitute and differentiate categories.

Financial realists
Accounting information:

> From the books . . . they tell you what's in the kitty . . . how much profit's been made or going to be made – they tell you how we are doing – you have to know that so as to know what's fair.

		Perception of accounting information	
		Veracious	Fallacious
Perception of intra-organizational relations	Unitary	Financial realist	A theoretically possible orientation unencountered in the field
	Dichotomous	Financial cynic	Financial sceptic

Figure 3.2 **Accounting orientations of senior shop stewards**

Intra-organizational relations:

> We're a team management and shopfloor . . . we've all got our different jobs to do and we'll argue a bit . . . but really we all win or lose together.

Financial cynics
Accounting information:

> It [DAI] tells you what's going on . . . it tells us what we can get out of them, what they've got . . . after all profit is profit . . . the figures can't lie, unlike management.

Intra-organizational relations:

> Really it's the books that tell us what's going on . . . it tells us how much they've got in the bank . . . but look it's a dog eat dog world and if I think the books put us on a loser – sod them, I'll ignore them . . . what I'd then justify our claim on would be standards of living or average pay rises locally or nationally – whatever's best – anything that supports the interests of my members I'll use . . . if management don't like it it's tough . . . my lads will back me.

Financial sceptics
Accounting information:

> All this twaddle about how much profits . . . costs, overheads . . . they [management] try to blind you with science . . . but I know they've got some prat with a sharp pencil to fiddle the books . . . It's like bloody Newspeak . . . once you start talking like them you begin to think like them . . . then they've got you.

Intra-organizational relations:

> That's what we base a claim on – what we need to keep house and home together and if those bastards [management] won't pay up they've got a fight on their hands and they know it.

Phase III: case features and causal analysis

Although the primary aim of the first interviews had been to gather data about variability in orientation and thereby construct a taxonomy of categories, a secondary aim was to provisionally elucidate case features so as to facilitate the development of an explanatory framework. This process entails movement down the 'funnel structure' of 'progressive focusing' (Hammersley and Atkinson, 1995: 206) with a shift of concern from description to the development of grounded theory regarding the categories by explicit reference

> to their involvement in a complex of inter-connected variables that the observer constructs as a theoretical model . . . which best explains the data . . . assembled. (Becker, 1970: 196)

From the data elicited it was possible to initially compare accounting orientation categories so as to identify which case features were unique to a category and which were shared by two or more. For Bloor (1976; 1978), case features shared by all three categories might be ruled out as influences upon their variability. Similarly, if case features appear to be randomly distributed between categories it is possible to infer that they are not exerting any systematic influence upon the categories. Some of the commonalities were outcomes of the research strategy adopted, while others serendipitously emerged during fieldwork; both types are described below.

Shared case features
All informants were men who defined themselves as 'lay' elected senior shop stewards and as skilled manual workers employed in private sector engineering. They all worked in organizations with between 600 and 1000 employees. Trade union membership varied within each category, but since members of the (then) AEU, GMBATU and TGWU were to be found amongst both 'realists' and 'sceptics' while the two 'cynics' were members of the AEU and GMBATU, membership of a particular trade union did not seem to influence category membership. Moreover no pattern within or between categories emerged regarding subjects' ages or length of experience as a senior shop steward.

All informants worked in organizations with a lengthy history of trade unionism with management recognition often having been acquired after protracted and attritious campaigns. Thus it was unlikely that they belonged to managerially sponsored shop steward organizations (see Willman, 1980). As incumbents of very similar offices all had been involved in significant areas of negotiation including collective bargaining over domestic rates of pay, changes in working practices, the introduction of new technology, redundancies, grievances, and the enforcement of collective agreements as well as custom and practice norms.

During fieldwork, several informants had claimed that they had not been exposed to DAI; they were therefore excluded from the sample. The remaining 16 were all familiar with employee reports and said that management also provided plant-level disaggregated information during collective bargaining. The latter included things such as output per worker (often juxtaposed with that of major competitors), plant operating accounts, costing information, state of the order book details, simplified balance sheets and predictions of future plant and company financial performance.

In this context, Jackson-Cox et al. (1984) have noted the significance of management's disclosure strategies in mediating the impact of DAI. They differentiate an 'integrated' strategy, with routine but selective provision of information, from an *ad hoc* strategy characterized by the piecemeal and intermittent provision of information. Of the informants in this research, two-thirds felt that management regularly provided information pertaining to specific issues with the remainder claiming that DAI was temporally intermittent and substantively haphazard. But since there was no pattern to the distribution of these phenomena between categories, I had to conclude that they exerted no systematic influence upon the development of the accounting orientations expressed by informants.

While they all had undergone some financial training through the education services of the trade union movement, a pattern between and within categories was apparent when I questioned them about in-company financial training provision. Only one 'sceptic' had admitted to some in-company financial training whereas all the 'cynics' and 'realists' did admit to this training. Although the form and content of these programmes varied, all the relevant informants remembered discussions and presentations of the missions and goals of their firm with a focus upon the current and future financial situation. All alluded to an emphasis upon issues such as the need to invest in current and fixed assets, sources of investment, profit and loss, value added, interest rates and the implications of these issues for the current and future financial management of the firm.

Therefore in-company financial training seemed to be an important case feature that might explain the development of informants' accounting orientations. But it was shared by two categories, 'realists' and 'cynics', and therefore could not account for their apparent differences. This implied that some unique case feature must account for this differentiation – but what?

During the first round of fieldwork I began to suspect that variations in informants' roles *vis-à-vis* constituents might constitute a battery of unique case features. These suspicions developed out of various comments such as that of a 'realist' who claimed:

> I tell the lads the plain facts, it's then their decision as to what we should do . . . it's only right to be democratic.

At this point I decided that it might be wise to obey Glaser and Strauss's (1967) injunction, regarding the application of the constant comparative method, to use the library to further develop what Blumer has called 'sensitizing concepts' or suggestions of 'directions in which to look' (1954: 7). While there was a variety of ideal-type categorizations of shop stewards' roles available, it was the one provided by Marchington and Armstrong (1983) which appeared most helpful for sensitizing concepts regarding shop stewards' roles, especially since it had developed out of a critique of earlier

		Representative	Delegate
	High	Leader	Cautious supporter
Orientation to unionism			
	Low	Workgroup leader	Populist

Figure 3.3   **Shop stewards' role (adapted from Marchington and Armstrong, 1983: 42)**

models (e.g. Batstone et al., 1977). Their fourfold taxonomy of role ideal-types is illustrated by Figure 3.3.

According to Marchington and Armstrong (1983) the 'leader' is highly committed to trade unionism and espouses wider political aims such as socialism or workers' control. In this s/he is willing and able to lead members. In contrast the 'populist' is neither committed to trade unionism and its wider political aims nor able to lead members; rather his/her role is perceived as the 'mouthpiece' or 'spokesperson' of constituents. 'Work-group leaders' share this parochialism, but they display strong leadership over constituents by agenda setting with reference to what they define as being in the best interests of their particular members. Finally the 'cautious supporter' was identified as a more transient role, containing various people who shared a wider commitment to trade unionism but were extremely cautious since they also perceived their role as being a delegate mandated by members. The potential for role conflict and ambiguity made this ideal-type a stopping-off point prior to a move into the 'populist' or 'leader' roles.

Senior stewards revisited: the search for unique case features
Armed with the sensitizing concepts developed out of both primary and secondary data, I returned to the field with the aim of elucidating their status as case features. This entailed a shift from describing informants' accounting orientations to explaining their occurrence through exploration of their perceptions of their roles as senior stewards and their definitions of and commitment towards trade unionism. This entailed more structure during interaction so as to direct dialogue towards the themes identified as potential unique case features. This progressive focusing was facilitated by grounding each second interview in the informants' frames of reference and terminology elicited in the prior round of interviews. The increasing complexity of the comparative analysis of emergent case features sometimes necessitated reinterviewing informants for a third time so as to check and develop elements of my emerging theoretical scheme. Again space precludes a full rendition of the subsequent accounts, so below I will provide only some

examples of the data elicited during progressive focusing which illustrate some pertinent aspects of case features.

Although informants were all senior shop stewards it emerged that relative to both 'cynics' and 'realists', 'sceptics' had appeared to be highly committed to a similar definition of trade unionism articulated as solidarity to 'fellow workers' in other workplaces. Typically one 'sceptic' claimed that:

> Many of the lads can't see beyond their own noses . . . If they think that something doesn't affect them then they're not interested . . . [but] we're all in this together . . . us, the miners, nurses, dockers, teachers . . . we're all workers . . . I have more in common with a German steelworker or a French miner than I have with the plant manager . . . we share economic conditions, all I share with management is the English language.

Another 'sceptic', when discussing the 1984–5 miners' strike, argued that:

> A few years ago we'd have taken the Tories on . . . we did at Saltley . . . the miners won in '74 because we stood together . . . you need the support of others otherwise you'll be crushed . . . many can't see that.

All 'sceptics' emphasized being a representative in the sense of having a proactive role as protector and leader of their constituents in what they considered to be a continual struggle against the excesses and arbitrariness of management. This entailed much agenda setting so as to protect or advance what they perceived as their members' best interests:

> Some of the lads are not too bright . . . they read rubbish like *The Sun* and listen to Radio Hallam . . . when it comes to knowing what's best for themselves they need help . . . that's my job . . . If I didn't . . . sometimes stop them from doing stupid things . . . management would twist them around their little fingers . . . most of the lads can't see beyond Page Three.

In contrast 'realists' were ambivalent towards the trade union principles of the 'sceptic'.

> One good thing that Thatcher has done for industrial relations is to stop secondary picketing . . . at one time my members were continually being laid off because of disputes elsewhere – things that had nothing to do with us.

Meanwhile 'cynics' also displayed an ambivalence towards such trade union principles but this was overlaid by a highly combative parochialism:

> I'll only support the JSSC [Joint Shop Stewards Committee] when it doesn't go against my members' interests – I have to fight to protect their interests sometimes from other unions and sometimes even from our own . . . in this world you have to look after yourselves – nobody else will.

What further differentiated between 'cynics' and 'realists' was how they arbitrated and defined constituents' interests. The former typically assumed a proactive representational role and perceived themselves as arbiters of what was best for their members:

> My members come first but they often make mistakes, they don't think about the consequences of what they might want to do or say . . . so I've got to be careful

about what I let through . . . they don't have the experience to deal with some issues.

In contrast 'realists' adopted a delegate role *vis-à-vis* constituents. This emphasized being a spokesperson for constituents, passing on their views to management and communicating management's position to members:

I don't try to tell the lads what they should do, rather I just give them the facts and let them decide . . . I then pass their decision to management . . . I'm just piggy-in-the-middle.

From the interviews, no 'cautious supporters' appeared to be evident in my sample. I decided that this was hardly surprising given that all informants were experienced senior shop stewards and that the 'cautious supporter' role was seen to be a transient role often adopted by neophyte shop stewards.

In sum three important associations emerged: the populist/realist, the workgroup-leader/cynic and the leader/sceptic. Although this covariance between unique case features and categories was important to any theoretical explanation, it was also important to explore what kind of rationale might underpin these apparent conjunctions in my data and elucidate the directions of causation.

Phase IV: theorization

Populist/realist association
It was plausible that informants' populism might exacerbate their suscepti-bility to accounting renditions of reality since such apparently objective information enabled them to 'rationally' transmit the 'facts' to constituents and facilitated their avoidance of taking unmandated decisions. If con-stituents wilfully chose to ignore those financial 'facts' and adopt 'irrational' courses of action, informants were personally divorced from any responsibil-ity in their role as delegate. However it was plausible that 'realism' could cause 'populism'. For instance 'realism' might abrogate them from the responsibility for defining constituents' interests and engender the role of reactive messenger because DAI constituted immutable facts that had to be transmitted regardless of their palatability.

The only way I could test the direction of causation was to investigate whether or not 'realists' had been 'populists' prior to their exposure to in-company financial training. Despite one exception it appeared that financial training was a possible case feature that differentiated 'sceptics' from both 'realists' and 'cynics', but the varying use of accounting information by 'cynics' and 'realists' implied the influence of some further discriminating factor. Therefore in a third round of interviews, with all the 'realists' I attempted to elucidate whether they had always adopted a 'populist' role, particularly with regard to delegacy, and especially prior to their exposure to in-company financial training. From the resulting data it appeared that 'populism' preceded 'realism'. The following statement was typical:

I've always been a go-between . . . At first I didn't have much of an opinion about the messages . . . but since I've gained more experience I think that sometimes the lads won't face up to the [financial] facts . . . but that's up to them isn't it.

The workgroup-leader/cynic association

The 'cynic' shares the realist's assumptions about the veracity of DAI; moreover they have also been exposed to in-house training. But these factors do not explain their very different negotiating strategies with management. For the 'cynic', although veracious, DAI does not define constituents' interests; rather it is taken as a lexicon that might be applied in their furtherance or discarded when it appears to be incommensurable. While these artful bargainers share with 'realists' an ambivalence towards trade union notions of solidarity, this is overlaid by a combative and parochial image of the 'us', while the 'them' pertains to anyone outside that immediate constituency.

The 'cynic's' parochialism creates a perceived need to defend constituents from the ever present threats from other groups. This concern appears to override the immanent implications of their acceptance of DAI as veracious and their exposure to in-company financial training. Although DAI may be the harbinger of an immutable financial reality, the intercession of this imagery prevents the translation of these 'truths' into the attitudes and practices of the 'realist'. Instead the cynic's 'war' leads to their Machiavellian pursuit of perceived interest by any available means, regardless of the moral imperatives deriving from an accounting rendition of organizational reality. Such training therefore appears to provide the 'cynic' with one more tactically deployable weapon in his arsenal. His proactive representative predilections enable and legitimate the implementation of this strategy as they insulate him from the impediment of constituents' sanction.

The leader/sceptic association

Excluded from the 'cynic's' conception of 'us' are broader constituencies of trade unionists. Although these 'others' are not necessarily perceived in the combative gaze that guides the 'cynic's' perception of management, there is a parochial ambivalence that coincides with the 'cynic's' orientation towards trade union principles of solidarity etc. In contrast the 'sceptic' invokes solidarity with groups, outside their immediate constituency, engaged in a shared 'class war'. However another factor unique to the sceptics, save for one subject, is a lack of exposure to in-company financial training. Hence, which of these case features was the most important in explaining the 'sceptic' accounting category?

Treasuring my exception, I carefully reanalysed the case of the one 'sceptic' who had experienced some in-company financial training and confirmed his original categorization. Unfortunately this subject refused to be interviewed for a third time, so from the data I had already collected, I left with the tentative conclusion that any exposure of 'sceptics' to in-company financial training would have little impact upon their view of DAI.

Presumably the tenure of solidaristic trade union principles, and the radical imagery that this implies, could prevent the acceptance of the messages disseminated through such training. For instance this imagery led to a perceived association between accounting information, accountants and management. As one 'sceptic' typically argued:

> they are all in it together . . . [DAI] tells us what they like so as to get us to do what they want us to – accountants and managers they are all the same . . . con men with company cars out to screw us.

In sum, from the primary data inductively collected throughout this field-work, the social phenomena and processes that influence informants' propensity to refer to particular accounting orientations are diagrammatically illustrated by Figure 3.4.

For Bloor (1976; 1978) AI will usually end at this stage – the proposal of a theoretical explanation inductively grounded in empirical data. However I decided to try to further test my grounded theory by interviewing six new informants. I reversed the data collection processes I had undertaken so far by firstly elucidating the shared and unique case features which, according to the above model, explain variation in accounting category. By analysing those data I then predicted which accounting category each subject would be

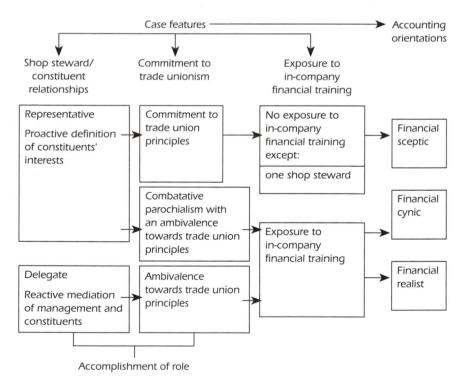

Figure 3.4   **Summary of the influences on senior shop stewards'
propensity to hold particular accounting orientations**

in, and then I conducted a second round of interviews to elucidate the accuracy of those expectations. The aim of this process was to try to further deal with the criticisms levelled by Robinson (1951) of Cressey's approach. As Hammersley (1989: 196–7) points out, it implies that AI should investigate cases where the conditions specified by the hypothesis hold, and if the phenomenon does occur, AI may then stop.

For the six informants, data referring to their relationships with constituents, their commitment towards trade union principles of solidarity, and their exposure to in-company financial training suggested that three would be 'sceptics' and two 'realists'. However, from his interview, the sixth informant displayed the case features of a 'cynic' except he had not been exposed to in-company financial training. During fieldwork he had expressed Machiavellian representative propensities and a combative parochialism couched in an ambivalence towards trade union principles. This suggested that his espoused accounting orientation would show a potential for 'cynicism' which could lie dormant until he was exposed to financial training.

In the subsequent round of interviews my expectations regarding the three sceptics and two realists were accurate. Moreover the potential for cynicism in the sixth informant is illustrated by the selections below:

> *Potential cynic*: I try to ignore it [DAI]. My maxim is that if you don't know the rules of the game . . . change the game to one that you know the rules for . . . so when I'm negotiating with management . . . I ignore their figures . . . I stick to things that I understand and which backs up giving us a good deal . . . If something doesn't, or you are not sure what it means, my advice is to ignore it and find something else . . . If you don't, management will piss all over you and you deserve it.
>
> *Researcher*: If you did understand what the accounts/books meant and if you felt that they supported your case, would you use them?
>
> *Potential cynic*: Yes . . . I think so . . . as I've said if I know the rules of the game and there's a good chance of winning . . . I take the bastards on . . . but if I think that I might lose I'll change the game . . . My job is to get the best for the lads, that's why they elected me . . . I call it looking after yourself and your own – them that elected me to the job in the first place and just them.

This potential for 'cynicism' illustrates how factors that relate to the senior shop steward's accomplishment of his role mediate the potential impact of any in-company financial training intervention. Moreover, these data seemed to corroborate my earlier speculations about the significance of those factors for mediating the potential impact of such training upon 'sceptics'.

Conclusions

This example of the application of AI illustrates how it seeks to capture aspects of the social world from the perspective of actors and allows the revision of hypotheses and conceptual structures through the analysis and elimination of negative cases. In doing so it attempts to maintain a faithfulness to empirical data gathered from a relatively small number of cases as the research process moves from those data to the construction of categories and from the elucidation of their case features to theorization and generalization. However underlying these processes are a number of epistemological and ontological ambiguities which are worth outlining.

Firstly, a criticism of AI argues that owing to the small samples used, the method can rarely make claims about the representativeness of its samples and therefore any attempt at generalizing is tenuous. For Mitchell (1983) such a criticism shows a confusion between the procedures appropriate to making inferences from survey research and those which are appropriate to case study work. He argues that analytical thinking about survey data is based upon both statistical and logical (i.e. causal) inference and that there is a tendency to elide the former with the latter in that 'the postulated causal connection among features in a sample may be assumed to exist in some parent population simply because the features may be inferred to co-exist in that population' (1983: 200). In contrast inference in case study research can only be logical and derives its external validity not from its representativeness but because 'our analysis is unassailable' (1983: 200). Such analytical thoroughness is achieved in AI by eliminating exceptions and revising hypotheses so that statistical tests are actually unnecessary once negative cases are removed (Fielding and Fielding, 1986: 89). Thus in AI extrapolation is derived from logical inference based upon the demonstrated power of the inductively generated and tested theoretical model 'rather than the representativeness of the events' (Mitchell, 1983: 190).

Secondly, AI's procedures entail the movement from the 'thick' description and categorization of actors' phenomenological worlds to propounding theoretical explanations of those categories. This entails an initial (re)presentation of actors' internal logics grounded in *verstehen* in order to formulate categories. However, in order to avoid analytic interruptus AI requires the researcher to shift to a form of analysis that entails his/her imposition of an external logic which exists independently of, and explains, the actors' internal logics. Clearly this shift entails an overt form of what Burrell and Morgan term 'ontological oscillation' (1979: 266) – the initial adoption of a subjectivist stance with the subsequent introduction of incommensurable objectivist assumptions. Now the question for AI is whether, as Burrell and Morgan claim, such oscillation poses a contradiction which should be avoided, or, as Weick (1995: 34–8) argues, such oscillation is a vital element in sense making that helps us understand the everyday actions of people. Basically the latter view would support AI as it is presented here, whereas the former would necessitate either the discarding of a phenomenological starting point for AI, or its dissolution through a limitation to phenomenological 'thick description'.

Finally there remains a basic question regarding the extent to which 'pure' induction is possible. Ironically, the claim that it is possible shares with logical empiricism the implicit assumption that there exists a theory-neutral observational language in which the researcher is construed as a neutral conduit of cultural experience who can objectively elucidate and present the 'facts' of a cognitively accessible empirical world. For Rorty (1979: 46) this view inevitably relies upon the received wisdom that the facts of an external objective social reality can be 'mirrored' in the 'glassy essence' of the observer. To ground AI or any methodology in such a mirror metaphor construes the relationship between the researcher and his/her area of interest in terms of a subject–subject (or indeed subject–object) dualism. In Rorty's terms this dualism entails the assumption that there is a mirror inside the mind of the researcher that can be methodologically polished so as to allow their mind's eye to gaze upon accurate reflections of reality – regardless of whether those reflections are of the cultures of knowing subjects or of the behaviour of non-sentient objects. But the assumption of such a dualism (re)constructs an epistemic privilege which ignores the processes by which any observer inevitably projects background preconceptions embedded in his/her own language and life-world (Spinelli, 1989). For Hammersley (1992) such issues are especially problematic for any approach which is committed to accessing members' phenomenological worlds so as to reveal their subjectivities. It creates a contradiction between an objectivist impulse that emphasizes how phenomenological accounts should correspond with members' subjectivity and a phenomenological impulse that suggests that people socially construct versions of reality – culturally derived epistemic processes to which researchers are not immune. Perhaps a key task for any methodologist with a subjectivist agenda is to resolve the problems posed by these epistemological ambiguities while avoiding the spectre, and quagmire, of relativism.

References

Banister, P., Burman E., Parker, I., Taylor, M. and Tindall, C. (1994) *Qualitative Methods in Psychology: A Research Guide*. Buckingham: Open University Press.

Batstone, E., Boraston, I. and Frenkel, S. (1977) *Shop Stewards in Action*. Oxford: Blackwell.

Becker, H.S. (1970) 'Problems of inference and proof in participant observation', in W.J. Filstead (ed.), *Qualitative Methodology*. Chicago: Markham.

Becker, H.S. (1973) *Outsiders: Studies in the Sociology of Deviance*. London: Free Press.

Berreman, G. (1962) *Behind Many Masks: Ethnography and Impression Management in a Himalayan Village*. Monograph 4, Society for Applied Anthropology. Ithaca, NY: Cornell University Press.

Beynon, J. (1983) 'Ways-in and staying in: fieldwork as problem-solving', in M. Hammersley (ed.), *The Ethnography of Schooling: Methodological Issues*. Driffield: Nafferton.

Bloor, M. (1976) 'Bishop Berkeley and the adenotonsillectomy enigma: an explanation of variation in the social construction of medical disposals', *Sociology*, 10 (1): 43–61.

Bloor, M. (1978) 'On the analysis of observational data: a discussion of the worth and uses of inductive techniques and respondent validation', *Sociology*, 12 (3): 545–52.

Blumer, H. (1954) 'What is wrong with social theory?', *American Sociological Review*, 19 (1): 3–10.

Bogdan, R. (1974) *Being Different: The Autobiography of Jane Fry*. London: Wiley.

Bulmer, M. (1975) 'Some problems of research into class imagery', in M. Bulmer (ed.), *Working Class Images of Society*. London: Routledge and Kegan Paul.

Burrell, G. and Morgan, G. (1979) *Sociological Paradigms and Organizational Analysis*. London: Heinemann.

Cressey, D. (1950) 'The criminal violation of financial trust', *American Sociological Review*, 15: 738–43.

Cressey, D. (1953) *Other Peoples' Money*. Glencoe, IL: Free Press.

Denzin, N. (1978) *The Research Act: A Theoretical Introduction to Sociological Methods*, 2nd edn. London: McGraw-Hill.

Douglas, J.D. (1976) *Investigative Social Research: Individual and Team Field Research*. London: Sage.

Douglas, J.D. (1983) *Creative Interviewing*. London: Sage.

Fielding, N.G. and Fielding, J.L. (1986) *Linking Data*. Qualitative Research Methods Series 4. London: Sage.

Geertz, C. (1973) *The Interpretation of Cultures*. New York: Basic Books.

Giddens, A. (1976) *New Rules of Sociological Method*. London: Hutchinson.

Gill, J. and Johnson, P. (1997) *Research Methods for Managers*, 2nd edn. London: Paul Chapman.

Glaser, B.G. (1978) *Theoretical Sensitivity*. San Francisco: Sociological Press.

Glaser, B.G. and Strauss, A. (1967) *The Discovery of Grounded Theory*. Chicago: Aldine.

Glesne, C. and Peshkin, A. (1992) *Becoming Qualitative Researchers: An Introduction*. London: Longman.

Goffman, E. (1969) *The Presentation of Self in Everyday Life*. Harmondsworth: Penguin.

Goffman, E. (1972) *The Interaction Ritual*. Harmondsworth: Penguin.

Hammersley, M. (1989) *The Dilemma of Qualitative Method: Herbert Blumer and the Chicago Tradition*. London: Routledge.

Hammersley, M. (1992) *What is Wrong with Ethnography?* London: Routledge.

Hammersley, M. and Atkinson, P. (1995) *Ethnography: Principles in Practice*, 2nd edn. London: Routledge.

Hansen, E.C. (1977) *Rural Catalonia under the Franco Regime*. Cambridge: Cambridge University Press.

Jackson-Cox, J., Thirkell, J.E.M. and McQueeney, J. (1984) 'The disclosure of company information to trade unions', *Accounting, Organizations and Society*, 9 (3/4): 253–73.

Johnson, P. (1995) 'Towards an epistemology for radical accounting: beyond objectivism and relativism', *Critical Perspectives on Accounting*, 6 (4): 485–509.

Jones, G.R. (1983) 'Life history methodology', in G. Morgan (ed.), *Beyond Method*. London: Sage.

Kidder, L.H. (1981) 'Qualitative research and quasi experimental frameworks', in M.B. Brewer and B.E. Collins (eds), *Scientific Inquiry and the Social Sciences*. San Francisco: Jossey-Bass.

Knights, D. and Willmott, H.C. (1993) 'It's a very foreign discipline: the genesis of expenses control in a mutual life insurance company', *British Journal of Management*, 4 (1): 1–18.

Kolb, D.A., Rubin, I.M. and McIntyre, J.M. (1979) *Organizational Psychology: An Experiential Approach*. London: Prentice-Hall.

Lessnoff, M. (1974) *The Structure of Social Science*. London: Allen and Unwin.

Lindesmith, A. (1947) *Opiate Addiction*. Bloomington, IN: Principia Press.

Loftland, J. (1970) 'Interactionist imagery and analytic interruptus', in T. Shibutani (ed.), *Human Nature and Collective Behaviour: Papers in Honour of Herbert Blumer*. Englewood Cliffs, NJ: Prentice-Hall.

Loftland, J. (1971) *Analysing Social Settings: A Guide to Qualitative Observation and Analysis*. Belmont, CA: Wadsworth.

Lyman, S.M. and Scott, M.B. (1970) *A Sociology of the Absurd*. New York: Appleton-Century-Crofts.

Manning, P.K. (1982) 'Analytic induction', in R.B. Smith and P.K. Manning (eds), *Qualitative Methods: Volume 11 of Handbook of Social Science Methods*. Cambridge, MA: Ballinger. pp. 273–302.

Marchington, M. and Armstrong, R. (1983) 'Typologies of shop stewards: a reconsideration', *Industrial Relations Journal*, 14 (1): 34–49.

Mitchell, J.C. (1983) 'Case and situational analysis', *Sociological Review*, 31 (2): 187–211.

Plummer, K. (1983) *Documents of Life: An Introduction to the Problems and Literature of an Humanistic Method*. London: Allen and Unwin.

Robinson, W.S. (1951) 'The logic and structure of analytic induction', *American Sociological Review*, 16 (6): 812–18.

Rorty, R. (1979) *Philosophy and the Mirror of Nature*. Princeton, NJ: Princeton University Press.

Shaw, C.R. (1966) *The Jack Roller: A Delinquent Boy's Own Story*. Chicago: Chicago University Press.

Shotter, J. (1975) *Images of Man in Psychological Research*. London: Methuen.

Silverman, D. (1993) *Interpreting Qualitative Data: Methods for Analysing Talk, Text and Interaction*. London: Sage.

Spinelli, E. (1989) *The Interpreted World*. London: Sage.

Spradley, J.P. (1979) *The Ethnographic Interview*. New York: Holt, Reinhart and Winston.

Trice, H.M. (1956) 'Outsider's role in field study', *Sociology and Social Research*, 14 (1): 27–32.

Wallace, W. (1971) *The Logic of Science in Sociology*. Chicago: Aldine-Atherton.

Weick, K.E. (1995) *Sensemaking in Organizations*. London: Sage.

Whyte, W.F. (1955) *Street Corner Society: The Social Structure of an Italian Slum*. Chicago: University of Chicago Press.

Willman, P. (1980) 'Leadership and trade union principles: some problems of management sponsorship and independence', *Industrial Relations Journal*, 11 (4): 39–49.

Wiseman, J.P. (1978) 'The research web', in J. Bynner and K.M. Stribley (eds), *Social Research, Principles and Procedures*. London: Longman.

Znaniecki, F. (1934) *The Method of Sociology*. New York: Farrer and Reinhart.

4   Critical Incident Technique

Elizabeth Chell

The critical incident technique (CIT) was first devised and used in a scientific study almost a half-century ago (Flanagan, 1954). The significance of this timespan is that then the assumption of a *positivist* approach to social science investigations was largely unquestioned. It was the dominant paradigm in the social sciences as it was in the sciences. The idea that some research questions can be pursued with validity by non-positivistic means is growing, as this volume and its predecessor demonstrate (Cassell and Symon, 1994). However, the pertinent point is that the CIT was originally used as a scientific tool and it now tends to be used as an investigative tool in organizational analysis from within an interpretive or phenomenological paradigm (Chell and Adam, 1994a). Thus, the potential varied adoption of CIT nicely cuts across the (simplistic) notion that quantitative methods assume positivism while qualitative methods make non-positivistic assumptions. The fact is that the CIT *may* be used within either paradigm! Therefore it is critically important that the researcher examines his/her own assumptions (and predilections), considers very carefully the nature of the research problem to be investigated, and thinks through *how* the technique may most appropriately be applied in the particular researchable case.

In this chapter, I shall dwell initially on those background assumptions as they have important implications for the choice of method. I shall then discuss the background to CIT in relation to three different approaches to its use which have been taken, drawing out the assumptions underlying the interpretation and development of the method. I will then select my own usage of CIT with a detailed exposition of the method adopted. This will be illustrated by means of a detailed case example of the use of the method from within an interpretive paradigm.

Background assumptions

The starting point for any investigative work is curiosity and sometimes puzzlement at a phenomenon which appears to be inadequately understood or explained. There are two ways in which the research can then proceed: (a) examine how the phenomenon has hitherto been defined and presented in the literature and attempt to identify further the researchable aspects of the problem; (b) consider that the phenomenon and associated issues need to be redefined. A part of this process which is often omitted is the one which asks what assumptions are being made in so framing those questions. That is, what assumptions are being made about the nature of organizational reality, how knowledge of organizational behaviour is arrived at, and the relationship between theory and method? A seminal paper (Morgan and Smircich, 1980) has enabled the researcher to consider these issues very carefully.

The first observation to make is that the assumptions are not dichotomous but form three continua. The first comprises the ontological assumptions concerning phenomenal versus 'concrete' reality. The second concerns the methodological assumptions of the subjective versus the objective approaches to the subject under investigation. The third is the assumption about human nature: on the one hand voluntarism, that is where persons have free will and are active constructors of their reality; and on the other hand determinism, that is where behaviour is structured and determined and the person is the passive responder to reality. Between such extremes there are definable positions which Morgan and Smircich (1980) have labelled (from the subjective position) phenomenology, ethnomethodology, social action theory, cybernetics, open systems theory, social learning theory and behaviourism. The question then arises as to what methods the social scientist may adopt in order that they might investigate a particular social/ organizational situation which is appropriate to the theoretical position they are assuming, and more particularly where the critical incident technique might be placed.

Background to the method

The CIT has been used in six distinct studies and in each case the method adopted has specifiable differences. These studies are: (1) the critical incident technique within the field of occupational psychology, initially developed in order to discover the reasons for pilot failure in learning to fly (Flanagan, 1954); (2) the behavioral event interview (BEI), developed in order to differentiate superior and average performers (McClelland, 1976; 1987; Spencer, 1983); (3) in management, the use of CIT in the measurement of 'trust' (Butler, 1991); (4) in entrepreneurship, a social constructionist approach to the application of CIT to distinguish different types of business owners according to their approaches to the development or maintenance of their business venture (Chell et al., 1991); (5) a grounded theory approach, using CIT and a computer package (NUD•IST) to investigate the impact of culture on the entrepreneurial/managerial behaviour of small firm owner-managers (Chell and Adam, 1994a; 1994b); (6) in interdisciplinary work, the critical incident analysis of business development activity of a sample of self-employed and microbusiness owners in the business service sector in the UK (Wheelock and Chell, 1996).

Flanagan defined the critical incident technique as

a set of procedures for collecting direct observations of human behavior in such a way as to facilitate their potential usefulness in solving practical problems and developing broad psychological principles . . . By an incident is meant any specifiable human activity that is sufficiently complete in itself to permit inferences and predictions to be made about the person performing the act. To be critical the incident must occur in a situation where the purpose or intent of the act seems fairly clear to the observer and where its consequences are sufficiently definite to leave little doubt concerning its effects. (1954: 327)

The studies reviewed by Flanagan (1954) assumed a 'concreteness' about reality such that (a) the general purpose of the activity being undertaken could be specified, (b) the criteria of what constitutes effective or ineffective performance of the activity could be identified, and (c) observers could be given explicit criteria for judging/evaluating observed behaviours as reaching the standard or not. The studies reviewed sampled specified occupational groups in defined situations. Observations were deemed 'objective' (i.e. 'fact') if a number of independent observers made the same judgement. Clearly fundamental to the method is the ability to classify the critical incidents. Ideally, it is desirable to observe a comprehensive set of incidents and to develop a classification system from such data. This classification then presents the analyst with objective criteria for application to a fresh study. Of course, as the classification has been arrived at inductively it can never be assumed to be fully comprehensive; there is always the possibility of making an observation which falls outside the existing criteria.

An example of one study reviewed by Flanagan was that of 'disorientation while flying'. The pilots were asked to describe what they 'saw, heard or felt that brought on the experience'. The study led to a number of changes in cockpit and instrument panel design. Another study was of combat leadership. Veterans were asked to make observations of specific incidents of effective and ineffective behaviour in accomplishing the mission. This was a large scale study and resulted in several thousand incidents describing officers' actions. The outcome of the research was a set of descriptive categories – 'critical requirements' – of effective combat leadership. By the use of expert observers whose independent judgements were compared, the essentially subjective nature of this process was converted into an objective set of criteria which could be rigorously applied to further groups.

The work of McBer using the 'behavioural event interview' (BEI) developed by David McClelland and colleagues was derived from the Flanagan critical incident method. It was known that measurable skills like verbal fluency and cultural content knowledge did not predict the performance of diplomats in the Foreign Office. Thus a key difference was that the study involved the identification of the less tangible aspects of behaviour, specifically 'soft' skills and competencies. The interviewees were asked to identify the most critical incidents they had encountered in their jobs and to describe them in considerable detail. McClelland additionally used thematic apperception test probes to elicit data about the interviewee's personality and cognitive style. The interview transcripts were content analysed to identify behaviours and characteristics which distinguished superior from average job performance. Cross-validation tests were also used. The outcome of this work was the development of a job competence assessment process to identify 'soft skills' which predict performance in more than 50 professions (Spencer, 1983).

Whilst work such as that of Butler (1991) has demonstrated the use of CIT in organizational analysis, in particular in trust relations, there has been a predominant use of the technique in the study of entrepreneurial behaviour. For example, a study by Chell et al. (1991) sought to distinguish behavioural differences between business owners of small to medium enterprises (SMEs) across a range of business sectors. The specified activity was business development (or not as the case may be) and as such the critical incidents identified by the interviewee could have facilitated or inhibited development. Thus the *outcome* was business development (measured in terms of growth indicators) whilst the inputs were behaviours carried out by the interviewee in relation to the identified incidents. The questions were: what incidents in the opinion of the business owner shaped business outcomes in terms of performance, and how did s/he handle those incidents? Could the behaviours by which s/he handled the events be construed as evidence of entrepreneurship? The outcome, which the team labelled 'growth orientation' (GO), was found to follow four different trajectories: expand, rejuvenate, plateau or decline. The patterns of behaviour identified from the description of the management of the incidents associated with business development were categorized. A profile of eight behavioural characteristics emerged as differentiating consistently between business owners. Criteria of what constituted 'prototypical instances of behaviours' were sought. Each business owner's strategies and tactics were assessed against this profile of entrepreneurial behaviours. A business owner whose profile constituted the eight behavioural characteristics was termed an 'entrepreneur', whereas different combinations of those characteristics gave rise to the 'quasi-entrepreneur', the 'administrator' and the 'caretaker'. The methodology of the application of neural networks was developed to demonstrate that once the criteria were so determined it was possible to use such technology to categorize business owners according to type (Chell et al., 1991; Haworth et al., 1991).

A subsequent study of the behavioural characteristics of business owners in four business sectors (catering, food processing, viniculture/winery and hotels) in New Zealand was carried out (Chell and Adam, 1995). The critical incident method was used to elicit 'evidence' associated with incidents which impacted business development. The respondents (all of whom were owner-managers) were asked to identify two incidents which affected the business positively and to identify one negative incident. They were asked to give detailed descriptions of how they handled the incident in each case and, where appropriate, what they felt, who else was involved, what part they played and what the outcome was for the business. The interviews were tape recorded, transcribed and coded using grounded theory (Glaser and Strauss,

1967; Strauss and Corbin, 1990). This method has been replicated in three other studies in Finland, Hong Kong, and the UK.

Whilst such work was being undertaken, a further study which focused upon inter-regional comparisons in locations in the north-east and south-east of England was carried out, the aims and objectives being to examine the interaction between business and household and the implications for each (Wheelock and Chell, 1996). Here the focus was on microbusiness owners (defined as a person or persons owning and managing a business which employed 0–10 full time equivalent employees). In this example, the business owner could select 'domestic' incidents if he/she wished in order to explain business development activity or inactivity.

Comparison with other qualitative methods

CIT may be used in case study research but is more often used in multi-site studies. The question arises as to whether other methods, for example participant observation and unstructured or semi-structured interviews, might not be more effective as research tools.

The CIT has in common with participant observation and the unstructured interview the fact that they are all examples of qualitative techniques used by the researcher to 'get closer to the subject' (Bryman, 1989). However, participant observation has a number of disadvantages: covert participant observation raises ethical issues (for example of deception), it focuses upon the 'here and now' (though it enables the researcher to build up a picture of organizational process, for example) and it presents difficulties for the observer in terms of recording observations. CIT is overt in that the subject is aware of being interviewed. Once assurances have been given of confidentiality and anonymity, the interviewee usually relaxes and is able to recount his or her story. One disadvantage is that the accounts are always retrospective; however, the fact that the incidents are 'critical' means that subjects usually have very good recall. Moreover, unlike the unstructured interview, there is a focus which enables the researcher to probe aptly and which the interviewee can concentrate on – a 'hook' upon which they can 'hang' their accounts. As is the case with participant observation, CIT is context-rich, but unlike participant observation the context is developed entirely from the subject's perspective. Some things can be checked. It is therefore usual to use documentary sources to check factual statements, and if possible to interview at least one other significant person. Further the fact that the CIT is used across multiple sites means that the researcher can look for evidence of commonalities in themes, that is, 'incidents' which increase the generalizability. A further advantage of the CIT is that the analysis enables the researcher to relate context, strategy and outcomes, to look for repetition of patterns of ways of doing, and thus to build up a picture of management tactics for handling difficult situations (see later section). This gives first hand evidence of the relationship between context and outcome, whereas a technique like participant observation, whilst context-rich, is likely to need more work in order to make the connections with outcomes.

Detailed breakdown of the method

The method, as developed by the author, assumes a phenomenological approach. It is intended through the process of a largely unstructured interview to capture the thought processes, the frame of reference and the feelings about an incident or set of incidents which have meaning for the respondent. In the interview the respondent is required to give an account of what those incidents meant for them, their life situation and their present circumstances, attitudes and orientation. This same approach may be used in the in-depth case study as well as the multi-site investigation. Thus, this method assumes an alternative definition:

> The critical interview technique is a qualitative interview procedure which facilitates the investigation of significant occurrences (events, incidents, processes or issues) identified by the respondent, the way they are managed, and the outcomes in terms of perceived effects. The objective is to gain an understanding of the incident from the perspective of the individual, taking into account cognitive, affective and behavioural elements.

There are eight distinguishable aspects of the method: (i) preliminary design work and determination of the sample, (ii) gaining access, (iii) introducing the CIT method and getting the interview under way, (iv) focusing the theme and giving an account of oneself as researcher to the respondent, (v) controlling the interview, by probing the incidents and clarifying one's understanding, (vi) concluding the interview, (vii) taking care of ethical issues, (viii) analysing the data.

Preliminary design work and determination of the sample

Conducting a critical incident interview is time consuming. Some preliminary investigative work is needed prior to the CIT interview proper. This usually comprises the compilation of a sampling frame, use of Companies House or other documentary sources of data on the companies, and then a telephone interview in order to collect some general descriptive information about the organization and the business. At this stage the telephone interviews are concluded and the information obtained processed. This means effectively that where there is (and there usually is) a criterion for inclusion of particular business and/or business owners, the ones which do not fit that criterion are deselected. Once the sampling frame is 'cleaned up' in this way the respondents are targeted, usually by randomization (though purposive selection may be appropriate in some studies).

Gaining access

Gaining access to an organization requires skills, patience and perseverance. Once the ice has been broken by means of the telephone interview it is often easier to gain further access. However, it is wise not to take such access for granted. A useful device therefore is the letter of introduction which sets out more formally the project's aims and objectives (briefly stated), and explains why the research team would like to carry out a follow-up interview. It should indicate that the letter will be followed up by a telephone call within the week. This means that letters should be sent out in small batches so that the telephoning and arrangements for a follow-up interview are manageable within the interviewer's diary.

Once a batch of interviews has been arranged the allotted time for any one interview will approach quickly. The interviewer needs to be prepared, for example, by reading up the background material. The location of the interview is a further important consideration. There may be more than one context where critical incidents have occurred and so whilst the organization might be the most obvious first choice, it is not always the most appropriate. For example, if the aim is to understand how business development decisions impact family life and vice versa, then it may be appropriate to interview both spouses at home. This of course may complicate the access problem as one cannot automatically assume the cooperation of both spouses. A further consideration is the security of the researcher. There are circumstances where the researcher may feel uncomfortable, intimidated or threatened by a domestic context which was not anticipated.

Researchers are not always treated well by business owners: for example, they may be kept waiting, sometimes on doorsteps; interviews may be postponed at the last minute; and announcements may be made abruptly that the respondent has only half an hour as something has 'come up'. Such obstacles and trying circumstances may tax the patience. The researcher needs to take it all in his or her stride and to know when to persist and at what stage to call a halt (where it appears that they may be being given the run-around). However, if procedures are followed meticulously good access is usually the result. The odd respondent with 'only half an hour to spare' is often the one you spend most time with as they realize that their coping mechanism for hiding their anxiety was unnecessary.

Introducing CIT

Once the researcher has gained access and is facing the interviewee s/he should explain succinctly the nature of the critical incident interview, and outline the purposes of the research and any possible benefits, particularly where there may be practical and/or policy implications. Whilst it may sound unconvincing on paper, there is no reason why the experienced researcher will not be able to point to the fact that this type of interview is often enjoyed and viewed by the respondent as an opportunity to take 'time out', to review and reflect upon a number of key issues and events. It is wise to raise issues of confidentiality at this juncture and to give assurances as necessary. The interview will appear to the respondent to be more like a conversation and therefore establishing a rapport of trust and confidence is clearly important. Conducting the interview where the respondent is uncomfortable or tense does happen but should not be as a consequence of the interviewer's presence. Handling the interviewee's feelings is thus an important skill.

Focusing the theme

The interviewer must focus the attention of the respondent on the interview and be able to explain succinctly the CIT in the context of the topic to be discussed. The interviewer must be ready for the odd respondent who will deny that 'anything has happened' to them or the organization. One ploy is to get the respondents to think graphically about the events which have transpired over the past (say) five years by offering them a sheet of paper containing a double arrow-headed line centrally along its length. The respondent is then encouraged to mark the position of the 'here and now' and then work backwards year by year, marking critical events along its length. This visual aid serves several purposes: it focuses attention, enables the interviewee to relax, jogs the memory and enables the researcher to get a sense of the nature of the critical events which have been impacting the organization. The initial stages of the interview may be characterized by an attempt to establish a chronology of events. Typical comments from the interviewer are:

> So that was 1994.
>
> Right, OK. So you were saying at the back end of 1993 there were three clients . . .
>
> Anything else, Betty, that has a significant effect on the household due to the business, because we're particularly interested in this interrelationship?
>
> When was that then?
>
> So before all these bad debts hit . . .?
>
> OK. Anything else happened in your sort of family life?
>
> Right, and has that had a major effect on you and the business?

The interviewer will then ask the respondent to 'select three critical events – two positive and one negative – which in his/her opinion have impacted the business/organization' (the wording will clearly differ according to the aims and objectives of the research questions). It may be that the respondent indicates that all the incidents have been either negative or positive. The interviewer must accept this initial statement as reflecting the respondent's frame of reference and evaluation of those events. The interviewee will commence his/her story by recounting one of the events. Some events may be interwoven both in time and in the mind of the respondent; therefore the interviewer must listen carefully and probe appropriately to ensure that he/she has fully grasped the essential details of the incident.

Controlling the interview

Generic probes seek answers to the following types of question: *What* happened next? *Why* did it happen? *How* did it happen? *With whom* did it happen? *What* did the parties concerned *Feel*? *What* were the consequences – immediately and longer term? *How* did the respondent cope? *What* tactics were used?

Such generic probes are translated into specific questions which relate to the context, language and rapport of the specific interview. For example, some interjections by the interviewer may seek *clarification*: 'And he came in as a partner?' 'Was this on the leisure consultancy side?', 'Are we about 1992 now?' Such interjections help control the flow of the interview and keep the interviewer alert. They also give a breathing space to the respondent to gather her/his thoughts. In highly critical incidents with high emotive content for the respondent the interview may otherwise become a monologue. This is not usually desirable as the interview may ramble and lose focus and the interviewer may lose the sense of what is being recounted. It is worth underlining that the purpose of the interview is to attempt to gain a genuine understanding of the other person through language. It is essential to elucidate the nature of the context which gives the words their particular meaning. Thus the interviewer may seek *further information* until they are satisfied that they do understand. It is important however that the interviewer does not dominate the discussion or interrogate the respondent; a balance must be struck.

Concluding the interview and taking care of any ethical issues

The interview tends to come to an end naturally as the respondent concludes their account. Usually the interviewer will simply thank the respondent for their time and energy in giving such a complete and vivid account of the incidents in question. It may be that the researcher aims to feed back the results of the work in a short report or a business seminar. Certainly the researcher must leave the impression that the interview was valuable and that any information revealed will be treated strictly confidentially. Thus issues such as the anonymity of respondents, the disguising of companies etc. must be addressed before the researcher departs. It is both a morale booster in respect of the interviewer's job satisfaction and very useful from the point of view of the research project if the interviewer can leave with a genuine and realistic feeling that s/he will be welcomed if s/he returns.

Analysing the data

The analytic process is likely to be based on a grounded approach; alternatively the researcher may have developed or adopted a conceptual framework which he/she wishes to test in the field. Grounded theory assumes, on the whole, that the researcher abandons preconceptions and, through the process of analysis, builds up an explanatory framework through conceptualization of the data. Thus there emerge categories of behaviour, contexts and types of outcomes associated with the particularities of the context and the strategies adopted for dealing with it. The evidence of patterns of categorical behaviours builds up within a transcript and also in the body of transcripts to enable a theory to be developed. Only after the accumulation of a considerable body of material can the theory move from the substantive to the level of a formal theory. An extant conceptual framework, on the other hand, suggests a set of preconceived categories – a coding frame – for which evidence may be sought in the data. Such a framework may be not only tested but also extended using the CIT methodology.

The unit of analysis may be the individual, the group or the team, but the CIT allows for the focus to shift, for example, to the organization, the industrial sector or the location – region or community, country or nation. Thus, for example, one may explore overarching concepts like 'climate', 'culture', 'style', etc. by examining the categorical data across the sample as a whole.

The research project has a set of aims and objectives from which a set of central themes is deduced. For example, if the central theme is *business development*, then the coding technique works by first identifying the central idea, in this case business development. This forms the core category. The link between the core category and its subcategories is by means of relational concepts: the conditions in which the action took place, the strategies adopted for dealing with the phenomenon, and the outcomes of the action. The conditions which obtain may be, for example, the need to establish a client base, or to firm up relations with suppliers, or, as in the case which ensues, to strengthen the top management team. The next question (in the coder's mind) is: what strategy did the interviewee adopt in order to achieve the desired outcome? The case shows that the interviewee's initial strategy was to take on a business partner. The CIT enables the coder to examine how this was handled and what the outcome was.

To examine how this was handled is to identify *what events took place*. Thus the condition or critical event identified by the coder in the case to follow is: setting up a business partnership. Further analysis seeks to identify what the *properties* of this event were. In the case in point these might be the quality of the relationship, the individual's performance, the change in business fortunes, etc. The question arises as to how much detail is needed; the answer to this question will clearly depend upon the aims and objectives of the project. However, a further level of detail where required is to examine the dimensions of properties. Thus, a relationship may be categorized as close or distant, fun or miserable, firm or fickle, etc.; the individual's performance as effective or ineffective, persistent, insightful or whatever; the business performance as declining, expanding, rejuvenating, plateauing, etc.

Each event also adds evidence in relation to the central theme. In each case, the business development theme raises the question of *how* the incumbent conducts his/her business. The categories which might suggest themselves are, for example, naively, deviously, opportunistically, etc. Thus the subcategories may code at a level of considerable detail.

Case study: a business owner's account of incidents impacting his business activities, their consequences for his family and subsequent business behaviour

Aims

The aims of the project were broadly to focus upon the internal dynamics of microbusiness households and to examine the interaction between business and family, with particular reference to entrepreneurial behaviour.

Method

The fieldwork was conducted in two contrasting economic environments: a prosperous location, Milton Keynes; and a non-prosperous location, Newcastle upon Tyne. All the businesses were in the business services sector and employed between none and nine employees. The sampling frame was compiled from multiple sources and access was gained by an initial telephone interview which enabled the researcher to establish a profile of the business including some demographics associated with the business owner. A detailed semi-structured interview was conducted with 102 business owners from which a subset were interviewed further using the CIT. This yielded a rich data set with considerable detail of the type of critical incidents which were impacting both the development of the microbusiness and where appropriate its consequences for the household. The case being considered here shows starkly how a set of critical incidents could have a devastating effect on both business and family. The CIT was conducted at the family home where the business owner also located his business. Both the business owner and his wife (who worked part time in the business in very much a supportive capacity) were present at the interview, and both responded to the interviewer's questions.

Background to the case study

Prior to setting up his present microbusiness in the business service sector, 'Bernard' owned three businesses employing up to 50 people. All three businesses were in the service sector but were unrelated. The events which unfolded in 1991 were dramatic and in every sense critical both to the demise of those concerns and to the establishment, structure and size of the current microbusiness. Although this is a complex case in which much of the detail has had to be omitted, it illustrates how the critical incident technique may be used to reveal the particular construction placed on events by the incumbents, how they handled those incidents and what the consequences were. In other words the CIT enables one to understand the context of action, the tactics, strategies and coping mechanisms adopted, and the outcomes, results or consequences of people's actions, and the new situation with which they are faced. In this case, the discussion is presented from the business owner's perspective of a series of negative incidents which impacted upon his business activities (and indeed his domestic and personal life).

The critical incidents which 'Bernard' identified were: (a) bringing in a business partner who operated at the wrong level, was unable to settle in and was unable to relate to the 'husband and wife team'; (b) taking up a leasehold property from '[a] landlord [who] was actually a crook'; (c) a fraud which resulted in loss of turnover from one business and the dismissal of seven staff; and (d) the asset stripping and loss of the business at the hands of a less than honest solicitor. In describing these critical incidents Bernard also highlighted other associated problems.

Focusing the interview initially

Essentially the interviewer had little difficulty in focusing this interview and, after a very short preamble, established a chronology of events from which ensued an account of the first critical incident.

Initially the interviewer reintroduced herself (a semi-structured interview had already taken place some six months previously) and she briefly explained the purpose of this interview. She then asked the interviewees if they would give an account of the development of the business over the preceding five years, focusing upon anything that had happened which they believed changed the fortunes of the business for either good or ill.

To aid this process, the interviewer presented the interviewee with an A4 card containing a double arrow-headed line running centrally along its length. She suggested that they regard this arrowed line as representing the preceding five years. She then asked them to mark along its length the significant events which had occurred in the order in which they had occurred. The events were named (i.e. labelled) as far as possible on the card, and thus a brief account of the chronology of what took place was presented.

This is an important first stage because the interviewer must be absolutely clear in her mind what in general terms has happened, and in what sequence. Thus the interviewer sought clarification of the respondents until she was clear, and then asked the interviewees to select and name three of the incidents for more detailed discussion.

Controlling the interview thereafter

The speech of the interviewees was recorded in detail and punctuated occasionally by probes which refocused the attention. For example,

Was this on the leisure consultancy side?

What was the situation with your (business) partner at this time?

Are those figures the turnover figures?

Are we about 1992 now?

The interviewer continued to use probes related on the one hand to the details of the situation being described, and on the other to the central theme (business development) being discussed. For example,

So you're not a gambler?

Do you want to make a lot of money?

So all these ideas and the running of your business – what's it all for?

About halfway through the interview, evidence that a relaxed relationship of trust had been established was shown in this quip by the interviewer: 'So, what do you do when you're not working – apart from cutting the grass and hitting Bill?' (The business owner had by now described in graphic detail his frustrations with his former business partner whom the couple blamed by and large for the demise of the previous business.) Laughter ensued and the interview continued.

Concluding the interview and taking care of ethical issues

Towards the latter stages of the interview, the discussion broadened out, and refocused briefly on the present business which was run from a shed at the bottom of the garden. Owing to his (indeed the whole family's) dire experiences during the failure of the previous business, this new business was set up using the latest technology and avoided as far as possible dependence on others, be they business partners, landlords or 'bent' solicitors. The interview was concluded in this particular case on a light-hearted note and discussion of the location of each person's (including the interviewer's) place of birth!

The key ethical issues that the interviewer had to concern herself with were ensuring that the couple, the business partner and other details of their case were sufficiently well disguised to assure anonymity. In the project as a whole the question of whether the business owner or the couple should be interviewed together or separately, or indeed whether to interview only the business owner and not include the spouse, was addressed.[1] It was decided that where a spouse was involved in the business in some capacity, then on balance it was better to include them and to interview jointly. In the case being presented, it was judged appropriate to interview both spouses together. Indeed, although the daughter was not present, her feelings were discussed in the course of the interview as being relevant to the judgement to restructure business activities in such a way as to minimize the impact on the family.

Detailed examination of the incidents

Partnership and fraud

Bernard and Bill had worked together before but not as business partners. The actual setting up of the business partnership was bungled by a reputable, well known firm of accountants. Bill's performance in the business quickly came under question as 'we got graphs coming out of our ears in terms of performance . . . which means absolutely nothing, if you don't get the business in.' Bill wished to switch his attention from one of the businesses to another. Turnover had dropped and Bill was offered a managing directorship with another company. 'So now he was leaving the ship, sort of thing.' He was given a two year contract with the company and he then

> decided he would do a management buy-out . . . Up until then he'd felt rather guilty about the state he'd left us in and we were really backs against the wall. And he then came on the phone drunk at night wanting the remainder of his money. But we'd paid him back and starved ourselves of cash . . . and the next thing that occurred . . . we think [was that] he'd been to bed with the manageress and as a result of that seven of them were involved in fraud . . . we had the police in . . . but they couldn't prove who'd actually done it . . . The result was seven members of staff left, and we lost two and a half thousand pounds worth of turnover . . . So now we'd got losses [in all three businesses] . . . that's when the home pressure was at its most . . . we started to look at the options [with our accountants] and clearly one of the options was to bin it. Er, but you're very reluctant to do it cos it's like chopping your arm off, in a way, it's still painful.

It is not difficult to discern in this brief abstract the different types of information which are given in the course of the interview: contextual and tactical information and outcomes are all apparent. So too is affective information. Occasionally, of course, what might appear as context could also be construed as an outcome. For example, the initial discussion above in respect of Bill's involvement in the business was interpreted as contextual information; it elucidates Bill's decision to join another business which developed into the disastrous attempt to defraud the company. The outcome of this incident was the dismissal of seven staff, a loss of turnover and the undermining of Bernard's business affairs.

Landlord, accountant and solicitor

In the midst of this crisis the renegotiation of rental on the leasehold of a property in village Y blew up. After 18 months, the landlord

> sacked his solicitor and the next thing was he fabricated an invoice and faxed us at half past four on a Friday afternoon . . . We either pay seventeen and a half grand tomorrow . . . or he's going to put the bailiffs in . . . We had a conflict of interests with our accountants . . . so we decided you know almost on the spur of the moment to go for [a solicitor] down in X-town . . . He was up in twenty minutes . . . He arrived on the scene, said don't worry about it . . . I'll teach this landlord a lesson . . . What you need to do is tomorrow morning be at the court in X-town . . . Incidentally, what's in the company? . . . We suddenly you know sort of sat there and said we wished we'd done this before, just such a relief that you know someone is helping us . . . We got down to the court, and just before going in I said, look Mr Black, you still haven't told me how much this is going to cost me. And he said, well you'll just have to trust me, won't you? And as soon as he said that I thought, God I've been had. So he said, well you can walk away if you like . . . well I mean I couldn't do that . . . and cutting a long story short, basically he robbed us of the company . . . He took *x* thousand pounds out in fees, he flogged the company to his mate, asset stripped it and they're now trading, and we got nothing . . . He screwed the paperwork up, didn't serve notice on the landlord . . . He cleared off to Australia for his holidays. The bailiffs came up . . . the landlord broke in with two heavies . . . So emotionally it was like devastating.

Bernard complained to the Institute of Chartered Accountants and also got his MP involved but to no avail.

> So, you can imagine what that was like, to deal with that, and there's a lot of bitterness, resentment, anger that comes out of that . . . [It] was like three years ago now . . . [Mary's attitude was] good riddance. My attitude is – this is wrong . . . Now I feel impotent that I can't deal with this.

This second set of incidents is presented largely in the interviewees' own words. It commences with an account of the situation facing them (context) and then proceeds to the tactics adopted by the couple in an attempt to manage their affairs ('so we decided . . .'). Interspersed throughout the account of what happened next is a description of their feelings, followed by a statement of the outcome of the incident. Next, an account of what happened further is given, again followed by an outline of Bernard's tactics (he complained to the Institute of Chartered Accountants). This is finally rounded off by an indication of further outcomes including attendant feelings: 'now I feel impotent'.

During the course of these revelations, the interviewer probed in order to seek clarification. The interviewees were forthcoming throughout. In many cases, however, the interviewer would need to probe rather more by following up leads and asking more questions. In the next excerpt of the CIT interview, the flow is much more interactive, with the interviewer checking out her understanding, and posing questions in order to clarify.

Controlling the interview

Once the overall story had been given, the interviewer probed for the additional information and reflections of the interviewees. In this excerpt, Bernard discusses the effect on the family (his wife Joan and young child) and then he reflects on the 'cause' of the problem – Bill, who had put the business into jeopardy.

> *Interviewer*: Do you blame it on him or . . .?
> *Bernard*: No, cos I blame myself.
> *Interviewer*: Was he partly responsible?
> *Bernard*: We could have coped with him, we could have coped with the fraud, no problem, we could have coped with them together. What we couldn't cope with was the lot. We couldn't cope with him, the fraud, the leasehold property deal, that's what brought us down, it was a combination of all those things.

Bernard reflected further on the effect that these incidents had had on him, for example, how he'd lost respect for institutions and other systems of authority and how his attitude and feelings in respect of the new business start-up had changed. After two years his enthusiasm was returning.

> *Joan*: It was quite amazing how one's mistakes have such knock-on effects, that was the frightening thing.
> *Interviewer*: What was the mistake?
> *Joan*: Bill.
> *Interviewer*: Did you have any doubts about Bill?
> *Joan*: No . . . I thought Bernard was getting a bit bored . . . and wanted to do something else. And I just don't have the same drive and I actually thought Bill would be the motivational tool . . . we knew the downside but we didn't look at that – but you don't when you're on the crest of a wave.
> *Interviewer*: Was it because of Bill that you took the leasehold in Village Y?
> *Bernard*: Yeh, it was his plan . . . which I swallowed, stupidly, you know.
> *Interviewer*: So how do you cope with stress?

Bernard then described help that he got over a period of eight months from a reflexologist.

> *Bernard*: It was almost like physical venom. It was almost like being sick. It sounds awful, but it was almost solid, and I felt this terrific badness . . . coming out, and at the end of it she said, now think of something nice. And I did . . . so she helped me enormously.
> *Joan*: You went and thumped Bill and that helped as well didn't it?

Bernard actually described this event in detail and how the family all felt about it. The interviewer asked: 'Did it make you feel better?' The answer was in the affirmative from both spouses.

Discussion

The above excerpts from a transcripted interview with a business owner and his wife are heavily edited. In describing in vivid detail four critical incidents which impacted his business undertakings the respondent painted a context out of which arose his present business – a microbusiness which he runs from his garage at home. His motivation to develop that business to the size of his previous business undertakings had been dashed, and he has operated with extreme caution when it was a question of with whom he would do deals. It became clear in the second part of the interview (not reported here) that Bernard as a person had all the characteristics of a highly entrepreneurial individual (Chell et al., 1991) and it was possible to construct a coherent explanation as to why such an individual was operating on such a small scale.

Reading through the 40 page transcript, one has to disentangle the chronology of events, as the respondent has not (and is unlikely to) recount in a neatly packaged form each critical incident. In the case in question they overlapped in time and, as the respondent points out himself, it was having to cope with all four that eventually brought them and the businesses down. In analysing these incidents, it is important to note the type of incident. They were: a problem with the business partner, rental of a leasehold property, fraud perpetrated by employees, and a dishonest solicitor. This finding can be extended by asking: are such incidents typical of the development activities of microbusinesses in the business services sector? We have detailed critical incidents for 33 other cases and so are able to answer that question.

A further useful observation is the timescale and duration of the incidents, in other words, over how long a period the events took place. In general the longer the period the more lasting the effect. In the case described above, it was over a two year period. Being unable to get along with one's business partner is not untypical. As with a marriage, severing the ties may be difficult, and it is during the period of separation that the real damage is done. The business partner Bill, we are told, did not fit in, became aggressive and is alleged to have become involved in fraud. Whilst we have not got the whole story (nor could we have!) we have sufficient detail of the nature of these incidents to be confident about their detrimental effect upon the business. Both spouses appeared to be taken in by Bill, believing him to be a useful addition who would give a growth spurt to at least one of the businesses. What we do not know is how Bernard handled Bill, or indeed if he was frozen out of this close-knit husband and wife team. We have evidence from other cases with such a team that exclusion can occur.

The incident over the leasehold and the 'crooked landlord' appeared on the face of it to be sheer bad luck. But was it? Bernard's eight year old daughter had said, 'Daddy, why do you deal with these people?', and he commented at one point, 'you make your own work.' In other words, people create their own luck; they can create a situation which increases the probability of a particular outcome. In this case, by associating with people who tended towards dishonesty (even in the professions) the likelihood of one of them 'doing him' was thereby increased. As a consequence of this glimmer of self-awareness Bernard changed his lifestyle, his business activity and his friends. Other outcomes of this case were that Bernard addressed the issue of the impact that such events were having on his family – his wife and his daughter as individuals. He set up a much smaller scale operation which relied less on other people and rather more on new technology. He and his wife increased their leisure and holiday activities and time spent at home.

Advantages and disadvantages of the method

This method enables a focused discussion around issues which are under investigation. Further it facilitates the revelation of those issues which are of critical importance to the interviewee. This was evident in the above case where the central theme was business development, with the incidents which unfolded showing a strong negative relationship to the development of the business. The actual incidents could not have been anticipated; the choice of what incidents to recount is under the control of the interviewee, although the skilled interviewer will attempt to ensure that there is a thorough coverage of actual incidents, with the interviewee then being required to select the incidents which he or she deems to have been the most important.

The CIT has the further advantage that it enables the issues to be viewed in context and is also a rich source of information on the conscious reflections of the incumbent, their frame of reference, feelings, attitudes and perspective on matters which are of critical importance to them. Bernard, for example, recounted how they were cheated of their company and what that felt like. Both he and his wife were able to put the incidents in perspective, for example, as they contemplated the 'knock-on effects' of the various incidents: how 'frightening' this all was. The information revealed from the CIT interviews enables a fine-grained analysis and detailed explanation of the behaviour of the incumbent and the outcomes of behavioural and managerial processes. Whilst other methods (such as the interview) may also enable the researcher to achieve this, the advantage of the CIT is that the linkage between context, strategy and outcomes is more readily teased out because the technique is focused on an event which is explicated in relation to what happened, why it happened, how it was handled and what the consequences were. An unstructured interview does not require the respondent to focus in this way.

Whilst phenomenology assumes the uniqueness of individual consciousness, the CIT enables the researcher to gain insights both into particular cases and across a sample of cases. For example, if the subset of cases is self-employed women with children, single parents, business owners at start-up, etc. then what are the typical issues which are raised by the particular subset? Is there a common set of problems? What do they need to know in order to be able to handle those problems? And so on. In the case study outlined above, the questions arise: are problems with business partners typical or rare? Do problems with other relationships typically occur, for example with subordinates?

Even where an extant conceptual framework is adopted, there is scope not only to test but to extend theory. Thus the CIT enables inductive theory development by adopting a grounded theory approach (Strauss and Corbin, 1990).

Finally, the CIT is particularly useful for comparative work. Case studies may be built up of specifiable organizational contexts, critical incidents, the strategies adopted to handle them and the outcomes. This compares with clinical work in the sense that whilst cases are examined individually, patterns of behaviour may be discernible which may inform theory, policy and practice. It can, however, be used where there is more than one interviewee, as was true in the above case study.

There are some aspects which may be construed as disadvantages. For example, the fieldwork is both expensive and time consuming, as is the coding and analysis of the transcripted material. There are confidentiality issues which must be respected, as respondents may name other people and/or their businesses concerns, putting them in a light which may constitute slander, or in some cases hint at criminal activity. (This was very evident in the case study.) In such cases a strict code of ethics and a procedure for handling tape-recorded and transcripted material are essential in order to protect all parties and the integrity of the research process.

The security of individual researchers is a consideration where the interview is to be carried out at the interviewee's home or in a context or location where common sense would suggest caution.

A view may be taken that research which is not based on large quantitative sample surveys is insufficiently generalizable to be of value in the creation of management/organizational knowledge for academic or policy purposes. This view is being challenged by qualitative researchers. The heterogeneity of populations of business organizations and of their owner-managers suggests that smaller samples tightly controlled for size, structural and other relevant dimensions are likely to have greater explanatory power than could be revealed by a large scale survey, although of course the latter may be useful for some purposes. In management and organizational behaviour/psychology, understanding the detail of the processes and behaviours is paramount and a technique such as the CIT enables such an objective to be accomplished.

The CIT interview is not easy to conduct well. It requires a skilled and mature researcher who can manage the respondent, directing the interview to achieve clarity of understanding, and who can handle the expression of emotion including distress. Of course not all respondents will reveal negative incidents and here the interviewer must be able to probe sensitively and not be carried away by the wave of success which the respondent may be putting across. In other words the interviewer must try not to allow himself or herself to be treated as an 'audience' but under all circumstances must try to establish a rapport of trust, honest and open exchange, and equality. In the above case study, the interviewer probed with relevant questions, (a) to ensure her understanding, and (b) to ensure that the account did not become a monologue. Thus the interaction between interviewer and interviewee is important in the CIT; the interviewer can help control the pace, add light relief and steer the interview so that it remains focused.

A further difficulty of conducting the interview well is attempting to ensure that all the critical incidents have been captured. Clearly in an inductive situation, whether they have or not cannot be 'proved'. Techniques such as the arrow diagram help assure this part of the process. However, critics evaluating this method might argue further that it is difficult if not impossible to test for reliability. There are several things which can be done in order to improve reliability. For example, the possibility of conducting more than one interview with the subject should always be considered. Time, budget and access considerations are likely constraints. The key issue is whether additional interviews are likely to improve reliability and whether they should be conducted under the same circumstances. Would it be desirable (that is, improve the quality of the research outcomes) were the same incidents to be discussed with a 'relevant other'? Clearly the answer to this question is a matter of judgement according to the particular issues and circumstances. It may well raise some ethical issues. For example, it is likely to be resisted by an employer in relation to an employee, and spouses in relation to each other. However, the point is that one is trying not to find a 'single truth' but to understand the respondent's perspectives and actions which affected specifiable outcomes. The reliability therefore is largely built into a quality interview process in which there is coherence. It may still be thought desirable to triangulate the results of the CIT with other sources of data, particularly where there may be tangible evidence (for example, as in the case of business growth or demise).

Concluding remarks

The creation of management knowledge relied upon the scientific method for the earlier part of this century. Phenomenology was considered to be an approach associated with esoteric areas of sociological or cultural anthropological enquiry (Burrell and Morgan, 1979). Now management researchers recognize the need to identify and explain processes which go on within organizations and result in particular kinds of outcome. There is no textbook answer to what is a dynamic process and real life is messy; the people immersed in those situations and circumstances are trying to make sense of their reality. Their accounts are partial; but partial or not, biased or not, such accounts constitute *their* reality, and arguably it is the way they view the world which shapes their future actions. How, if those closest to the events have only a partial view which they may not have clearly articulated, can we as researchers hope to collect valid data by use of extensive survey techniques? How can we hope to gain a genuine understanding of the persons involved in an organizational drama if we do not know anything of the context, that is, where they are coming from? The case of Bernard illustrates graphically this point. The CIT enabled us to focus upon those incidents which from his perspective were critical in the demise of his previous businesses and which were shaping his present strategy not only in the development of a new business but in relation to his private life, that is his family and domestic situation. Had we not known about his previous business undertakings and the circumstances surrounding their unfortunate demise we would not be able to understand him and his present business activity.

Critics question the reliability and the validity of research carried out using qualitative techniques. Some have even been known to question the integrity of qualitative researchers: 'How do we know that they haven't made it up?' Such a criticism misses the point. The point is that the qualitative researcher can only present an interpretation of the events recounted to them. The worth of this approach is that it yields genuine insights into the processes which shape behaviour, and as a coherent account it makes sense, that is, it has face validity. Furthermore, the integrity of research is maintained by either permitting public access or disseminating sufficiently widely, so enabling wider public debate and critical appraisal.

The advantage of adopting the critical incident technique is that this technique permits a degree of replication. Whilst the individual firm's circumstances may be unique, the type of incident and the context, strategy and outcomes as a pattern of related activities may in general terms be apparent in other businesses. The method enables the development of case based theory grounded in actual critical events which shape future actions. The insights gleaned and the conclusions drawn facilitate the development not only of theory but also of policy. In combination with the application of grounded theory (Strauss and Corbin, 1990) and NU•DIST – the software designed for the handling of coded, qualitative data (Richards and Richards, 1991) – the critical incident technique is capable of extending our theoretical understanding and our ability to explain organizational behaviour.

Notes

The case study material was collected and developed from a research project funded by the Economic and Social Research Council (ESRC) grant no. R00234402. I would like to acknowledge the particular assistance of Dr Sue Baines and Dr Alison Abrams for their part in the data collection process and subsequent discussion of the particularities of the case.

1   The sample of business owners included: sole female; sole male; husband and wife; joint male; joint female; and joint non-related male and female.

References

Bryman, A. (1989) *Research Methods and Organization Studies*. London and New York: Routledge.

Burrell, G. and Morgan, G. (1979) *Sociological Paradigms and Organizational Analysis*. London: Heinemann.

Butler, J.K. (1991) 'Toward understanding and measuring conditions of trust: evolution of a conditions of trust inventory', *Journal of Management*, 17: 643–63.

Cassell, C. and Symon, G. (1994) 'Qualitative research in work contexts', in C. Cassell and G. Symon (eds), *Qualitative Methods in Organizational Research: A Practical Guide*. London: Sage. pp. 1–13.

Chell, E. and Adam, E. (1994a) 'Exploring the cultural orientation of entrepreneurship: conceptual and methodological issues'. Discussion Paper 94–7, School of Business Management, University of Newcastle upon Tyne.

Chell, E. and Adam, E. (1994b) 'Researching culture and entrepreneurship: a qualitative approach'. Discussion Paper 94–9, School of Business Management, University of Newcastle upon Tyne.

Chell, E. and Adam, E. (1995) 'Entrepreneurship and culture in New Zealand'. Discussion Paper 95–8, Department of Management Studies, University of Newcastle upon Tyne.

Chell, E., Haworth, J.M. and Brearley, S. (1991) *The Entrepreneurial Personality: Concepts, Cases and Categories*. London: Routledge.

Flanagan, J.C. (1954) 'The critical incident technique', *Psychological Bulletin*, 51 (4): 327–58.

Glaser, B. and Strauss, A. (1967) *The Discovery of Grounded Theory*. Chicago: Aldine.

Haworth, J.M., Brearley, S. and Chell, E. (1991) 'A typology of business owners and their firms using neural networks', *Entrepreneurship and Regional Development*, 33 (3): 221–35.

McClelland, D.C. (1976) *A Guide to Job Competency Assessment*. Boston: McBer.

McClelland, D.C. (1987) 'Characteristics of successful entrepreneurs', *Journal of Creative Behavior*, 21 (3): 219–33.

Morgan, G. and Smircich, L. (1980) 'The case for qualitative research', *Academy of Management Review*, 5 (4): 491–500.

Richards, L. and Richards, T. (1991) 'The transformation of qualitative method: computational paradigms and research processes', in N.G. Fielding and R.M. Lee (eds), *Using Computers in Qualitative Research*. London: Sage.

Spencer, L.M. (1983) *Soft Skill Competencies*. Scottish Council for Research in Education.

Strauss, A. and Corbin, J. (1990) *Basics of Qualitative Research: Grounded Theory Procedures and Techniques*. London: Sage.

Wheelock, J. and Chell, E. (1996) *The Business-owner Managed Family Unit: An Inter-Regional Comparison of Behavioural Dynamics*. Ref. No. R000234402. London: Economic and Social Research Council.

5 Attributional Coding

Jo Silvester

Although attribution theory has proven popular among organizational researchers, one might be surprised to find it described in a book concerned with qualitative methods. Of the many studies which have explored the influence of attributions on organizational behaviours, including sales performance and employee turnover (Corr and Gray, 1996; Seligman and Schulman, 1986), job satisfaction and commitment (Furnham et al., 1994), job seeking behaviour (Prussia et al., 1993) and attributions for subordinate performance (Kipnis et al., 1981; Knowlton and Mitchell, 1980), most, if not all, have employed quantitative methods. It has generally been assumed that attributions are internal and essentially private cognitions which require methods such as questionnaires, behavioural vignettes and hypothetical or laboratory simulations in order to render them open to investigation. Unfortunately, an important consequence of this has been that little attention has been paid to the 'public' or spoken attributions that are produced when people share their understanding of the causes of important events with one another.

The aim of this chapter is to discuss a method known as 'attributional coding'. This method enables the researcher to extract, code and thereby analyse patterns of public attributions, defined here as attributions communicated through either discourse (e.g. conversations, team meetings, speeches) or written material (e.g. company reports, letters, e-mail). Attributional coding is unusual in that it is a method which can be used in qualitative or quantitative research depending upon the theoretical perspective and objectives of the researcher. Qualitative material can be coded using a prespecified coding frame in a way which permits statistical analysis and consequently comparison across groups. Alternatively, researchers can choose to focus upon the content of the attributions which are extracted and explore the unique ways in which different individuals explain why particular events have occurred. In this chapter I have chosen to focus upon some material from my own research into candidates' impression management during selection interviews as a means to illustrate how attributional coding can be used. Consequently, my emphasis will be on use of the prespecified coding system and the identification of common patterns of attributions typical of successful and unsuccessful candidates.

Background to attributional coding

Attribution theory concerns the everyday causal explanations that people produce when they encounter novel, important, unusual or potentially threatening behaviour and events (Baucom, 1987; Weiner, 1985; Wong and Weiner, 1981). According to attribution theorists, people are motivated to identify the causes of such events, because by doing so they render their environment more predictable and potentially more controllable (Heider, 1958). Organizational researchers have been especially interested in attributional 'sense-making' because the way in which an individual explains an event can have a powerful influence upon how that person chooses to respond (Fincham and Jaspars, 1979). For example, when a sales person attributes their failure to secure a sale to the choice of a wrong sales strategy (an internal controllable cause) they are less likely to become demotivated or experience lowered self-esteem because they believe that they are capable of changing their behaviour and achieving a more successful outcome in future (Sujan, 1986). However, the sales person who attributes failure to lack of ability (an internal uncontrollable cause) or their client's lack of interest (external uncontrollable cause) may be less motivated to strive for future success because they perceive themselves less able to influence sales outcomes.

Particular attention has been paid by attribution researchers to individual differences in the way people typically explain outcomes. Such differences are known generally as 'attributional style' and are seen by many as representing a cognitive personality trait (Furnham et al., 1994; Peterson and Seligman, 1984). The most common means for exploring attributional style has been the questionnaire, for example, the Attributional Style Questionnaire (ASQ: Peterson et al., 1982) and the Occupational Attributional Style Questionnaire (OASQ: Furnham et al., 1992). Both questionnaires require subjects to consider a series of hypothetical positive events (e.g. 'you secured the promotion you were looking for') and hypothetical negative events (e.g. 'your presentation went badly'), identify a possible cause for each event and then rate that cause on a number of causal dimensions. Another popular approach has been to use behavioural vignettes describing a particular outcome where subjects are required to 'guess' possible causes. Similarly, role-play situations have required individuals to rate possible causes for their own and their partner's behaviour along a number of causal dimensions.

From a research perspective there are clear advantages to using questionnaires and vignettes: they are easy to administer and analyse, and they are consistent across subjects. Yet they also have important limitations which are frequently, and somewhat conveniently, 'overlooked' by researchers in their search for rigorous psychometric properties. For example, by using hypothetical events attention is focused on examples which the experimenter rather than the individual considers meaningful or important.

Moreover, events are frequently presented as isolated incidents which lack the additional contextual information one might expect to be present when an event is witnessed directly. Finally, the experimental 'subject' has little or no freedom to negotiate the meaning or relevance of the attribution with the researcher (Antaki, 1994).

Increasingly, however, attributional activity is being recognized as a 'social' and not just a private phenomenon (Doise, 1980; Wells, 1981) and consequently more attention is being paid to causal attributions produced spontaneously during communication. It would appear that individuals not only are motivated to 'make sense' of their world for their own private understanding and mastery of the environment (Kelley, 1973), but also need to share this understanding if they are to interact effectively and cooperate successfully with others. According to Snyder and Higgins (1988), individuals 'negotiate a shared reality' through conversation which enables them to understand the causes of events from the perspective of others. Furthermore, by listening to the causal attributions made by other people, those who have not witnessed an event can adopt attributions 'second hand'. Wells (1981) describes these as 'social attributions' and anyone who has taken part in organizational gossip should appreciate the prevalence of this form of attributional activity!

In recognizing that attributions occur regularly and frequently in everyday conversation, particularly when people discuss events which are unusual, important and mutually relevant (Antaki, 1988; 1994; Harvey et al., 1988; Wong and Weiner, 1981; Weiner, 1985), a number of areas which have traditionally escaped investigation are now open to more detailed exploration using the appropriate methodology. These include discourse and 'sense-making' during team meetings and appraisal situations, interpersonal decisions in selection interviews, and dialogue with customers or even letters to shareholders presented in organizations' annual reports.

Description of the method

A limited number of methods now exist for exploring public or spoken attributions, for example the 'content analysis of verbatim explanations' (CAVE: Schulman et al., 1989). However, this chapter focuses on a modified version of the Leeds Attributional Coding System (LACS: Stratton et al., 1988), a system which has a number of potential advantages over other similar methods, among them a more extensive coding framework. The LACS is also unusual in that rather than focusing simply upon a speaker's attributions for outcomes involving themselves, it enables researchers to explore attributions made by one person, but which concern the behaviour or actions of other people. The LACS was originally designed as an ecologically valid and less intrusive method for analysing the attributions produced by family members during therapy sessions (Munton and

Antaki, 1988). It has since been used in a variety of clinical (e.g. Brewin et al., 1991; Joseph et al., 1993; Silvester et al., 1995) and non-clinical contexts (e.g. Silvester, 1997; Silvester et al., 1997). I first became involved with attributional coding 10 years ago when I used it as part of my PhD to explore attributions made by abusive parents. At that time I was interested in whether attributions spoken by abusive parents *during* diagnostic family therapy sessions influenced therapists' decisions regarding prognosis for rehabilitation (see Silvester et al., 1995). This led to a later interest in candidates' attributions during selection interviews and interviewers' selection decisions. It is probably fair to say that my original approach to attributional coding was from a quantitative rather than a qualitative perspective. I was interested in using the method as a more ecologically valid 'questionnaire' with the aim of identifying universal patterns of attributions associated with particular groups and behaviours. My assumptions were that spoken attributions simply reflect internal cognitions: a view which is common to many attribution researchers, but which has recently been criticized by Edwards and Potter (1993). However, the experience of using attributional coding has certainly led me to question a number of these assumptions. Consequently, whilst the method can be used to support a more positivistic research approach, I would argue that an important advantage of attributional coding is the way in which it highlights the complex and dynamic way that people manipulate public attributions in order to convey particular impressions.

In many ways the selection interview is an ideal situation for exploring public attributions. Not only do candidates enter interviews assuming that they have to justify why they are suited to the job, but interviewers frequently ask candidates why they have acted in a particular way, or why they have applied to that company, in order to predict how the candidate might react in future work situations. Although there has been a tremendous amount of research concerned with the selection interview, I was especially surprised by two factors on first becoming interested in the area. First, virtually no research has looked in detail at what candidates actually *say* during interviews (Harris, 1989). Second, very few studies have used *real* selection interviews as opposed to simulated role-play scenarios. Given the difficulties facing the researcher who wishes to access and audio-tape selection interviews, this may not be so surprising, but it does leave an important gap in our knowledge of the selection process. Attributional coding is especially suited to analysing this type of material and in the next section I will explain the method using material from an ongoing investigation of graduate recruitment interviews in a multinational oil company. My main objective in conducting this research has been to follow up on an earlier investigation (Silvester, 1997) which found that candidates who made particular types of attributions during selection interviews (stable, personal and controllable for negative outcomes) were more likely to be rated favourably by interviewers in graduate recruitment interviews. The intention is to replicate these findings using a larger sample from a single company. In

Table 5.1   *Stages of attributional coding*

1   Identify source of attributions
2   Extract attributions
3   Identify agent and target
4   Code attributions on causal dimensions
5   Analysis

addition I am interested in exploring the questioning strategies adopted by interviewers given certain earlier indications that interviewers ask different types of questions of female and male candidates (Silvester, 1996). It is possible that the types of questions asked impact upon the types of attributions that candidates make. However, for simplicity, and because interviewers tend to keep their own attributions private and unspoken during interviews, I will concentrate on candidate rather than interviewer attributions in this chapter.

The five stages to attributional coding as defined by the LACS are illustrated in Table 5.1.

Identify source of attributions

Attributional coding focuses on the *exchange* of public attributions, extracted either from transcripts of discourse or from material already in written form. Any discourse which can be audio-taped and transcribed, such as a speech by a chief executive officer, team meetings, semi-structured research interviews (see King, 1994), or written archival material including annual reports or letters to shareholders (see Forster, 1994), can therefore be used as a potential source of attributions. However, whilst attributions are usually present in most types of material, certain sources may not be as rich as others. In my experience technical descriptions or selection interviews where factual or problem solving answers are requested tend to generate fewer attributions than material where individuals discuss important events (e.g. performance down-turn of an organization or group, failure to pass an exam) or justify decisions and behaviour (e.g. promoting one individual and not another, choosing to study abroad). The least rich source of attributions I have encountered proved to be written archive material and the most rich an interview with a sales director who generated a total of 350 attributions in one hour! Typically, semi-structured research interviews will generate one or two attributions per minute. In a 30 minute selection interview candidates can produce between 40 and 100 attributional statements, depending upon how much interviewers talk themselves (Silvester, 1997).

Negotiating permission to audio-tape interviews or other discourse material can in itself prove a challenge to the researcher (Silvester, 1996). In previous research I have had to approach several different organizations in order to gain access to just one or two for the final study. Of course, permission is likely to depend upon the sensitivity of the material being recorded as well as the context from which it is generated. The selection interview is a situation where it is unfair to audio-tape unless permission has been obtained from candidates in advance. Although in my experience the most reticent participants have been the interviewers, who are unwilling to have their interviews subjected to scrutiny! For these interviews, I have usually left the tape recorder with the company and relied upon interviewers to record the interviews themselves. Tapes have then been passed to me for analysis while interview report forms and other material such as candidate application forms are held by the company until after analysis has been completed.

Extract attributions

In the second stage attributions are extracted from verbatim transcripts of the material. Although attributions can be extracted by 'ear' simply by listening to audio-tapes of, for example, interviews (less time-consuming and costly), this can lead to a reduction in reliability and makes it difficult for coders to use the additional contextual information which is present in a transcript. Obviously the definition of a causal attribution is important. In their study of spontaneous attributions produced by survivors of the *Herald of Free Enterprise* disaster, Joseph et al. defined causal attributions as 'statements identifying a factor or factors that contribute to a given outcome' and where 'a stated or implied causal relationship has to be present' (1993: 249). An attribution is therefore defined as a statement which refers to a causal relationship where the speaker implies that a specific outcome (e.g. 'I got the job') is a consequence of a particular cause (e.g. 'because I had friends in that company'). In general, the LACS makes no distinction between reasons, justifications, causal accounts or hypothetical outcomes, although it would be possible to include a coding category which allows the researcher to differentiate between these. Finally, it is very important to remember that attributions are extracted and coded from the speaker's perspective. There-fore, although the attribution need not be one with which the coder agrees (e.g. 'I got the job, because I'm the best candidate they'll ever see'), all attributions made by the speaker, whether highly unlikely or even considered 'wrong' by the researcher, are extracted for later coding.

It takes a little practice to identify attributions quickly and reliably. Some attributions are more obvious than others and many will include a causal connective such as 'because', 'so', 'therefore', 'as a result'. But, there will also be causal attributions where the link is implied rather than stated explicitly. In the case of 'He's never been very good in cars, he had a bad experience when he was young', the bad experience (cause) results in not being very good in cars (outcome) but no link word is used. In selection interviews, interviewers often explicitly request a causal explanation (e.g. 'Why do you think you are suited to this particular job?) and in doing so they provide an outcome (being suited to the job) and request one or more causes from the candidate (e.g. 'Well, I've always been very good with people'). Similarly, although speakers do generate simple causal statements (e.g. 'I will get a good grade if my lecturer gives me feedback'), in many instances causal statements are complex and may be best described as a causal sequence. Take the following example:

> *Interviewer:* And what's the attraction to this company? I see you have applied to other interesting companies as well . . .
>
> *Candidate:* Yes well, it's a multinational, with works overseas, it's got a good reputation in the oil industry. I'm quite interested in working for a company which sells a particular product as opposed to working for a financial institution which is not so focused upon one thing and, you know, for me it's a tangible good, you know, oil and, you know, the, the things you develop from it and so that interests me. I had a friend that worked for [this company], he took a year out in his degree and said he had a good time.

Certain researchers (e.g. Brewin et al., 1991) have chosen to extract causal paragraphs rather than causal sentences, but while this can make extracting attributions easier, it does pose difficulties for later coding. In the above example, the speaker provides a number of different, even contradictory causes for the same outcome. The LACS suggests that in such cases the researcher should identify the outcome (e.g. failing an exam) and then list each of the stated causes separately (e.g. missing a bus, not revising enough, poor lecturer). These are treated as separate causal statements for later coding. A common convention when identifying causal attributions in transcripts is to use a pencil to underline a cause with an arrow pointing in the direction of the outcome, and a solidus / indicating approximately where the outcome ends (in the case of an outcome following a cause) or begins (when the outcome precedes a cause). This is shown in the following example:

> *Interviewer:* /And what's the attraction to this company? I see you have applied to other interesting companies as well . . .
>
> *Candidate:* Yes well I, (1) ←it's a multinational, with works overseas, (2) ←it's got a good reputation in the oil industry. (3) ←I'm quite interested in working for a company which sells a particular product as opposed to working for a financial institution which is not so focused upon one thing and, you know, (4) ←for me it's a tangible good, you know, oil and, you know, the, the things you develop from it and so that interests me. (5) ←I had a friend that worked for [this company], he took a year out in his degree and said he had a good time.

Here the interviewer provides an outcome in the form of a question which would be extracted as: 'I am attracted to this company, because . . .', and the individual causes would listed as:

1　it's a multinational, with works overseas;
2　it's got a good reputation in the oil industry;
3　I'm quite interested in working for a company which sells a particular product;
4　for me it's a tangible good, you know, oil and, you know, the, the things you develop from it and so that interests me;
5　I had a friend that worked for [this company], he took a year out in his degree and said he had a good time.

Identify agents and targets

Once all attributions have been extracted, the first stage of coding is to identify the 'agent' and the 'target' for each attribution. Kelley (1973) distinguishes between the person, entity or group which causes a particular outcome to occur, and the person, entity or group to whom something happens. Agent–target coding is essentially a content analysis of who or what the speaker nominates as causing an event to happen and who or what is being influenced by the cause. The LACS defines an 'agent' as the person, group or entity nominated in the *cause* of the attribution, and the 'target' as the person, group or entity which is mentioned in the *outcome* of the attribution. In order to simplify codings, agent–target categories are usually restricted to individuals, groups or entities likely to be of interest in that particular investigation. For example, a researcher interested in family attributions might code each family member as a separate agent and target. Theoretically, any number of agent–target categories can be coded, but as larger numbers can have the disadvantage of reducing inter-rater reliability, I have tended to use the following categories with material from selection interviews:

1　speaker;
2　speaker's family;
3　friends and work colleagues;
4　education (may include teachers at school or university);
5　company or employer;
6　other.

So, for example, in the following attribution: 'I decided to study law because several of my family are lawyers', the target or person involved in the outcome ('I decided to study law') would be coded 'self' (1) and the agent would be coded 'family' (2). In the attribution: 'My school was very proactive in securing work placements, several of my friends got work that way', agent would be 'education' (4) and target would be 'friends' (3). The second attribution illustrates one advantage that the LACS has over other similar coding schemes in that it allows the researcher to code attributions where the speaker is neither agent nor target.

　　Agent–target codings can be useful for a number of reasons. First, by counting the number of times a speaker mentions different agents or targets, it is possible, for example, to explore the extent to which the speaker describes themselves as an agent (i.e. causing events to occur) rather than a target (being influenced by a particular cause). A simple count provides insight into the extent to which the speaker considers or wishes to portray themselves as influencing of, rather than being influenced by, specific outcomes. Second, it is possible to identify those agents which the speaker nominates as most likely to influence certain targets. Third, it is possible to decide whether particular agents and targets are associated with negative or positive outcomes.

Code attributions on causal dimensions

There are a number of commonly accepted causal dimensions used for coding attributions. Heider (1958) originally distinguished between causes perceived as being 'internal' to a person and those perceived as being 'external'. This dimension together with 'stability' and 'globality' are included in the Attributional Style Questionnaire. They are also central to the attributional reformulation of the helplessness model of depression (Abramson et al., 1978) which proposes that negative outcomes attributed to internal non-changing and important causes are likely to be particularly debilitating. However, Weiner (1986) makes a distinction between causes which are internal and controllable (e.g. effort) and causes which are internal yet uncontrollable (e.g. personality). He proposes 'control' as a separate causal dimension. The LACS incorporates each of these four dimensions together with a fifth, 'personal-universal', which refers to whether or not the attribution describes something unique or idiosyncratic about the person. Each separate attribution is coded on each of these causal dimensions. Definitions of these dimensions together with examples are provided in the following. It is worth stressing again at this point that attributions are coded, as well as extracted, from the perspective of the speaker. The coder should use information present in the attribution or surrounding transcript to make a decision, rather than their own knowledge of what in their view might be a more 'true' representation of the situation. Antaki (1994) describes this as 'hearable as', that is the meaning that the individual wishes to convey irrespective of whether or not the listener believes or agrees with what is being said.

As a matter of convention when using the LACS all dimensions are coded on a three point scale, where, for example, a 'stable' attribution would be coded '3'; an 'unstable' attribution would be coded '1'; and when there is insufficient information for the coder to make a decision, or the cause is somewhere between 'stable' and 'unstable', the attribution would be coded '2'. As a rule of thumb, approximately 20 per cent of attributions will usually fall into this middle category. There is no reason why a researcher should not choose an alternative coding system, for example a 1–7 scale, although different systems are likely to have different consequences for inter-rater reliability.

Stable–unstable

This dimension refers to how permanent or long-lasting the speaker believes the *cause* of the attribution to be. 'Stable' causes are more likely to have an ongoing effect upon subsequent behaviour than 'unstable' causes, and a simple question to ask oneself when coding is: 'Does the speaker believe that this cause is unchanging or is it likely to have an ongoing effect on other outcomes?' If the speaker believes that the cause is likely to have an ongoing influence upon future outcomes, then code 'stable' (3). For example, 'I'm not particularly good in large groups of people, so I'm looking for a job which will allow me to work by myself' would be coded 'stable' because the speaker gives no indication that he (in this case the speaker is male) believes the cause (a personal characteristic) is likely to change. However, a 'stable' cause may also be a 'one-off' event which has continuing effects upon the speaker. In the example 'Deciding to go to America that summer really opened opportunities for me. I now know I want to become a geologist', although the cause (deciding to go to America) is an isolated event, it is continuing to have effects upon the speaker's choice of career.

If, however, the cause appears to be relatively short-term or to have a non-permanent effect upon subsequent outcomes, then code 'unstable' (1). For example: 'I decided not to apply to that company, because I wanted to go travelling that summer' would be coded 'unstable', because there is no evidence to suggest that the cause continues to have an effect. Similarly, 'I didn't do too well that year, because I had glandular fever' would be coded 'unstable' because the speaker describes the outcome in terms of a particular year. Realistically, having glandular fever could have had a more long-term influence on this individual's choice of university and subsequent job opportunities, but the task of the coder is to use *what information is present in the attribution*. In this attribution the speaker provides no additional information that having glandular fever has had long-term repercussions, and therefore it is coded 'unstable'. Where there is insufficient information to determine whether the attribution should be coded 'stable' or 'unstable', use code 2.

Global–specific

The 'global' dimension refers to the 'importance' or sphere of influence of the *cause* of a particular attribution. According to the reformulated depressive attributional style, a 'global' cause is one which can affect a large number of other non-trivial outcomes. However, this and the 'personal' dimension are best defined with respect to the aims and context of the study. For example, in a study concerned with employee attributions for the success of a culture change programme (Silvester et al., in press), 'global' causes were defined as those which resulted in outcomes at a company rather than a group or an individual level. In the case of graduate recruitment interviews, I have defined a 'global' cause as one which could reasonably be expected to influence a wide number of other important outcomes and have included causes which have influenced or are likely to influence later work opportunities or choice of career. For example, 'I think managing to get into Cambridge has opened doors for me' would be coded 'global' (3), as would 'I decided to study law because several of my family are lawyers', because they are both causes which have influenced career opportunities or are likely to influence them in future.

In contrast, a 'specific' cause is one which has a more limited and less important effect on outcomes, one which is unlikely to have a wide influence or is considered relatively unimportant by the speaker. For example, 'I go to quite a number of plays and films, because I belong to the university Arts Society' would be coded 'specific' (1), because there is no evidence that belonging to the Arts Society has any influence over other outcomes. Similarly, 'I do lots of sport, so I have to be organized' would be coded 'specific'. Again, if there is insufficient information for a decision to be reached, code 2.

Internal–external

In the case of the internal–external, personal–universal and controllable–uncontrollable dimensions, each attribution can be coded separately for speaker, agent and target when these involve different people or groups. For example, if a mother makes the attribution 'she [daughter] doesn't like school, because the other children bully her', her daughter would be identified as target and the other children as agent. The cause could then be coded separately for mother (speaker), daughter (target) and children (agent) on these dimensions. In order to keep things fairly simple in this chapter, however, I will focus on coding attributions for speaker only. The reader is referred to the LACS manual (Stratton et al., 1988) for further information.

An attribution is coded 'internal' (3) when the *cause* originates in the person being coded, for example, their behaviour, a personality characteristic or a skill. Thus, 'The company took me on, because I knew about that particular system' would be coded 'internal' (3) because the cause is the individual's knowledge, and 'I failed the exam because I didn't do enough preparation' would be coded 'internal' because the cause is the individual's failure to act. Alternatively, causes coded 'external' (1) originate outside the person being coded and may include the behaviour of someone else, situational constraints or circumstances in which the person finds themselves. For example, 'None of the class did very well on that particular exam, because the teacher gave us the wrong material to learn' and 'I learnt a lot from working alongside specialists in the area' would both be coded 'external' (1). As with the other dimensions, code 2 if uncertain or there is insufficient information to make a decision.

Personal–universal

The personal–universal dimension was originally created as a way of identifying attributions where family members identified something special or unique to a particular person. I find that the dimension can also be useful in a work context to distinguish between attributions where an individual seeks to set themselves apart from the group and attributions where they describe their actions in normative terms. An attribution is coded 'personal' (3) when either the cause or the outcome describes something unique or idiosyncratic about the person being coded and is not typical of that particular referent group. I have used other graduates as the referent group in the case of graduate recruitment interviews. For example, 'They chose me, because I had captained the school hockey team' would be coded 'personal' because the interviewee describes something about herself which she considers is distinct, or would not be typical of a majority of other graduates applying for a job. Similarly, 'Backpacking through Africa gave me a rare insight into other cultures' would be coded 'personal'. In contrast, an attribution is coded 'universal' (1) when there is nothing in the cause or outcome to indicate something distinctive about that person or where the cause or outcome might be typical of any other person in that referent group. For example, 'I wanted to do criminal law, I guess at that age you're rather naive and utopian' would be coded 'universal' because the candidate associates their behaviour with a 'group norm', that is, anybody of that age might have been expected to act similarly.

Again, it is worth remembering that attributions are coded from the speaker's perspective. Therefore, even though in the coder's opinion the action describes something highly idiosyncratic about the person, if the speaker is describing the outcome or cause in terms which are 'normative', the attribution would be coded 'universal'. Take the following rather extreme example and one somewhat unlikely in a selection interview: 'It was nothing special, my friends were taking soft drugs so I decided to get involved'. This attribution might be taken as indicating something highly 'personal' about the individual, but should still be coded 'universal' because the speaker considers it a fairly 'normal' behaviour.

Controllable–uncontrollable

According to Weiner (1986), the perceived controllability of a cause will influence an individual's motivation to act upon or change future outcomes. An attribution is coded 'controllable' (3) if in the speaker's opinion the cause could, without exceptional effort, be influenced or changed by the speaker so as to produce a different outcome. For example, 'I failed chemistry, because I spent too much time on my duties as secretary for the Athletics Society' would be coded 'controllable' because the speaker could have been expected to have influenced the outcome. It was within their sphere of influence. Similarly, 'I went on writing letters and in the end they decided to offer me the place' would be coded 'controllable'. The following attribution would also be coded 'controllable', because the speaker was able to influence the outcome: 'They were renovating the school library, so I asked if I could use the one at the local college'. In contrast, an 'uncontrollable' (1) attribution is one where the speaker perceives the outcome to be inevitable or not open to influence. For example, 'I missed the deadline for the application because I came down with flu' would be coded 'uncontrollable', as would 'None of my class did well in that subject because the teacher followed the wrong syllabus.' If there is not enough information to determine whether the individual considers themselves to have control over the cause or the outcome, code 2.

Valency

Finally, there is considerable evidence that people make different types of attributions for positive and negative outcomes, and consequently these should be coded and analysed separately (Brewin and Shapiro, 1984). Attributions referring to a positive, neutral or desired outcome are usually coded 'positive' (2) and those referring to a negative or undesired outcome are coded 'negative' (1).

Coded example

As an illustration the following short extract from a selection interview with a postgraduate applicant has been coded using the LACS. The extract is taken from an early part of an interview with a male applicant, where the interviewer asks the applicant to discuss his involvement with rowing at university. For all attributions the cause has been underlined and a / indicates the approximate end (or beginning) of an outcome.

Interviewer: I see that you mention rowing on your application form. Could you tell me /what motivated you to get involved with rowing?

Candidate: I'm not too sure, rowing just kind of appealed to me (1) ←it just seemed like part of university life, you know, the Oxford and Cambridge boat race. Also (2) ←I wanted to try a totally new sport, it's very different from what we've practised in the south of Ireland where we had no chance really to row.

Interviewer: OK, right. Have you continued with it at all?

Candidate: I have, yes. I rowed for my final two years as an undergraduate and then I rowed when I became a postgraduate. /I gave it up after my first year for a few different reasons.

Interviewer: Like what?

Candidate: (3) ←Well I didn't enjoy the club atmosphere that much. This will probably sound quite bad, but (4) not being from a public school→ made it quite difficult/. We were all asked where we came from and you know you'd have a guy saying 'Oh I rowed at Cambridge' or 'I rowed at Oxford' and it was 'Oh great a Cambridge man'. (5) Obviously where I studied was→ 'Oh OK'/. Also (6) there was no real structure in the club→ so I didn't see myself doing too well/. I got selected for the first crew initially but (7) the team didn't feel right,→ so I decided to give it up for a while/. (8) But now I kind of miss the structure in my life that rowing gave me→ so that's why I'm trying to get back into it at the moment./

Table 5.2   *Coding of attributions in rowing example*

	Stable	Global	Internal	Personal	Controllable
1 (I got involved with rowing because) it just seemed like part of university life					
	1	1	1	2	3
2 (I got involved with rowing because) I wanted to try a totally new sport.					
	1	1	3	3	3
3 I gave it up after my first year... Well I didn't enjoy the club atmosphere that much.					
	1	1	1	3	3
4 not being from a public school made it quite difficult.					
	3	3	3	3	1
5 Obviously where I studied was 'Oh OK'.					
	3	3	3	3	1
6 there was no real structure in the club so I didn't see myself doing too well.					
	1	1	1	1	1
7 the team didn't feel right, so I decided to give it up for a while.					
	1	1	1	1	3
8 But now I kind of miss the structure in my life that rowing gave me so that's why I'm trying to get back into it.					
	3	3	3	3	2

The attribution coding is shown in Table 5.2. The first attribution has been coded 'unstable' because there is little indication that the Speaker considers that the cause (that rowing seemed like part of university life) is likely to operate again in future. Similarly, it is coded 'specific' because there is no evidence in this attribution that the cause has an influence over a large number of other important areas of the speaker's life. It is coded 'external' because the cause originates outside the speaker, and 'controllable' because the speaker implies that he had influence over this particular outcome. The 'uncertain' coding has been used for 'personal' because it is difficult to establish whether the speaker is implying that his view – that rowing is part of university life – is something unique to him, or widely shared by other undergraduates.

The second attribution is coded 'unstable', 'specific' and 'controllable' for the same reasons as the first, but this time the cause is coded 'internal' because it refers to the speaker's wish to try a new sport. The attribution is also coded 'personal' because there is more evidence that the speaker is implying that the attribution refers to something which distinguishes him from other undergraduates.

The third attribution is coded 'unstable' because the cause 'not enjoying the club atmosphere' appears to be a 'one-off' occurrence and there is little indication that the speaker believes that this will be typical of other clubs that he joins. It is also coded 'controllable', because although the speaker may not have been able to influence the club atmosphere, he was able to take the decision to leave the club.

The fourth and fifth attributions, which relate to not being from a public school or not attending Oxford or Cambridge, have been coded 'stable' and 'global'; this is because not having attended such institutions, in this speaker's opinion, appears to have ongoing and potentially wide-ranging consequences. In addition, both of these attributions are coded 'uncontrollable' because there is little to indicate that the speaker believes that he could have influenced the outcome in either case, or changed either cause.

In the sixth and seventh attributions, the speaker appears to externalize responsibility for having left the club by stating that there was 'no real structure' in the club and that 'the team did not feel right'. Neither of these suggests that the speaker considers cause or outcome to reflect anything personal about himself. Attribution 6 is coded 'uncontrollable' because there is nothing to indicate that the speaker considered himself able to influence cause or outcome. Attribution 7, however, is coded 'controllable' because the outcome refers to a decision to give up rowing.

Finally, in the eighth attribution, the speaker implies that rowing provides a structure to his life which is likely to have an ongoing and important influence; hence the attribution is coded 'stable' and 'global'. It is also coded 'internal' and 'personal' because of the implication that the statement describes something which originates within him and is relatively idiosyncratic. However, the 'uncertain' coding is used for control, because, while there is evidence that the speaker is attempting to influence the outcome, he has not as yet succeeded.

Additional coding categories

It should be stressed that in addition to the coding categories specified here there is absolutely no reason why the researcher may not include other categories relevant to his or her data. In a recent investigation of cross-cultural organizational attributions (Silvester et al., 1997) we coded the topic of each attribution produced by German and UK engineers. In doing so our aims were to identify the areas of organizational functioning that engineers discussed during semi-structured interviews, as well as *how* they described them in terms of causal relationships. In practice, however, researchers using attribution theory as a paradigm are most familiar with specific attributional dimensions, including those used in the LACS. It is therefore fair to say that, although potentially enriching the field, adopting a more 'radical' approach and incorporating unfamiliar and less traditional coding categories is likely to result in more difficulties as far as peer review and the publishing process is concerned.

Analysis

The LACS differs from methods such as psychometric questionnaires and behavioural vignettes in another important way. Whilst in theory there is no reason why an individual should not code their own attributions, research using the LACS has generally used independent coders to extract and code attributions in much the same way as a researcher would content analyse discourse material. By adopting this approach, emphasis is placed not so much on 'accuracy', that is, whether or not the coder accurately assesses underlying cognitions, but on the extent to which these attributions convey the same meaning to different listeners. Thus, inter–rater reliability – the extent to which two or more coders working independently code individual attributions in the same way – becomes central to ensuring the validity of the method. This approach would be consistent with the aims of certain qualitative researchers when conducting a content analysis of discourse material and where inter-rater reliability is assessed. Of course the use of independent coders also increases the cost of the research. Not only must the researcher find people willing to act as coders and provide incentives, possibly payment, but coders must also be trained in the use of the LACS to ensure adequate levels of reliability. This will inevitably increase the amount of time a researcher will need to complete a project.

Achieving good levels of inter-rater reliability is important should the researcher's aim be a statistical analysis of coded attributions (an approach which would fit more closely with a quantitative use of the method). Yet the use of qualitative material of this type means that reliability similar to that achieved using structured questionnaires is unlikely. Good levels of reliability require clearly defined dimensions and coders who have had sufficient training and practice. Reliability is calculated using Cohen's kappa (see Fleiss, 1971) for approximately 20–30 per cent of the attributions extracted for a study. In general, Fleiss (1971) suggests that kappas above 0.4 are considered acceptable, whereas those above 0.6 are good. Typically, all causal dimensions have demonstrated acceptable or good levels of reliability (Stratton et al., 1986), although the 'global' and 'personal' dimensions usually prove least reliable. Moreover, 'control' can be difficult to code when the agent or target is inanimate, for example in the case of 'organization' or 'education'. Researchers may wish to further define dimensions to suit the needs of their particular research topic.

Similarly, if a researcher wishes to quantify patterns of attributions using this method, a further advantage of coding spoken attributions rests with the number of attributions it is possible to generate. In comparison with questionnaires which rely on six positive and six negative attributions, the focus on spoken attributions for real events means that several thousand attributions can be generated from a single research study. Moreover, as attributions are coded on each dimension, the resulting data set can prove large enough to permit investigation of both nomothetic and idiographic patterns. By entering the data into an SPSS data sheet, it is possible to select certain types of attributions, for example where the speaker is agent and outcomes are positive. However, because individuals produce different numbers of attributions, I usually convert the total number of attributions coded on a particular dimension (e.g. 15 'stable' and 35 'unstable' attributions) into percentage values (e.g. 30 per cent 'stable', 70 per cent 'unstable'), thus allowing comparison of patterns of attributions across different individuals or groups of individuals.

Advantages and disadvantages of the method

Researchers need to weigh the advantages and disadvantages of any method before they decide which one best suits their particular research question or theoretical perspective. The disadvantages of attributional coding lie with its complexity as well as the fact that it is time-consuming and therefore costly to undertake. It will also take time and possibly training before the newcomer feels entirely confident with the method and able to achieve adequate levels of reliability. Consequently, attributional coding should not be viewed as a method which can be learnt and then applied over a very short space of time. Similarly, attributional coding, like many other qualitative methods, depends upon transcribed material and, as a result, can prove costly in terms of either money required to pay someone to transcribe or time if one transcribes the material oneself. On a positive note, the growing body of transcribed material now being made available through groups such as the Economic and Social Research Council should provide one means of reducing costs, as could greater sharing of material by qualitative researchers. These problems aside, I have found attributional coding to be very rewarding and, despite the inevitable frustration encountered when trying to code unusual attributions, I am convinced that the method can provide a valuable means of exploring how individuals make sense of their world.

Attributional coding can be used by researchers working in either qualitative or quantitative disciplines. In fact, attempts to code public or spoken attributions sit somewhat uneasily between these two powerful camps. To my mind the fact that *both* qualitative and quantitative researchers can use the method is in itself a strong advantage of attributional coding. However, it does require the researcher to be clear about how he or she interprets these attributions. Coding and then quantifying individual attributions according to a prespecified coding framework can have more in common with a quantitative or reductionist perspective in that it enables the researcher to explore consistency and track change in the patterns of attributions produced by individuals or groups of individuals over a period of time. It is also possible to treat spoken attributions as a verbal equivalent to responses on an attribution questionnaire. Such approaches fit the traditional view of causal attributions as direct reflections of internal cognitions. As Marshall (1994) points out, however, the positivistic standpoint which accepts language as a transparent medium through which cognitions are transmitted unproblematically and without distortion is very much open to question. Clearly the analysis of spoken attributions alerts us to the proactive and complex ways in which individuals can manipulate attributions as part of impression management and negotiate desired outcomes.

The strength of attributional coding is that it can also provide researchers with the means to conduct a more intensive exploration of idiographic patterns of attributions produced by individuals as they make sense of the events they witness and attempt to share this understanding of causal relationships with others through conversation. It is not strictly necessary to employ the prespecified coding categories used in the LACS; researchers may prefer instead to use categories which emerge from their research and the discourse itself. In this way public attributions are viewed as an active and reflexive component of language, which can play an active and constructive role in enabling individuals to adapt to the needs of different situations (Marshall, 1994). For my own part, witnessing the richness of spontaneous accounts and the creative way in which people manipulate attributions in order to convey specific impressions has certainly influenced my own research perspective. Like many quantitative researchers, I would argue that spoken attributions must, at some point, reflect underlying cognitions. But I would also argue that it is equally important to acknowledge the sensitivity shown by speakers to the situations in which they find themselves, and their skill in adapting to these different situations, as well as cultural differences with respect to beliefs and expectations regarding how one should explain outcomes in public.

In conclusion, the advantages of attributional coding include a focus on naturalistic data and, more specifically, the attributions that individuals produce themselves for real events rather than hypothetical scenarios created by researchers. The sensitivity of the method means that areas previously beyond the bounds of more intrusive research methods can be explored, as can the dynamic interplay of negotiating the most likely causes of events between two people. The ability to quantify patterns of attributions also renders them open to further investigation and comparison, including how they change over time. Although attributional coding is not a technique which can be lifted from the shelf one day and applied the next, perseverance can be rewarded with a more detailed insight into the relationship between attributions and behaviour, such as the selection decisions reached by interviewers listening to candidates explain themselves (Silvester, 1997). Therefore, although attributional coding can be time-consuming, frustrating and nerve-wracking when it comes to calculating reliability kappas, I plan to continue using the method if only because it has forced me to *listen* to how people explain events in their own words. Attributional coding permits researchers a rich insight into the proactive and complex way in which people make sense of their surroundings as well as how they choose to communicate this understanding to others. I believe that attributional coding can contribute to and not detract from the more typical empirical enquiries into causal interpretation.

References

Abramson, L.Y., Seligman, M.E.P. and Teasdale, J. (1978) 'Learned helplessness in humans: critique and reformulation', *Journal of Abnormal Psychology*, 87: 49–74.

Antaki, C.R. (1988) *Analyzing Everyday Explanation: A Casebook of Methods*. London: Sage.

Antaki, C.R. (1994) *Explaining and Arguing*. London: Sage.

Baucom, D.H. (1987) 'Attributions in distressed relationships: how can we explain them?', in D. Perlman and S. Duck (eds), *Intimate Relationships: Development, Dynamics and Deterioration*. London: Sage.

Brewin, C.R., MacCarthy, B., Duda, K. and Vaughn, C.E. (1991) 'Attribution and expressed emotion in the relatives of families with schizophrenia', *Journal of Abnormal Psychology*, 100: 546–54.

Brewin, C.R. and Shapiro, D.A. (1984) 'Beyond locus of control: attribution of responsibility for positive and negative outcomes', *British Journal of Psychology*, 75: 43–50.

Corr, P.J. and Gray, J.A. (1996) 'Attributional style as a personality factor in insurance sales performance in the UK', *Journal of Occupational and Organizational Psychology*, 69: 83–7.

Doise, W. (1980) 'Levels of explanation', *European Journal of Social Psychology*, 10: 213–31.

Edwards, D. and Potter, J. (1993) 'Language and causation: a discursive action model of description and attribution', *Psychological Review*, 100: 23–41.

Fincham, F. and Jaspars, J. (1979) 'Attributions of responsibility to the self and other in children and adults', *Journal of Personality and Social Psychology*, 37: 1589–602.

Fleiss, J.L. (1971) 'Measuring nominal scale agreement among many raters', *Psychological Bulletin*, 76: 378–82.

Forster, N. (1994) 'The analysis of company documentation', in C. Cassell and G. Symon (eds), *Qualitative Methods in Organizational Research: A Practical Guide*. London: Sage. pp. 147–66.

Furnham, A., Brewin, C.R. and O'Kelly, H. (1994) 'Cognitive style and attitudes to work', *Human Relation*, 47: 1509–21.

Furnham, A., Sadka, V. and Brewin, C.R. (1992) 'The development of an occupational attributional style questionnaire', *Journal of Organizational Behaviour*, 13: 27–39.

Harris, M.M. (1989) 'Reconsidering the employment interview: a review of recent literature and suggestions for future research', *Personnel Psychology*, 42: 691–726.

Harvey, J.H., Turnquist, D.C. and Agostinelli, G. (1988) 'Identifying attributions in oral and written explanations', in C. Antaki (ed.), *Analyzing Everyday Explanation: A Casebook of Methods*. London: Sage.

Heider, F. (1958) *The Psychology of Interpersonal Relations*. New York: Wiley.

Joseph, S.A., Brewin, C.R., Yule, W. and Williams, R. (1993) 'Causal attributions and post-traumatic stress in adolescents', *Journal of Child Psychology and Psychiatry*, 34: 247–53.

Kelley, H.H. (1973) 'The process of causal attribution', *American Psychologist*, 28: 107–28.

King, N. (1994) 'The qualitative research interview', in C.Cassell and G. Symon (eds), *Qualitative Methods in Organizational Research: A Practical Guide*. London: Sage. pp. 14–36.

Kipnis, D.S., Schmidt, K., Price, K. and Stitt, C. (1981) 'Why do I like thee: is it your performance or my orders?', *Journal of Applied Psychology*, 66: 324–8.

Knowlton, W.A. and Mitchell, T.R. (1980) 'Effects of causal attributions on a supervisor's evaluation of subordinate performance', *Journal of Applied Psychology*, 65: 459–66.

Marshall, H. (1994) 'Discourse analysis in an organizational context', in C. Cassell and G. Symon (eds), *Qualitative Methods in Organizational Research: A Practical Guide*. London: Sage. pp. 91–106.

Munton, A.G. and Antaki, C. (1988) 'Causal beliefs amongst families in therapy', *British Journal of Clinical Psychology*, 27: 91–8.

Peterson, C. and Seligman, M.E.P. (1984) 'Causal explanations as a risk factor for depression: theory and evidence', *Psychological Review*, 91: 347–74.

Peterson, C., Semmel, A., Von Baeyer, C., Abramson, L.Y., Metalsky, G.I. and Seligman, M.E.P. (1982) 'The attributional style questionnaire', *Cognitive Therapy and Research*, 6: 287–300.

Prussia, G.E., Kinicki, A.J. and Bracker, J.S. (1993) 'Psychological and behavioural consequences of job loss: a covariance structure analysis using Weiner's (1985) attribution model', *Journal of Applied Psychology*, 78: 382–94.

Schulman, P., Castellon, C. and Seligman, M.E.P. (1989) 'Assessing explanatory style: the content analysis of verbatim explanations and the attributional style questionnaire', *Behaviour Research Therapy*, 27: 505–12.

Seligman, M.E.P. and Schulman, C. (1986) 'Explanatory style as a predictor of productivity and quitting among life insurance sales agents', *Journal of Personality and Social Psychology*, 50: 832–8.

Silvester, J. (1996) 'Questioning discrimination in the selection interview: a case for more field research', *Feminism & Psychology*, 6: 574–8.

Silvester, J. (1997) 'Spoken attributions and candidate success in graduate recruitment interviews', *Journal of Occupational and Organizational Psychology*, 70: 61–73.

Silvester, J., Anderson, N., Patterson, F. and Ferguson, E. (1995) 'Unlocking the quality culture: a socio-cognitive model of organisational culture and culture change', in *Proceedings of the British Psychological Society Occupational Psychology Conference*, Warwick.

Silvester, J., Bentovim, A., Stratton, P. and Hanks, H.G.I. (1995) 'Using spoken attributions to classify abusive families', *Child Abuse and Neglect*, 19: 1221–32.

Silvester, J., Ferguson, E. and Patterson, F. (1997) 'A cross cultural comparison of the attributions produced by German and UK engineers', *European Journal of Work and Organizational Psychology*, 6: 103–17.

Silvester, J., Anderson, N. and Patterson, F. (in press) 'Organizational culture change: An intergroup attributional analysis', *Journal of Occupational and Organizational Psychology*.

Snyder, C.R. and Higgins, R.L. (1988) 'Excuses: their effective role in the negotiation of reality', *Psychological Bulletin*, 104: 23–35.

Stratton, P., Heard, D., Hanks, H.G.I., Munton, A.G., Brewin, C.R. and Davidson, C. (1986) 'Coding causal beliefs in natural discourse', *British Journal of Social Psychology*, 25: 299–313.

Stratton, P., Munton, A.G., Hanks, H.G.I., Heard, D.H. and Davidson, C. (1988) *Leeds Attributional Coding System (LACS) Manual*. Leeds: LFRTC.

Sujan, H. (1986) 'Smarter versus harder: an exploratory attributional analysis of sales people's motivation', *Journal of Marketing Research*, 23: 41–9.

Weiner, B. (1985) 'Spontaneous causal thinking', *Psychological Bulletin*, 97: 74–84.

Weiner, B. (1986) *An Attributional Theory of Motivation and Emotion.* New York: Springer-Verlag.

Wells, G.L. (1981) 'Lay analyses of causal forces on behaviour', in J.H. Harvey (ed.), *Cognition, Social Behaviour and the Environment.* Hillsdale, NJ: Erlbaum.

Wong, P.T.P. and Weiner, B. (1981) 'When people ask "why" questions and the heuristics of attribution search', *Journal of Personality and Social Psychology,* 40: 649–63.

6 Qualitative Research Diaries

Gillian Symon

Generally speaking, we are familiar with the concept of diaries as either calendars in which we record planned future activities, or autobiographical accounts of events, thoughts and feelings we have experienced, usually recorded on a daily basis. In the latter case, there are many famous examples of published diaries, such as Samuel Pepys's or Anne Frank's diaries. While there are some studies of diary-keeping (e.g. examining what motivates people to keep diaries: Mallon, 1984), autobiographical diaries, in this familiar guise, are infrequently used for research purposes. While the diary is, in general, an under-utilized research method, in psychology, at least, the growing interest in conducting diary studies has tended to be from within a positivist paradigm, focusing on quantified measurements. In contrast, this chapter aims to encourage *qualitative* diary research by offering some practical design and implementation guidelines, as applied to organizational settings.

Uses of diaries in research

'The diary is the document of life *par excellence*, chronicling as it does the immediately contemporaneous flow of public and private events that are significant to the diarist' (Plummer, 1983: 17).

The diary study allows access to ongoing everyday behaviour in a relatively unobtrusive manner, which allows the immediacy of the experience to be captured, and also provides accounts of phenomena *over time*. Some claim it allows 'hidden' behaviours and events to be revealed, e.g. instances of violence in the workplace (Leadbetter, 1993). Whatever the reasons for conducting the study, and whether or not there is an explicit interest in time effects or changes over time, the distinctive feature of the diary (as a research tool) is that it is completed regularly over time by the respondent, gathering instances of events, feelings etc. as they happen.

In the 1950s and 1960s, diaries were the favoured research tool of the work activity school of researchers who were interested in the detailed study of managerial jobs (Mintzberg, 1973). In these cases (e.g. Carlson, 1951; Stewart, 1967), managers were asked to keep a record of their activities throughout each day so that the researchers could get a flavour of the range of tasks which comprise the typical working day of a manager. Currently, in occupational and organizational psychology, diaries are most often utilized to examine the effects of different shift systems and to record stressful events. Typically, in the case of shift work, respondents may be asked to monitor feelings of overload, eating patterns and mood before and after a change in shift schedule to establish disruptive effects and stabilization periods (e.g. Ng-A-Tham and Thierry, 1993; Williamson et al., 1994). In stress research (e.g. Douglas et al., 1988), respondents may be asked to identify stressors, evaluate the intensity of the stress impact, and record measures of other concurrent physiological and emotional experiences, thus allowing the description of variations in stress responses over time, links between stress responses and other 'symptoms', and the identification of 'everyday' stressors (i.e. daily hassles, e.g. Kenner et al., 1981).

More unusually, diaries may be used as an intervention tool, rather than purely for information-gathering purposes. In the occupational stress area, for example, respondents use 'stress logs' to monitor physiological symptoms of stress over time, the results of which can be analysed to identify patterns and formulate coping strategies (e.g. Ross and Altmaier, 1994). Indeed, there is a growing body of evidence which indicates that recording stressful and traumatic events may *in itself* have beneficial effects on health (e.g. Pennebaker, 1993). Diaries have also been utilized as a training tool for managers (e.g. Stewart, 1968; Jepsen et al., 1989), allowing them to reflect on their work habits and to work towards more effective personal strategies, e.g. better time management.

Diary designs

Diary studies, like interviews (King, 1994), have the advantage that most respondents are familiar with the concept and are aware of what 'keeping a diary' means. However, diaries used for research purposes may look very different from the kind of personal diaries individuals may keep. There are a number of different ways of categorizing types of diaries including: by format; by schedule of completion; and by content.

Diary formats

Many (published) diary studies in (occupational and organizational) psychology use structured and quantitative measures, i.e. they provide closed questions (e.g. requiring yes/no answers or ratings) and the emphasis is on repeated measures of phenomena specified by the researcher. For example, diarists may be asked to complete a series of rating scales or tick boxes in a checklist at the end of every day. In Carlson's (1951) study, a checklist of managers' daily activities was kept (see Figure 6.1).

Date: *3/11 49*   Telephone: In ☐   Out ☐

Time: *10:45–11.05*

Place (other than own office): _____

Person: _____

_____

Manuf. dir.	☐	Comptr.	☐	Adv. dir.	☐
Works man. A		Account.		Pers. dir.	
Works man. B	☒	Sales dir. Swed.		Assistant	
Organ. dir.		Sales dir. exp.		Secr.	

A. Question handled		Kind of action	
Finance, legal	☐	Getting information	☒
Accounting	☐	Systematizing information	☐
Buying	☐	Taking decisions	☐
Production	☒	Confirming or correcting	☐
Product research	☒	decisions of others	
Sales	☐	Giving orders	☐
Personnel	☐	Advising, explaining	☐
Public relations	☐	Inspecting, reviewing	☐
Organiz. planning	☐	Executing	☐
_____	☐	_____	☐
_____	☐	_____	☐
_____	☐	_____	☐
Private	☐	Personal development	☐

B. Question handled		C. Question handled	
Development	☒	Policy	☐
Current operations	☐	Application	☒

Figure 6.1   **Diary form for study of managing directors' working methods (Carlson, 1951: 46)**

There are diary studies where a combination of closed questions and/or rating scales and open-ended sections have been used (e.g. Duck and Miell, 1982). These 'open' sections are often calling for 'comments' (i.e. additional information on the event which has already been quantitatively described).

Diaries as intervention tools in coping with stress (as outlined above) tend to adopt a more open-format response style, i.e. allowing respondents to recount feelings about personally meaningful events. In these cases the diary format probably comes closest to that of the 'personal' diary. Thus, Burt (1994) asked a sample of students to keep a diary for seven weeks where they were required to simply recall events of the day in an unstructured and idiosyncratic way in order to investigate how daily recall of events related to measures of stress and anxiety. An interesting aspect of this study, from the point of view of this chapter, is that Burt made no examination of the diary material itself, but required all the respondents to describe their daily responses using seven provided codes (e.g. 'thoughts, feelings and emotions', 'problems and hassles'; 1994: 333). All further (quantitative) analysis conducted by Burt was carried out using these codes. While ethical considerations are clearly important here, there also seems to be some waste of potentially insightful material. Of course the author's objective was to test hypotheses, and from a positivist perspective this requires standard (quantitative) measures of phenomena. Other researchers working in this area have chosen to analyse the actual content of the diaries kept in this way in more detail (although usually as an additional 'extra' to largely quantitative measures). For example, Spera et al. analysed the content of the daily diaries kept by unemployed professionals and found themes across the diaries relating to 'emotions surrounding and problems of finding a new job', 'conflicts surrounding family and love relationships' and 'general feelings of rejection' (1994: 727).

Mintzberg (1973) rejected diaries as a research method in his study of managerial activity because he felt that their structured nature (as illustrated in Figure 6.1) constrained the research material that could be gathered. Furthermore, Stewart (1967), despite having conducted a large diary study, dismissed the material as 'unreliable' because she judged that diarists were interpreting the categories of activities in different ways. Mintzberg concludes that 'the difficulty appears to be with the diary method itself' (1973: 24). Indeed, from within a positivist paradigm, these problems must seem insurmountable. However, from interpretivist or constructivist perspectives, these concerns are less of an issue, given the rejection of a realist position and the acceptance of the relevancy of individual accounts (e.g. Woolgar, 1996). The 'problem', therefore, does not lie with the method but rests on the epistemological assumptions of the researcher. Thus, in line with the key characteristics of qualitative approaches to research (Cassell and Symon, 1994), 'qualitative' diaries (if based on an interpretivist epistemology) do not pre-specify activities, events, attitudes or feelings but allow the respondent to record subjective perceptions of phenomena of relevance to themselves at that point in time. The objective of the researcher is to understand the respondents' reactions and descriptions from the respondents' per-spectives and within the context of their own worlds.

Schedule of completion

Parkinson et al. (1996) distinguish three strategies for prompting diary completion across time: interval contingent; event contingent; and signal contingent (also termed experience sampling). In the first case, *interval contingent*, respondents are asked to complete the diary at specified times (for example, at the end of the day). This is most like our 'normal' conception of a diary and is a strategy often utilized in activity diaries (see below) and more discursive methods. *Event contingent* studies require respondents to note experiences, feelings etc. after pre-specified events (e.g. after a family visit). Parkinson et al. argue that such studies are 'less suitable for studying unfolding processes' (1996: 309), however, it would be possible to use such a strategy in the workplace, for example to analyse the progress of a set of activities after each of a series of meetings.

In the case of *experience sampling*, respondents will be prompted to complete the diary by an alarm (e.g. a beeping watch) either at specific intervals (e.g. every two hours) or randomly throughout the day. For example, Williams et al. (1991) used 'wrist terminals', which beeped eight times a day, to investigate how working mothers manage their multiple roles on a daily basis. These beepers prompted the women involved in the study to indicate their present activity (from a list provided), whether they had been juggling more than one task in the previous 30 minutes, their evaluation of their present task ('task enjoyment') and their current mood. A more recent innovation in this line is the use of computerized diaries or personal organizers (e.g. Totterdell and Folkard, 1992). While such tools have not as yet been utilized to gather the more discursive material common to qual-itative research approaches, there is no obvious reason why they should not be used for this purpose. As an alternative to pencil-and-paper methods, and as a convenient way to record qualitative data, Dictaphones could also be utilized.

Content

Diaries can be used to investigate a wide range of subjective phenomena. Diarists may be asked to record: reactions and feelings (e.g. mood research); specific behaviours (e.g. research into diet); social interactions (e.g. personal relationship research); activities (i.e. activity logs, e.g. Carlson, 1951; Stewart, 1967; Harvey, 1990); and/or events (i.e. event recording,[1] e.g. Stone et al., 1991). In these latter two cases, although a time for completing the diary is usually specified (e.g. at the end of the day), the measures are not time dependent, the objective being to record the activities in which the respondent has been engaged over a period of time (e.g. watching the television, washing up) or events they may have experienced (e.g. having an argument, computer malfunction). In these kinds of studies the researcher may be less interested in how the respondent perceives or feels about these events or activities. A checklist is usually provided in activity diaries but there has been some argument for allowing respondents to record their own examples (e.g. Harvey, 1990), which are later coded.

Design considerations

I have suggested below some questions aspiring diary researchers should ask themselves before and during their diary study, together with some hints and tips in partial answer to these questions. It is, of course, impossible (and probably not desirable) to provide step-by-step instructions – all contexts are different and researchers and their respondents need to decide what is desirable and feasible in any particular situation – but these questions may at least provide a starting point.

What are you interested in finding out and do you need a diary study to do this?

I have already outlined some uses that have been made of the diary study. The research objectives (What is the phenomenon of interest? What do you want to investigate?) should come well before considerations of method-ology. If you are clear about why you want to conduct a diary study in particular, the design of the study and the analysis will be much easier. This may seem like an obvious point to make, but the precedence of methodology is often the weakness of quantitative studies (where a concern with statistical analysis obscures the experience and meaning of the phenomena being studied) and the lack of guiding questions the weakness of qualitative studies (where many data are generated but analysis is confused).

Who should fill it in?

The available literature on diary design, as it is predicated on the collection of quantitative data, assumes the need to gather a representative sample (Stone et al., 1991). However, the rather different underlying assumptions of an interpretivist paradigm may suggest a different strategy. The major consideration therefore, particularly as oriented to organizational research, might be to ask yourself, who is *relevant*? It may be the case, for example, that you are interested in a particular process within an organization (e.g. selection). Your sample of diary recipients might therefore be those involved in this process (e.g. interviewers, candidates, recruitment consultants, personnel staff). In some cases, it may be only one or two particular individuals.

Most qualitative diaries are likely to be pen-and-paper and require a certain amount of discursive material from the respondent (however, as suggested above, Dictaphones may also be a possibility). This does have implications for the likely literacy level of participants (see Carp and Carp, 1981 for other demographic factors which might affect diary completion, e.g. socio-economic status, age). Considerable variation between respondents in articulation of answers will be found for a variety of reasons (e.g. degree of commitment to the diary study).

How often should respondents fill it in and over what period of time?

This rather depends on the objectives of the research project. To take our selection example again. You may want to identify a particular recruitment drive (perhaps for a particular job) and your data collection is therefore defined by the start and end dates of this particular example. Diary-keeping may begin during job evaluation and finish with the appointment of a particular candidate.

You should be aware of the context in which diary completion is taking place: for example, will the diary be completed during a time of organizational upheaval (which does not form part of your research interests) and what implications does that have for the reporting of events and attitudes? If the diary study is related to a particular organizational project, is there any specific stage of that project when diaries might prove most fruitful?

What questions should you ask, how should the diary be formatted, and what is the best medium?

Again, these depend on the purpose of the research study. You should bear in mind that you will not be present to explain completion requirements (although, as suggested below, you should have spent some time with the respondents at the outset demonstrating the diary). Therefore the method of completion should be as self-explanatory as possible and the questions clear.

You (in collaboration with the respondents?) have to decide what degree of structure is required in the diary. Are there particular issues you want to see covered? Or is it particular events you are interested in? Can the respondents note any information they feel is relevant? Or do you want to orient them to specific aspects of the event, experience etc.?

Most diary studies are pen-and-paper but you could consider Dictaphones or computerized personal organizers (there are clearly cost issues here, including programming the personal organisers). When using booklets, it makes intuitive sense to keep response pages to one page (or, at the least, one double page) so as not to overburden the respondent (one page looks less daunting) or cause omissions (when people fail to turn over the page).

You might find it helpful to pilot the diary before giving it out to your main respondents in order to check whether the questions you want to ask or the general format of the diary make sense and it is feasible to complete the diary in the timespan.

How should the diaries be distributed?

A major concern in diary-based research is participant attrition (although some debriefing material suggests this may be less serious than is often assumed, e.g. SAM Consultants, 1993; Verbrugge, 1980). Quite apart from obvious ethical considerations, one way of retaining participants is to explain the requirements of the study as thoroughly as possible from the beginning, including the likely demands. In this way, the participants know what to expect and are not caught unawares or feel as if they have been deceived.

Explaining the instructions very carefully is also of the utmost importance. You will not be at hand to advise your respondents (although you should leave a telephone number or e-mail so that they can contact you with queries).

Explain the objectives of your research plan. Apart from being ethically appropriate, this allows respondents to properly understand the importance of regular and comprehensive completion (*if these factors are important to your study*). It may also be helpful to the participant to give some indication of the amount of time you would expect diary completion to take on a daily basis. This will give some idea of the time commitment required and also the depth of response sought (e.g. an hour's writing every evening suggests quite a different kind of response than 10 minutes).

What happens over the course of diary completion?

It has been suggested that the first week of diary-keeping is most susceptible to attrition (Stone et al., 1991), and consequently it is a good idea to keep in particularly close contact with participants during this time. For example, phone up to check how their diary is progressing. This gives the respondents a chance to ask you any questions that might have arisen since your initial briefing. It has also been observed (Stone et al., 1991) that if respondents fail to complete their diary on one or two occasions they may assume that they are no longer appropriate for the study and give up. You may not be aware this has happened and it may be useful to reassure respondents at this point. Indeed, it is a good idea to keep in regular contact throughout the period of the diary study (say once a week if the diary is to be kept for a few months), thus avoiding the respondent feeling they have been abandoned or that you are no longer interested in them. However, the degree of contact must be a case for personal discretion: there should be no question of 'pestering' the respondent or 'forcing' them to complete their diary. If the respondents are sufficiently committed to the study itself then you should be able to rely upon self-motivation.

What should I do when it's time to collect the completed diaries?

It is essential that participants are properly debriefed after the study. As suggested above, the diary study can be a serious commitment on the part of the respondent and this should not go unacknowledged. Participants are entitled to proper feedback about the study in which they have invested so much time and effort, and in the outcomes of which they may well have a vested interest. Spend some time with the participant discussing how they felt about completing the diary and any issues that arose during the study. This kind of information is also important to the interpretation of the diarist's responses and may have implications for future similar studies. Once you have formed a view of the results of the overall study, go back to the respondents and discuss that interpretation with them. Do they see it the same way? If not, why not? Valuable insights can be gained in this way and some check on possible researcher excesses of imagination provided.[2] In essence, this approach is similar to the 'diary-diary interview' advocated by Zimmerman and Wieder (1977), in which respondents are taken through their diary entries in a step-by-step manner post-completion.

What can I do with the responses?

This is something that might be most helpfully considered *before* designing the diary. Again this seems like an obvious point but often we find ourselves at the end of a research project with a mound of data by which we feel overwhelmed. The manner of analysing the data is largely dependent on the purposes of the research and the format of the diary, and it is not the purpose of this chapter to describe all potential forms of analysis. The case study outlined below gives one specific example.

It is possible that a 'thematic' analysis is required (looking for common themes in the data either across instances with one individual or across individuals). This method of analysis is not confined to the diary study and advice could be sought from general guidelines (on analysing interview transcripts, for example, see King, Chapter 7 in this volume; Silverman, 1993).

One of the potential benefits of conducting diary studies in organizations is the ability to collect different perspectives from different individuals on the same event. You might find it helpful to draw on stakeholder analysis in interpreting these kind of data (e.g. Burgoyne, 1994).

As mentioned above, one of the motivations for conducting diary studies is the ability to collect information about patterns of and changes in behaviour over time. This is perhaps most commonly carried out where repeated measures have been used (most usually in quantitative studies).

However, it is possible to look for patterns and changes across time in qualitative data using, for example, event listing and time-ordered matrices (Miles and Huberman, 1994).

Case study example: IT project team diaries

In this example study, diaries were utilised as one of a number of (qualitative) research techniques within the overall framework of a case study (see Hartley, 1994). The purpose of the study was to examine the development and implementation of individual workstations in a public service organization. In the early stages of this research, I was focusing on the work of the development team as they tried to formulate a statement of requirements for the new system (using some structured project management techniques) and demonstrated a prototype of a potential system to users.

In this case I was not *specifically* interested in the 'time' element of the study. The diaries were a qualitative form of activity diaries (see above) and I was interested in identifying reported activities and subjective interpretations of those activities.

I have not debated organizational access issues here although I will describe gaining individual agreement to participate. I had negotiated access to study the design and implementation process in general terms with the CEO, the user project manager (UPM) and the UPM's line manager some months earlier and had a free brief as to how I conducted the research, with the expectation that I would negotiate specific research activities with relevant individuals as the study proceeded.

Objectives of the diary study in this research

I had already conducted interviews with members of the development team but I felt that in order to appreciate the ongoing *detail* of development work, information about the *flow of activity* as the project progressed would be helpful. I felt that the literature on the work of technical experts concentrated too much on their (so-called) 'technical' work (e.g. designing software, testing hardware) and I suspected they had a wider range of activities given their potential roles as organizational change agents (Keen, 1981). So I wanted to get a picture of the sorts of activities they were engaged in on a daily basis. I was also aware that many (superficially trivial) decisions were made and unpredictable events occurred on a daily basis which could change the direction of the IT project and have future repercussions. I wanted to record some of those moments, partly to capture the complexity of the technological change process as it happened, but also because I was planning a longitudinal study and thought I might find these data useful in interpreting future events.

Participant observation might have fulfilled these objectives more completely. However, one researcher can only be in one place at any one time and, even if I had been permanently in the organization, I could not have known what was happening to all the (geographically disparate) members of the team at the same time. Furthermore, I was interested in each individual's account of what was occurring (see Henwood and Pidgeon, 1992) – sometimes different perceptions of the same events.

Another important consideration in deciding to conduct a diary study was my relationship with the members of the development team. I had been involved in this research for several months before the diary study took place, and had established a fairly good relationship with (most of) the potential diary respondents. Consequently, I felt that I *could* ask them to keep diaries for me (which, as indicated above, can be quite an onerous task). This may not always be a concern when considering conducting a diary study, but it is worth keeping in mind. While this overcame the initial hurdle of gaining agreement to keep the diary (everyone I asked agreed to do it), and my relationship was such that the task did not seem threatening to any of the team members, this does not mean that I did not have to keep in touch with them over the course of the study, or that our relationship was such that they necessarily felt *obliged* to keep a comprehensive account.

Diary respondents

The group of participants was, to a great extent, predetermined, defined by their membership of the development team. However, this is not as unproblematic as it first appears. For example, who is a member of the development team and who is not? For the purposes of the larger study, I had already formulated a definition of 'the development team' which was more inclusive than many previous assumptions (i.e. including some line managers responsible for advising and monitoring the team). Furthermore, it should be borne in mind that, over time, the constitution of the team can change. In my case, some of the respondents had been working on the project for some months and some had only just been appointed. No-one joined or left mid-way through this particular diary study – but this eventuality should be considered in the design of any similar study. In all, 10 members of the development team kept diaries over the period studied.

Schedule of diary completion

Given my objectives for this particular study, time of day effects were not of particular significance. Similarly, I did not feel it was necessary that the diaries be updated every couple of hours during the day and expected a daily completion, at the end of the day, would be sufficient for most respondents. However, given the disparate roles of the team members, it was clear that some would be working full-time on the project (and thus have many activities to report) while some would be also working on other projects (and thus have fewer activities to report). Consequently, in order to encourage completion and be sensitive to the demands on and different circumstances of the respondents, I asked some respondents not to complete the diaries on a daily basis but as and when they were engaged in a (self-defined) 'relevant' activity.

I decided to conduct the study over a period of a month which I felt was long enough in the context of this particular project to allow all the team members to have been engaged in a number of project relevant activities. This period covered the middle to end of one project phase and the beginning of the next, thus potentially including a variety of activities.

The most dedicated respondent in this case – the project manager – was commuting to and from work and filled in his diary on the train on the way home every day, i.e. he had a specified time and place for completion which suffered from few distractions and rarely varied. I think this illustrates a more general point. While I did discuss with participants when they should complete the diary at the time of distribution, it might have been helpful if I had worked on specifying a *particular* time and place with them.

Diary format

In this research study, I did not want to pre-specify activities (in contrast to most activity sampling studies, e.g. Harvey, 1990) – I neither knew *nor wanted to assume* what activities might constitute a 'day in the life' of a systems developer – and I wanted to understand the concerns of the participants from their perspective. So my diaries consisted of open-ended questions, as shown in Figure 6.2.

Each A4 page represented one activity. Rather than simply providing blank sheets, I did ask some specific questions for each activity. Requiring the respondents to note date and other participants in the activity meant that I could later match up accounts of events from the perspectives of different project team members. I was interested in the purpose of the activity in terms of how the respondent saw this activity as contributing to the overall project and what they were expecting to achieve. I asked about outcome to ascertain whether this was an ongoing activity and because I thought that might help me to link activities recorded here to future activities (as I have already indicated, I expected the research project to be a lengthy one, of which the diary study was one part). Their evaluation of the activity I thought would give some indication of whether the purpose they had identified was achieved and some idea of *why* they regarded activities as successful or not.

Despite the fact that I had visited each of the respondents individually and explained the diary study to them, I still included a front page (see Figure 6.3) detailing how often they should complete the diary, how long they should take on the task and some examples of likely entries. In this latter

Date:

Activity:

Participants:

What is the purpose of this activity from your point of view?

Outcomes of the activity (e.g. problems solved, new activities revealed, activities completed, activities postponed/cancelled)?

Has this been a straightforward or a difficult activity? Why?

Figure 6.2   **Page from diary**

case, I had to weigh up the disadvantage of unduly influencing the participants' responses against the advantage of giving the participants some guidance so they felt more comfortable with the task. In the end, I decided to provide the examples, and it seemed that the respondents did provide examples different from those I suggested.

Pilot study

I felt it was important to pilot the diary to make sure that the questions made sense and that it was a feasible proposition to keep a diary of this type. I decided the best way to test it was to ask a member of the organization to try keeping the diary for a limited period. At the time of the diary study, my key contact within the organization was the user project manager, who agreed to 'road-test' the diary for me for a week. At the end of that week, I collected

---

Name ....

<Project Name> Project Diary

At the end of each day, please spend 15 minutes describing your major activities over the day in relation to the <project name> project. The activities may include: a telephone conversation; writing a document; attending a meeting; discussion with colleagues; devising diagrams etc. The nature and number of the activities will largely depend on your role in the project(s).

When describing these activities, please try to answer as fully as possible.

The completed record will be considered confidential.

Figure 6.3   **Diary frontispiece**

the diary from him and we had some discussion about his perceptions of diary-keeping. These discussions did forewarn me that at particularly busy periods, respondents might be less conscientious in regularly updating the diaries, so I was prepared to try to negotiate this point with individuals at the time of diary distribution (see below). Otherwise, the user project manager did not report any problems in understanding or answering the questions.

Diary distribution

As I have already mentioned, I already knew most of the members of the development team and either phoned them up directly to ask them to take part in the diary study or (more usually) asked them in the context of some other concurrent contact (e.g. an interview or a site visit). I visited each of the respondents individually (sometimes in pairs) to give out the diary and explain the requirements of the diary study. I explained that I was interested in understanding, in relative detail, the day-to-day work of system development. As I recall these occasions, my impression is that they were very happy to 'help me out' with my project as long as it did not interfere too much with their everyday activities, and consequently I 'sold' the diaries with that view in mind, bearing in mind that I did not want to alienate them by overtaxing their commitment to the research process. This may have had implications for individual attitudes to diary completion, and I summarize strategies for encouraging diary completion in the evaluation section.

Monitoring diary completion

Over the timespan of the diary study, I was regularly visiting the organization to attend system demonstrations (as an observer) and conduct interviews (with other key actors in the organization outside the development team, e.g. senior managers). Consequently, I was often in touch with members of the development team and would enquire about their experiences of diary completion. Generally speaking, they would claim to be completing the diary regularly, although many pointed out that this was not always on a daily basis. Clearly, this was rather a casual form of monitoring and is certainly something I would have done differently with hindsight – leading me now to emphasize regular contact as an important component of the diary study research design.

Diary collection and debriefing

At the end of the month, I visited each respondent at work and collected their diaries. On collecting the diary, I had a general discussion of their experiences around the following matters:

1 how they had selected what activities to record (i.e. what constitutes a relevant project activity) and what was omitted;
2 the ease (or otherwise) with which they were able to record activities;
3 the degree to which they felt keeping a diary changed the activities under review;
4 how often they recorded events (i.e. whether they often did not record things they themselves regarded as important);
5 the degree to which they found the diaries useful.

Most claimed to have recorded their major activities concerning the project, excluding phone calls or brief discussions between colleagues working closely together (although a few respondents *did* record this material). Respondents varied according to whether they thought recording the activities actually changed their perceptions of that activity or their methods of pursuing the activities. About half felt that the diaries had had no impact. However, three others reported that the process of keeping a diary made them more reflective (e.g. 'made me consciously deliberate over shortcomings', 'made me use my time better') and gave them insight on their activities: 'you realize [in meetings] you didn't make a decision – so woolly it was a waste of time.'

The important thing to note about this debriefing material is that it is an *integral part* of the research study which aided my interpretation of the actual diary material.

Data analysis

All 10 diaries were returned. Given the open-ended nature of the task, it was hardly surprising to find considerable differences in response 'styles'. Some respondents made very brief entries, while others were much more expansive. Some stuck to the 'facts' as they saw them, while others provided more political/symbolic accounts of their activities.

Each of the diaries was then transcribed as an 'activity diagram'.[3] Figure 6.4 comes from the project manager's (PM's) diary and Figure 6.5 from the user project manager's (UPM's) diary. Figure 6.6 is from a recent recruit to the team. In all of the figures, only a subset of the material is reproduced here to ease presentation.

The major activities identified form the central 'bubbles' and surrounding these are specific instances of these activities.[4] In some cases, these are identified by date because I wanted to be able to look across the diaries and compare different perspectives on the same occasions. In other instances, distinctions were made by content or type (e.g. meetings for the PM were distinguished as: strategic/planning; project assurance; informal). These kinds of distinctions do not function as general categories: in reading the diaries it was clear that individual examples were often very distinctive and I did not want to lose any detail by grouping these together. The distinctions were sometimes common across individuals but more often idiosyncratic, reflecting their different roles and experiences on the project. Spanning out from the bubbles are the perceived objectives and evaluations of the activities, with any additional comments.

I used very large sheets of paper for these transcriptions which allowed me to capture all the information from one diary on one sheet. I found being able to scan the whole month's work at one time helpful. This kind of diagrammatic form (or picture) allowed me to take in patterns and distinctions just by looking at it. And by putting two sheets side by side I could see where commonalities and distinctions lay between respondents.

While it is not the objective of this chapter to provide a discussion of my specific research project, I think it is illuminating in terms of explaining the research method to look more closely at some of the information I gathered. I found a lot of interest and relevance to the objectives of my research project.

Looking at the PM's diary, he construes many of the events he experiences and his own activities in political terms – more specifically, in terms of his need to manage the image of the project in a political environment. For example: using a meeting to 'determine responsiveness' of the users to advancing more money for the project; 'receiving advice' at that meeting on how to present the issue to the CEO in the most effective light; and suggesting that an intervention during a system demonstration might have damaged the project's image of 'caring for our users'. He seems to see system development as a political activity and is portraying himself as

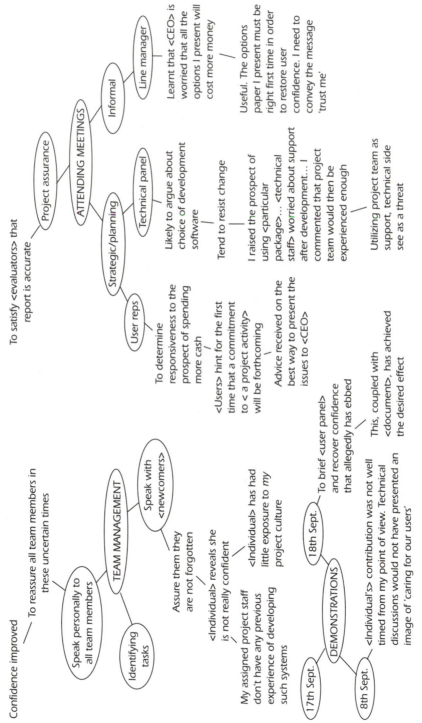

Figure 6.4   **Diary of the project manager**

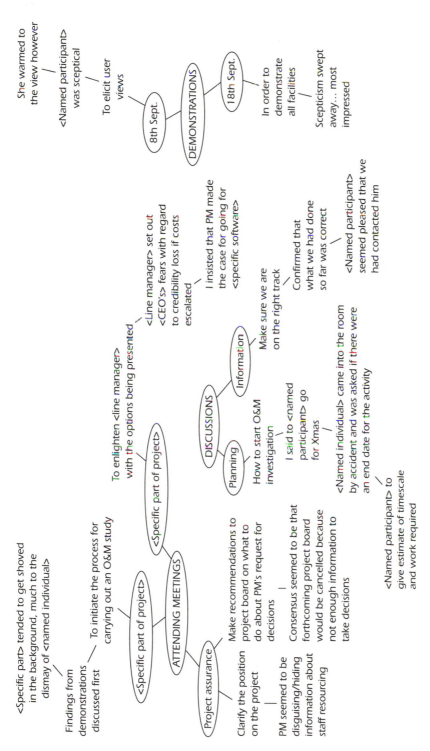

Figure 6.5 **Diary of the user project manager**

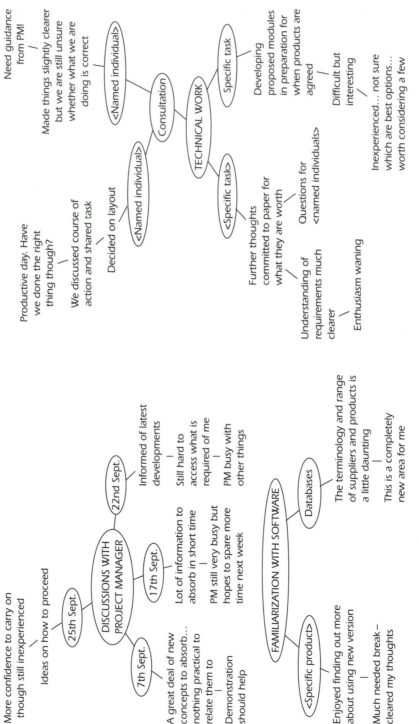

Figure 6.6 **Diary of the new recruit**

someone politically astute, thus establishing his credibility as a project manager in this particular environment.

The UPM's accounts mainly centre around issues of control; system development is depicted as an uncertain activity. For example, in both formal meetings and more informal discussions, he reports 'seeking to clarify the position on the project' and 'making sure we are on the right track'. Note the contrast between his account of the project assurance meeting – 'PM seemed to be disguising/hiding information about staff resourcing' – with the PM's account of the same meeting, where he is seeking 'to satisfy [evaluators] that the report is accurate'.

Turning to the diary of the new team member, there is again a great deal of uncertainty portrayed in her account: she interprets her difficulties in terms of both her own lack of experience in this area and the lack of guidance from the PM. For example, on completing an activity, 'Have we done the right thing though?', and after a meeting with the PM, 'still hard to access what is required of me'. This system development project is portrayed as a difficult and unfamiliar activity. Indeed this team member left the project some months later.

Taking all three accounts together, system development comes across as a potentially dangerous enterprise, where any moment a carefully constructed image of control and expertise may be destroyed, with possibly serious repercussions for those involved.

How does any of this differ or add anything to what might have been gained from interview research? In interviews, I would suggest, the participants would have to spend several hours on a weekly basis with the researcher to acquire this level of detail about events as they are experienced. Nor could changes in perceptions, or the identification of specific instances of interaction, events etc. (as opposed to generalized views) be captured in the same way.

I am aware that the diaries mean more to me than they will to the reader. This is because of my knowledge of the context – to some extent gleaned from other sources. In this particular case example, I used material from the diaries to inform my understanding and interpretation of the overall IT project (which I followed for about four years), in the context of other information I had gathered or to which I had access (e.g. interviews, observations and documentation). I doubt that the diary method (or any method) should be used in isolation – in as much as an understanding of context is recognized as paramount in enabling interpretation.

Overall the study provided many insights for me into how IT projects unfold, for example, challenging idealist and rationalist perceptions of the IT development process. Furthermore, the assumption of much IT research is that there is inherent conflict between technical staff and users. While this might be the case in this example, the PM also reports arguments *within* the technical function. Indeed, this turned out to be a major issue in the light of ongoing events in the organization. On Figure 6.4, the software package mentioned under the 'technical panel' meeting turned out to be ineffective.

The internal IT debates about the suitability of the software at the time allowed the IT department to distance itself from the PM's choice once the software was implemented. This demonstrated for me the importance of differentiating between different subgroups of technical staff. In addition, the material illustrates the pragmatics of system development in context, where new staff come in and out of the project and have to be inducted into the 'culture' of the team.

Evaluating diary studies

I have already referred to the many positive benefits of the diary study, which can be found in the immediacy of the account of events and feelings generated and the degree of detail which can be recorded, which all contribute to an understanding of complex organizational processes. Additionally, the charting of events over time allows the identification of patterns and changes in diarists' accounts of these processes.

A potential drawback is the extent to which diarists are committed to recording events, reactions etc. on a regular basis. I have suggested a number of ways in which respondents could be encouraged to provide 'full' accounts: by carefully explaining project objectives; by keeping in regular contact; by involving respondents in the design; by working on specifying a regular time and place for completion; and by ensuring the diaries are personally useful. However, one must also avoid the situation of 'forcing' respondents to provide 'answers' to 'questions' that are not really relevant. In my case example, some shorter diaries were probably an accurate reflection of the respondents' degree of involvement in the IT project. In this way, diaries may have the advantage over some methods in that they do not necessarily force research participants to respond – depending, of course, on the particular design of the diary and the nature of the 'contract' between the researcher and the diarist.

Which leads me to another issue which I think should be considered in the design of diary studies: the degree of structure imposed on diary responses. One could argue that, by providing specific questions, I was influencing diarists' responses too much, structuring their accounts for them. Although the participants were free to define 'activity', even providing separate pages for each activity is an assumption on my part of some notion of (relatively) fragmented events. Reflexively, this illustrates for me the 'implicit theories' that the researcher brings to the research process. The diaries indicate some preconceptions on my part (e.g. that activities can be regarded as separate events; and that activities have objectives and outcomes), some of which were challenged by the diarists' responses themselves. It is, of course, possible to use much less structured materials (e.g. a blank sheet for each day). In doing this, one may want to be careful about finding a balance between depicting participants' everyday experiences and fulfilling research objectives. The diary researcher should be aware of these issues in the design of their own research.

There are probably other disadvantages that could be described for the diary approach – and these will differ according to one's epistemological position. However, while I would not claim that my case study example is 'perfect' (and there are changes I would have made with hindsight), it certainly revealed for me the potential of the qualitative diary as a method of gaining insight into complex, ongoing organizational processes.

Conclusion

Stewart (1967) and Mintzberg (1973) concluded that diaries were inappropriate tools for gathering the kind of detailed information they were seeking. In this chapter, I have tried to illustrate that this conclusion was based on a rather restricted perception of potential uses of the diary method, and that the qualitative diary study can be a very useful and insightful information source.

While I have drawn on my use of a qualitative *activity* diary to demonstrate the potential of diary studies, there are many more psychological and organizational phenomena which might benefit from this kind of detailed, longitudinal approach. The guidelines provided here are not definitive but may act as a starting point for those unfamiliar with the method – particularly, perhaps, from a qualitative perspective. It is certainly my hope that more researchers and practitioners may be encouraged to explore the possibilities of diary studies in their own areas of interest.

Notes

Thanks to the CEO of the public service organization and Cathy Cassell for their comments on an earlier draft of this chapter. Thanks also to Rob Briner for providing helpful references.

1   Not to be confused with 'event contingent' sampling as described above.
2   This does not mean that the researcher's view counts for nothing. There is, however, the possibility of negotiation between participants in the research process (all of whom have different perspectives) as to the meaning of events etc.
3   This technique of organizing data was not one with which I was familiar; it just seemed the best way to represent the diary responses, retaining the respondents' original words and styles as much as possible. In style, it may come closest to Jones's (1985) account of 'cognitive mapping'.
4   I have had to provide general terms in some instances in the figures to maintain anonymity.

References

Burgoyne, J. (1994) 'Stakeholder analysis', in C. Cassell and G. Symon (eds), *Qualitative Methods in Organizational Research: A Practical Guide*. London: Sage. pp. 187–207.

Burt, C. (1994) 'Prospective and retrospective account-making in diary entries: a model of anxiety reduction and avoidance', *Anxiety, Stress and Coping*, 6: 327–40.

Carlson, S. (1951) *Executive Behaviour: A Study of the Work Load and the Working Methods of Managing Directors*. Stockholm: Strömbergs.

Carp, F. and Carp, A. (1981) 'The validity, reliability and generalizability of diary data', *Experimental Aging Research*, 7: 281–96.

Cassell, C. and Symon, G. (1994) 'Qualitative research in work contexts', in C. Cassell and G. Symon (eds), *Qualitative Methods in Organizational Research: A Practical Guide*. London: Sage. pp. 1–13.

Douglas, R., Blanks, R., Crowther, A. and Scott, G. (1988) 'A study of stress in West Midlands firemen, using ambulatory electrocardiograms', *Work and Stress*, 2: 309–18.

Duck, S. and Miell, D. (1982) 'Charting the development of personal relationships', paper presented to the International Conference on Personal Relationships, Madison, Wisconsin, July 1982.

Hartley, J. (1994) 'Case studies', in C. Cassell and G. Symon (eds), *Qualitative Research Methods in Organizational Research: A Practical Guide*. London: Sage. pp. 208–29.

Harvey, A. (1990) 'Time use studies for leisure analysis', *Social Indicators Research*, 23: 309–36.

Henwood, K. and Pidgeon, N. (1992) 'Qualitative research and psychological theorizing', *British Journal of Psychology*, 83: 97–111.

Jepsen, L., Mathiassen, L. and Nielsen, P. (1989) 'Back to thinking mode: diaries for the management of information systems development projects', *Behaviour and Information Technology*, 8: 207–17.

Jones, S. (1985) 'The analysis of depth interviews', in R. Walker (ed.), *Applied Qualitative Research*. Aldershot: Gower.

Keen, P. (1981) 'Information systems and organizational change', *Communications of the ACM*, 24: 24–33.

Kenner, A., Coyne, J., Schaefer, C. and Lazarus, R. (1981) 'Comparison of two modes of stress measurement: daily hassles and uplifts versus major life events', *Journal of Behavioral Medicine*, 4: 1–39.

King, N. (1994) 'The research interview', in C. Cassell and G. Symon (eds), *Qualitative Research Methods in Organizational Research: A Practical Guide*. London: Sage. pp. 14–36.

Leadbetter, D. (1993) 'Trends in assaults on social work staff: the experience of one Scottish department', *British Journal of Social Work*, 23: 613–28.

Mallon, T. (1984) *A Book of One's Own: People and Their Diaries*. New York: Ticknor & Fields.

Miles, M. and Huberman, A.M. (1994) *Qualitative Data Analysis*, 2nd edn. Thousand Oaks, CA: Sage.

Mintzberg, H. (1973) *The Nature of Managerial Work*. New York: Harper & Row.

Ng-A-Tham, J. and Thierry, H. (1993) 'An experimental change of the speed of rotation of the morning and evening shift', *Ergonomics*, 36: 51–7.

Parkinson, B., Totterdell, P., Briner, R. and Reynolds, S. (1996) *Changing Moods: The Psychology of Mood and Mood Regulation*. Harlow: Longman.

Pennebaker, J. (1993) 'Putting stress into words: health, linguistic and therapeutic implications', *Behaviour Research Therapy*, 31: 539–48.

Plummer, K. (1983) *Documents of Life: An Introduction to the Problems and Literature of a Humanistic Method*. London: George Allen & Unwin.

Ross, R. and Altmaier, E. (1994) *Intervention in Occupational Stress*. London: Sage.

SAM Consultants (1993) *Manual and Procedures for Diary Studies and Mood Assessment*. Unilever Research, Port Sunlight Laboratory.

Silverman, D. (1993) *Interpreting Qualitative Data: Methods for Analysing Talk, Text and Interaction*. London: Sage.

Spera, S., Buhrfeind, E. and Pennebaker, J. (1994) 'Expressive writing and coping with job loss', *Academy of Management Journal*, 37: 722–33.

Stewart, R. (1967) *Managers and Their Jobs*. London: Macmillan.

Stewart, R. (1968) 'Diary keeping as a training tool for managers', *The Journal of Management Studies*, 5: 295–303.

Stone, A., Kessler, R. and Haythornthwaite, J. (1991) 'Measuring daily events and experiences: decisions for the researcher', *Journal of Personality*, 59: 575–607.

Totterdell, P. and Folkard, S. (1992) '*In situ* repeated measures of affect and cognitive performance facilitated by use of a hand-held computer', *Behaviour Research Methods, Instruments and Computers*, 24: 545–53.

Verbrugge, L. (1980) 'Health diaries', *Medical Care*, 18: 73–95.

Williams, K., Suls, J., Alliger, G., Learner, S. and Wan, C. (1991) 'Multiple role juggling and daily mood states in working mothers: an experience sampling study', *Journal of Applied Psychology*, 76: 664–74.

Williamson, A., Gower, C. and Clark, B. (1994) 'Changing the hours of shiftwork: a comparison of 8- and 12-hour shift rosters in a group of computer operators', *Ergonomics*, 37: 287–98.

Woolgar, S. (1996) 'Psychology, qualitative methods and the ideas of science', in J.T.E. Richardson (ed.), *Handbook of Qualitative Research Methods for Psychology and the Social Sciences*. Leicester: BPS Books. pp. 11–24.

Zimmerman, D. and Wieder, D. (1977) 'The diary–diary interview method', *Urban Life*, 5: 479–97.

7 Template Analysis

Nigel King

What is template analysis?

Template analysis is a very widely used approach in qualitative research, although it is often referred to by other terms such as 'codebook analysis' or 'thematic coding'. Quite frequently (especially in student projects) authors do not give any name to the approach they are taking; they merely say that they 'looked for themes' in the texts they analysed. In this chapter I will use the term 'template analysis' (following Crabtree and Miller, 1992), if only to remain consistent with my own previous usage (King, 1994). The essence of the approach is that the researcher produces a list of codes (a 'template') representing themes identified in their textual data. Some of these will usually be defined *a priori*, but they will be modified and added to as the researcher reads and interprets the texts.[1]

The template approach can thus be seen as occupying a position between content analysis (Weber, 1985), where codes are all predetermined and their distribution is analysed statistically, and grounded theory (Glaser and Strauss, 1967), where there is no *a priori* definition of codes. Within this middle ground, there is scope for wide variation in analytical techniques, from those which are very close to content analysis, with codes tightly defined and largely predetermined, allowing statistical as well as qualitative analyses of the same data, to those which start with only a few defined codes, and which use the template in a highly flexible way to produce an interpretation of the texts. Such differences reflect differing philosophical orientations of researchers using template analysis techniques, from 'soft-nosed logical positivism' (Miles and Huberman, 1984) to a purely phenomenological position (Hycner, 1985). Given the overall objectives of this volume, my emphasis will be on using template analysis in research which is towards the latter end of this spectrum.

Why should anyone about to embark on a qualitative research project choose to use template analysis? In particular, why should they choose it over grounded theory, which it resembles in many ways and for which there is a wealth of instructional material available (e.g. Strauss and Corbin, 1990; Strauss, 1987)? One reason for such a preference is philosophical; while it may be argued that grounded theory is not wedded to one epistemological approach (Charmaz, 1995), it has been developed and utilized largely as a realist methodology. That is to say, its users have mostly claimed to be uncovering the 'real' beliefs, attitudes, values and so on of the participants in their research. Those qualitative researchers taking a social constructionist (Burr, 1995) or phenomenological (Kvale, 1983) view are sceptical of the existence of 'real' internal states which can be discovered through empirical research, and may therefore feel that template analysis is more conducive to their position.

Template analysis may also be preferred by those who are not inimical to the assumptions of grounded theory, but find it too prescriptive in that it specifies procedures for data gathering and analysis which *must* be followed:

> The procedures must be followed in doing research. . .It is only by practicing the procedures through continued research that one gains sufficent understanding of how they work, and the skill and experience that enables one to continue using the techniques with success. (Strauss and Corbin, 1990: 26)

While practice and experience are also essential to developing skills in template analysis, on the whole the technique is more flexible with fewer specified procedures, permitting researchers to tailor it to match their own requirements.

Defining codes

Put simply, a code is a label attached to a section of text to index it as relating to a theme or issue in the data which the researcher has identified as important to his or her interpretation. To take a hypothetical example, in the transcript of an interview with a work-based counsellor, the researcher might define codes to identify the points in the text where the interviewee mentions particular groups of staff ('senior managers', 'middle managers', 'clerical staff' etc.), or particular categories of presenting problem ('workload problems', 'relationships at work', 'relationships outside work'). Codes such as these are essentially descriptive, requiring little or no judgement by the researcher of what the interviewee means. Many codes will be more interpretive, and therefore harder to define clearly; in our hypothetical example, these might include codes relating to the counsellor's feelings about the mismatch between their own and clients' perceptions of their role.

Hierarchical coding

It is usual in template analysis for codes to be organized hierarchically, with groups of similar codes clustered together to produce more general higher-order codes. Returning to the workplace counselling example, separate codes relating to 'unrealistic client expectations', 'uncertainty about availability of resources' and 'confusion in relationships with outside agencies' might be incorporated into a single higher-order code: 'effects of lack of role clarity'. Hierarchical coding allows the researcher to analyse texts at varying levels of specificity. Broad higher-order codes can give a good overview of the general direction of the interview, while detailed lower-order codes allow for very fine distinctions to be made, both within and between cases. There can be as many levels of coding as the researcher finds useful. Most templates fall within the two to four level range, and it is worth bearing in mind that too many levels can be counter-productive to the goal of attaining clarity in organizing and interpreting the data.

Parallel coding

Template analysis usually permits parallel coding of segments of text, whereby the same segment is classified within two (or more) different codes at the same level. Parallel coding is only likely to be problematic in research which is located strongly towards the positivistic end of the qualitative research spectrum, where researchers may wish to combine template analysis with elements of quantitative content analysis. The study I described in the predecessor to the present volume (Cassell and Symon, 1994) is an example of such a case (King et al., 1994; Bailey et al., 1994).

The study: managing mental health in primary care

People with mental health problems constitute a substantial proportion of the patients seen by British general practitioners. For instance, Freeling and Tylee (1992) report that as many as half of all general practice attendees may be suffering depressive episodes, and both research and anecdotal evidence (Goodwin et al., 1989) suggests that such patients are often difficult for GPs to manage. There are several reasons why this might be the case. GPs may be unsure about which service is most appropriate for a particular patient, because of the large number of services which deal with mental health problems and/or a lack of clarity about what some of these services offer. Uncertainty has been increased by policy and organizational changes, such as the move to care in the community, with a changing role for both GPs and local authorities. Mental health has long been a 'Cinderella' service within the NHS, with the result that a GP's clinically preferred option might be unrealistic because of the length of waiting lists. People with mental health problems, by the very nature of their condition, may be difficult for GPs to interact with, especially where the patient is unwilling or unable to recognize their problem as psychological rather than physical.

The project I will be describing here – the Managing Mental Health Study – set out to identify the key issues for GPs from one health district in making decisions about the management of patients with mental health problems. It was commissioned by the health authority, in collaboration with local GP representatives, in the hope that it would inform choices about the mental health services purchased on behalf of GPs by the authority. The research was carried out by myself and Julia Maskrey. Two main research questions were posed:

1   What factors do GPs perceive to be influential in their mental health treatment/management decisions?
2   What are GPs' experiences of and attitudes towards mental health service providers?

The study district was largely urban, but with a very mixed population in terms of class and ethnicity. The 13 participating GPs were recruited with the assistance of local GP representatives to include a cross-section of practice areas, including predominantly middle-class, predominantly white working-class and high ethnic minority (mainly Pakistani) populations. Three of the GPs were female and 10 were male. The average age of the GPs was 30 and the average length of time spent in the profession was nine and a half years.

The method chosen for this study was that of focus group interviews. Focus groups are a valuable way of gaining insight into shared under-standings and beliefs, while still allowing individual differences of opinion to be voiced. They enable participants to hear the views and experiences of their peers, and cause them to reflect back on their own experiences and thoughts (Morgan, 1993; Steyaert and Bouwen, 1994).

Before attending the focus groups, all GPs were asked to complete a standard recording booklet, giving brief details of all their mental health consultations over a period of two weeks, or until 20 consecutive cases had been recorded (whichever was the sooner). The identities of all patients were concealed by using a numbering system. The researchers then selected a small sample of these cases from each of the GPs' booklets. Care was taken to ensure that the cases selected were of a varied nature, regarding their presenting problem and management details. At the beginning of each focus group, each GP was asked to comment on these cases, focusing on any particularly difficult or notable experiences. Discussion of particular cases then led into a wider consideration of issues relating to mental health services. The interviewers used a set of broad topic headings to guide the interviews, but tried as far as possible to allow the participants to lead the discussion. Each of the focus group interviews lasted for approximately one and a half hours, and was tape recorded for later transcription.

Developing the template

In this section I will describe the development of the analytical template, illustrating throughout with examples from the Managing Mental Health study. It is crucial to recognize that development of the template is not a separate stage from its usage in analysis of texts. A useful contrast can be made with content analysis, where the researcher first constructs a coding scheme, then applies it to the texts to generate quantitative data for statistical analysis. In qualitative template analysis, the initial template is applied in order to analyse the text through the process of coding, but is itself revised in the light of the ongoing analysis.

Creating the initial template

Unlike the grounded theory approach, template analysis normally starts with at least a few pre-defined codes which help guide analysis. The first issue for the researcher is, of course, how extensive the initial template should be. The danger of starting with too many pre-defined codes is that the initial template may blinker analysis, preventing you from considering data which conflict with your assumptions. At the other extreme, starting with too sparse a set of codes can leave you lacking in any clear direction and feeling overwhelmed by the mass of rich, complex data.

Often the best starting point for constructing an initial template is the interview topic guide – the set of question areas, probes and prompts used by the interviewer. The topic guide itself draws on some or all of the following sources, depending on the substantive content and philosophical orientation of a particular study: the academic literature, the researcher's own personal experience, anecdotal and informal evidence, and exploratory research (see King, 1994 for a detailed discussion). Main questions from the guide can serve as higher-order codes, with subsidiary questions and probes as potential lower-order codes. This is most effective where the topic guide is fairly substantial, with the interviewer defining in advance most of the topics to be covered in the interview. In contrast, some research requires a more minimalistic approach to the construction of the topic guide, allowing most issues to emerge within each individual interview. This was the case in our Managing Mental Health Study; issues for discussion were identified during the first part of each group interview, where GPs described individual cases. We did produce a list of issues to raise ourselves if the participants did not bring them up, and this was added to as the study progressed, but it was not sufficiently detailed to serve as an analytical template in itself.

The approach Julia Maskrey and I used was to develop an initial template by each examining a subset of the transcript data (one group interview each), defining codes in the light of the stated aims of the project. We then considered each other's suggestions and agreed a provisional template to use on the full data set. This kind of collaborative strategy is valuable as it forces the researcher to justify the inclusion of each code, and to clearly define how it should be used. It serves as an important counter to the tendency to allow one's own assumptions and expectations to shape the way a template develops – a tendency that is by no means restricted to inexperienced researchers. If you are a sole researcher on a project using template analysis, I would strongly suggest the use of one or more outside advisers at this stage; ideally these would be people with some knowledge of the research area and experience of analysing qualitative data, though it often may not be possible to obtain both types of expertise in one person.

As can be seen in Table 7.1, the initial template consists of four highest-order codes, subdivided into one, two or three levels of lower-order codes. The extent of subdivision broadly reflects depth of analysis, with the second and third highest-order codes ('the consultation' and 'service contact') covering the central issues of the study: patient management decisions in the selected target cases, and GPs' wider experiences of the various mental health services available to their patients. (For the sake of clarity I will

Table 7.1 *Initial template from the Managing Mental Health Study*

1 Case background history
    1 Illness category
    2 Treatment history
    3 Patient's personal history

2 The consultation
    1 Presenting problem
    2 Treatment/management offered
        1 Prescription
        2 Advice
        3 Referral
    3 Factors influencing treatment/management
        1 Patient/GP interpersonal relationship
        2 The GP role
            1 GP's own perception of role
            2 GP workload/time pressure

3 Service contact
    1 Service(s) used
        Practice nurse
        Psychiatrist
        Clinical psychologist
        Community psychiatric nurse
        Social worker
        CAST (community assessment team)
        CRUSE (bereavement counselling)
        Relate
        Drug rehabilitation
        Other voluntary services
    2 Factors influencing GP use of service
        Role responsibilities of service
        Communication difficulties
        Availability of service
        Response time of service
        Personal familiarity with individual service provider
        GP knowledge about mental health services
        Flexibility of service
        Appropriateness of specific intervention(s)

4 Possible areas of improvement
    1 Areas identified in course of discussion
    2 Priorities for investment (responses to specific question)

henceforth refer to coding levels numerically, with the highest-order codes being 'level one' and the lowest 'level four').

The first level-one code is 'case background history', which comprises three level-two codes: 'illness category', 'treatment history' and 'patient's personal history'. It would have been entirely possible to further subdivide these codes; indeed this would have been essential if we had been concerned with systematically identifying how aspects of patients' medical and personal histories related to GPs' management decisions. However, as this was tangential to the main research questions of the study, and as time and resources were tight, no further levels were defined. Indexing to second-level codes enabled us to easily locate sections of transcripts where these background details were given, and left open the possibility of more detailed analysis through the addition of further coding levels if this was considered necessary as the template was developed.

The second level-one code ('the consultation') relates to accounts of specific consultations with patients from the first part of the interview. Level-two codes index references to the particular problem the patient presented with on the occasion in question, the treatment or management offered, and factors influencing the choice of treatment/management. This area – particularly the third second-level code – is of direct relevance to the study's aims, and therefore required a more finely grained analysis than the first level-one code: hence the inclusion of four levels of coding on the initial template.

'Service contact' is the third level-one code, and also encompasses key issues for the study. It is used to index accounts of mental health services used by the GPs in the study, mentioned either in the course of describing specific cases, or in the more general discussion of issues arising. The first level-two code here is purely descriptive, identifying sections of transcripts where references to services are made. Ten level-three codes specify particular services or types of service (e.g. 'voluntary services') used by the GPs. The second level-two code relates to factors influencing when and how they choose to utilize specific services.

Finally, 'possible areas of improvement' is the fourth level-one code. While this was an important issue, it was secondary to the main aims of the study in identifying influences on management decisions and experiences of mental health service providers. On the initial template the code was subdivided only as far as two second-level codes, the first identifying areas for improvement emerging in the course of the focus group discussions, the second covering comments specifically about how GPs would prioritize future investment in mental health services.

Revising the template

Once an initial template is constructed, the researcher must work systematically through the full set of transcripts, identifying sections of text which are relevant to the project's aims, and marking them with one or more appropriate code(s) from the initial template. In the course of this, inadequacies in the initial template will be revealed, requiring changes of various kinds. It is through these that the template develops to its final form. The researcher faces an important decision regarding the mechanics of this coding process: whether to employ a qualitative analysis software package (such as NUD•IST or Ethnograph), or to code by hand – typically by using colour coding in the margins of the transcripts or colour highlighting of text. Initial coding is probably faster done by hand than by computer, and it can be very helpful to be able to look at several pages of text with clear colour coding spread out on a large desk or floor. However, it is much less cumbersome to revise codes on a computer package and much more efficient when searching for instances of particular themes or combinations of themes. I would advise that the more data one has, and/or the more complex the template, the more worthwhile it is to use a computer package. In the Managing Mental Health Study we used the NUD•IST package, largely because of the complexity of our template.

Below I describe four main types of modification likely to be made whilst revising an initial template, illustrating with examples from our study.

Insertion

Where the researcher identifies an issue in the text of relevance to the research question, but not covered by an existing code, it is necessary to add a new code.

In many – perhaps most – studies, this is the commonest type of modification made to the initial template. Such was the case in the Managing Mental Health Study, where we found it necessary to add new codes at all levels. For example, 'GP lack of mental health training' was added as a subcategory of 'GP role', because it arose as an issue which some participants felt had affected their management of patients:

> it's either ask the psychiatrist to come and see them to help you sort this out, or deal with it yourself, and there's nothing really in-between, so training for that in-between area would be invaluable for most GPs.

Arguably the most significant insertion was the definition of 'inter-agency issues' as a level-one code, embracing a set of lower-level codes which either were new themselves or had initially appeared elsewhere in the template. This was in recognition of our increasing awareness over the course of the analysis that inter-agency issues were a key theme in much of the GPs' discussion:

> Sometimes, when there's a large team and you contact a central point [pause] the case is allocated, you tend to lose a bit of control and you're speaking to someone who's nameless.

Deletion

An initially defined code may be deleted at the end of the process of template construction simply because the researcher has found no need to use it. Alternatively, a code which had seemed to represent a distinct theme may be found to substantially overlap with other codes (perhaps as a result of redefinitions) and again will be deleted.

On our initial template, under the level-one code 'possible areas of improvement', we distinguished between suggestions arising in the course of discussion, unprompted by us as interviewers, and suggestions made in response to a direct question about participants' priorities for additional investment. On reflection we decided that there was so much overlap in the kinds of comments arising in these two contexts that it did not make sense to keep these as separate level-two codes. We therefore deleted both and replaced them with two new codes, identifying whether the suggestions were related to particular services or general improvements (such as 'better communication'). Both of these were subdivided into more specific level-three codes.

Changing scope

Where the researcher finds that a code is either too narrowly defined or too broadly defined to be useful, the code will need to be redefined at a lower or higher level.

We used this kind of modification extensively in developing our template. 'GP role' was initially a level-three code, defined narrowly as one of the factors influencing treatment/management decisions in specific consultations. It very soon became apparent that this was an issue of much wider relevance to the study, and we consequently revised the template to include it as a level-one code.

> I think you've also got to bear in mind that people have got an individual responsibility, so, my feeling would be that patients have an individual responsibility for themselves, and they can't just bring all their woes and offload them on their GP and expect them to give them answers.

At the same time, we decided to use 'the consultation' code simply to index descriptive details about patients discussed by participants, and therefore reduced it in scope to a level-two code, under 'case background history'.

Changing higher-order classification

The researcher may decide that a code initially classified as a subcategory of one higher-order code would fit better as a subcategory of a different higher-order code.

We used this modification in several places in our study's template, often in conjunction with other types of modification. For example, we initially included 'communication difficulties' (with service) as a third-level code, under 'factors influencing GP use of service':

> I've referred few patients to it because you don't have any feedback of any kind, I've never been able to assess how useful it's been and so I probably don't point as many in that direction as I might otherwise do.

We subsequently decided that it would be clearer if this second-level code was removed, and all the individual factors which had comprised it (including 'communication difficulties') were placed as third-level codes under each of the individual services identified. Later in the analysis, the higher-order classification of 'communication difficulties' was then changed again, as a second-level code under the newly defined level-one code 'inter-agency issues'. It was also redefined as referring to all kinds of communication issues, and not just 'difficulties'.

> What was good about the clinical psychologist is that you could grab her and say, 'I've got this lady, or gentleman, this situation, which direction do you think I should be going and is it worthwhile you seeing them?' So you could actually relate an actual scenario, and that was very useful.

Thus the process of finding a suitable location in the template for this code involved all four of the types of modification I have identified; the *deletion* of 'factors influencing GP use of service', two *changes to higher-order classification*, the *insertion* of 'inter-agency issues' and a *change in scope* from third to second level (from 'difficulties' to 'issues').

The 'final' template

One of the most difficult decisions to make when constructing an analytical template is where to stop the process of development. It is possible to go on modifying and refining definitions of codes almost *ad infinitum*, but research projects inevitably face external constraints which mean that you do not have unlimited time to produce an 'ideal' template. The decision about when a template is 'good enough' is always going to be unique to a particular project and a particular researcher. However, no template can be considered 'final' if there remain any sections of text which are clearly relevant to the research question, but remain uncoded. Also, as a rough rule of thumb, it is most unlikely that a template could be considered final if all the data have not been read through closely at least twice.

Commonly most or all of the texts will have been read through three or four times before you begin to feel comfortable with the template. It is generally easier to make a confident judgement that the point has been reached to stop the development of the template where two or more researchers are collaborating on the analysis. A solo researcher might again use one or more outside experts to help determine whether the template is sufficiently clear and comprehensive to call a halt to modifications.

In our study, Julia Maskrey and I took a pragmatic decision that we had reached an acceptable version of the template once we were both sure that there were no relevant sections of transcripts which were uncoded, and that we both had a clear understanding of what each code meant. Undoubtedly further development work would have resulted in some refinements, but (as is often the case) we were under pressure from the funding organization to

Table 7.2   *Final template from the Managing Mental Health Study*

1   Case background history
   1   The consultation
      1   Presenting problem
      2   Treatment/management decision
         1   Prescription
         2   Advice
         3   Referral
   2   Management/treatment history
   3   Patient's personal history

2   GP role and relationship issues
   1   GP role
      1   GP perceptions of role
         1   Changing role
         2   Inappropriate aspects of role
      2   GP workload
         1   'Shifting' patients to other agencies
         2   Reduction in amount of advice provided for patients
      3   GP lack of mental health training
   2   GP/patient interaction
      1   Quality of GP/patient relationship
      2   GP perceptions of patient
         1   Need to 'protect' other services
         2   Somatization
         3   Ethnicity
      3   Patient's cooperation/compliance
      4   Stigma of mental illness

3   Inter-agency issues
   1   Inter-agency communication
      1   Between GPs and other agencies
         1   Psychiatry
         2   Clinical psychology
         3   Community mental health team
         4   Practice-based counsellors
         5   Alternative therapists
         6   Voluntary agencies
         7   Other agencies in general
      2   Amongst other agencies
         1   Psychiatry
         2   Clinical psychology
         3   Community mental health team
         4   Practice-based counsellors
         5   Alternative therapists
         6   Voluntary agencies
         7   Other agencies in general
   2   GP's personal familiarity with other agencies
   3   GP's knowledge/understanding of other agencies
      1   Effects of changes in mental health services
      2   Formal information provided for GPs

Table 7.2   *Continued*

4   Specific services
  1   Psychiatry
  2   Clinical psychology
    1   Rapid access
    2   Other
  3   Community mental health team
    1   CAST
    2   Community psychiatric nurses
    3   Social workers
    4   Team as a whole
  4   Practice-based counsellors
  5   Alternative therapists
  6   Drug and alcohol services
  7   Voluntary agencies
    1   CRUSE
    2   Relate
    3   Drug rehabilitation
    4   Mind
    5   Others
  8   Child services
    1   Psychiatry
    2   Psychology
    3   Others

  1   Degree of use
  2   Specific skills
  3   Availability
    1   Via cross-referral
    2   Waiting times
  4   Flexibility of service
  5   Effectiveness of interventions
  6   Patient attitudes to service
  7   Comparisons between services
  8   Role responsibilities
  9   Appropriateness for particular
      problems
    1   Is appropriate
    2   Is inappropriate

5   Possible areas for improvement
  1   Specific services
      Clinical psychology
      Community mental health team
      Practice-based counselling
      Substance abuse services
      Child services
      Adult psychiatry
      Forensic psychology
  2   General areas for improvement
    1   Communication
    2   Definition of roles
      1   GPs'
      2   Others'
    3   Reduced frequency of organizational change

produce findings to a tight deadline. In fact the 'final' version of the template used to analyse the data for our report to the commissioning organization has since been modified further, as we have gone back to the data in the course of preparing academic publications from it. Qualitative researchers should beware the common temptation to feel that once a published version of a template has appeared it should not be tampered with any further.

Table 7.2 shows the 'final' template from the Managing Mental Health Study.

Interpreting and presenting template analysis

Interpretation

It is sometimes assumed that developing a template and using it to code a set of transcripts (or other textual data) constitute the process of analysis *in toto*. All that is left is to report which codes occurred where in which transcripts. Such an approach leads to a very flat, descriptive account of the data, providing little more depth than would be gained from quantitative content analysis, but without the rigorously consistent definition of units of analysis required to properly carry out *that* method. The template and the coding derived from it are only means to the end of interpreting the texts, helping the researcher to produce an account which does as much justice as possible to the richness of the data within the constraints of a formal report, paper, or dissertation.

It would be inappropriate to set out any general rules for how a researcher should go about the task of interpreting coded data; a strategy must be developed which fits the aims and content of a particular study. I will offer some guidelines and examples which may serve as a useful starting point, but urge readers not to view these as the only permissible strategies.

Listing codes

I usually find it useful at an early stage to compile a list of all codes occurring in each transcript, with some indication of frequency. Most qualitative analysis software packages enable you to do this very simply. If coding is entirely by hand, it is important that codes are marked very clearly in margins, ideally with some colour coding, to make it possible to list codes quickly and accurately. The distribution of codes within and across transcripts can help to draw attention to aspects of the data which warrant further examination. For example, if a theme occurs prominently in all but one of a set of interview transcripts, it may be revealing to look closely at the one exception and attempt to explain why the code was absent.

A word of warning about the counting of codes is required. There is a danger in such a procedure that the researcher will make the assumption that differences in frequencies of codes automatically correspond to meaningful differences within or between transcripts. Such an assumption is invalid in qualitative research, which by definition does not make any attempt to standardize and measure units of analysis, and for this reason some qualitative researchers argue that no attempt should be made to count codes. However, such an absolute regulation seems to me to be the kind of rigidity that qualitative research sets out to oppose. Comparisons of frequencies can be very helpful in suggesting areas which might repay close consideration by the researcher. What is crucial is that the researcher recognizes that quantitative patterns in coding in and of themselves can never tell us anything meaningful about textual data. The fact that code A appears in three out of ten transcripts whilst code B appears in seven out of ten *by itself* tells us nothing of interest in a qualitative study.

Selectivity

Perhaps the opposite danger to that of drifting into a quasi-quantitative approach through counting codes is that of unselectivity, where the researcher attempts to examine and interpret every code to an equal degree of depth. It is never possible – not even in the space of an 80,000 word PhD thesis – to say everything that could be said about every theme identified in a set of qualitative data. Novice researchers fall into the trap of unselectivity for the best of reasons, heeding exhortations to keep an open mind and not allow the analysis to be limited by their own prior assumptions. This is valuable advice, but it has to be followed realistically, which means that you must seek to identify those themes which are of most central relevance to the task of building an understanding of the phenomena under investigation.

Openness

The need to be selective in analysing and interpreting data must be balanced against the need to retain openness towards it. You must not be so strongly guided by the initial research questions that you disregard all themes which are not obviously of direct relevance. Themes which are judged to be of marginal relevance can play a useful role in adding to the background detail of the study, without requiring lengthy explication. More problematic are those themes which are clearly of great importance to participants, but which seem to lie well outside the scope of the study, and perhaps were even deliberately excluded from it. In such cases, you must carefully consider whether investigation of the 'excluded' theme casts any significant light on the interpretation of central themes in the study. If it does, then it should be included in the analysis.

An example of this occurred in the Managing Mental Health Study. From an early stage we had decided to avoid the topic of substance abuse, feeling that many of the issues raised by it were likely to be quite distinct from those raised in the management of other mental health problems. The subject really required a separate study to do it justice. We therefore did not select substance abuse cases as examples for discussion, nor did we include questions about substance abuse services in the interview guide. However, we found the topic occurred very frequently in the focus group discussions, and was evidently one which most of the GPs felt strongly about. Furthermore, some key themes emerging elsewhere in the data were particularly well illustrated in relation to substance abuse. These included the difficulties GPs had with patients who were unwilling, or unable, to follow their advice, and their feelings that they were being held responsible for dealing with social problems beyond their control. If we had been too hasty in excluding from our analysis all comments about substance abuse our understanding of these aspects of GPs' experiences would have been impoverished.

Presentation

The final task facing you is to present an account of your interpretation of the data, often in the limited space of a few thousand words in a report or academic paper. I firmly believe that writing up should be seen not as a separate stage from analysis and interpretation, but rather as a continuation of it. Through summarizing detailed notes about themes, selecting illustrative quotes, and producing a coherent 'story' of the findings, the researcher continues to build his or her understanding of the phenomena the research project has investigated.

As with other stages of template analysis, it is impossible to define one single correct or ideal way to present findings. The researcher needs to consider the nature of the data, the type of document to be produced (including its word length) and, critically, the intended readership. All the same, it is possible to identify three common approaches to presentation, any one of which might prove useful, at least as a starting point:

1   *A set of individual case studies, followed by a discussion of differences and similarities between cases*   This gives the reader a good grasp of the perspectives of individual participants, and can help to ensure that the discussion of themes does not become too abstracted from their accounts of their experience. However, where there are a relatively large number of participants, this format can be confusing for the reader, and it does rely on there being sufficient space to provide an adequate description of each case.

2   *An account structured around the main themes identified, drawing illustrative examples from each transcript (or other text) as required*   This tends to be the approach which most readily produces a clear and succinct thematic discussion. The danger is of drifting towards generalizations, and losing sight of the individual experiences from which the themes are drawn.

3   *A thematic presentation of the findings, using a different individual case study to illustrate each of the main themes*   This can be a useful synthesis of approaches 1 and 2 above; the key problem is how to select the cases in a way which fairly represents the themes in the data as a whole.

Whatever approach is taken, the use of direct quotes from the participants is essential. These should normally include both short quotes to aid the understanding of specific points of interpretation – such as clarifying the way in which two themes differ – and a smaller number of more extensive passages of quotation, giving participants a flavour of the original texts.

Advantages and disadvantages of the technique

Throughout this chapter I have alluded to a variety of advantages and disadvantages of using template analysis; I will draw them together here to present what I hope is a balanced summary. The greatest advantages of template analysis reside in the fact that it is a highly flexible approach that can be modified for the needs of any study in a particular area. It does not come with a heavy baggage of prescriptions and procedures, and as such is especially welcome to those who want to take a phenomenological and experiential approach to organizational research. At the same time, the principles behind the technique are easily grasped by those relatively unfamiliar with qualitative methods – in part because of the similarities to content analysis – and as such it can be a valuable introduction to the whole field. I have found students at undergraduate and master's level taking to the technique quickly and successfully, even where they have not previously used qualitative methods. Finally, the discipline of producing the template forces the researcher to take a well-structured approach to handling the data, which can be a great help in producing a clear, organized, final account of a study.

Regarding disadvantages, the lack of a substantial literature on this kind of technique, compared with that on grounded theory or discourse analysis, can leave the lone novice researcher feeling very unsure of the analytic decisions he or she has to make. This can result in templates which are too simple to allow any depth of interpretation, or (more often) too complex to be manageable. It can also result in the dangers of over-descriptiveness and of 'losing' individual participants' voices in the analysis of aggregated themes, which I discussed above. Networking with experienced researchers and with fellow novices is highly recommended to tackle such difficulties. The Internet is an increasingly useful tool for this, as there are several discussion lists devoted to issues around qualitative research.

Concluding comments

A fundamental tension in template analysis (indeed in most qualitative research) is between the need to be open to the data and the need to impose some shape and structure on the analytical process. Too much openness and the product is likely to be chaotic and incoherent; too much structure and the researcher can be left with all the drawbacks of quantitative research but none of its advantages. I have tried to offer guidance as to how the reader may cope successfully with this tension throughout this chapter. If anything, I have tended to veer towards an over-structured rather than under-structured approach, because in my experience newcomers to this type of research more often suffer from too much openness than too little. You must remember that there are no absolute rules here; in the end you must define an approach to analysis that suits your own research.

Notes

1 Template analysis can be used on any textual data, including organizational documents, participant observation notes, and research diaries, but it is most often used on transcripts from individual or group interviews.

References

Bailey, J., King, N. and Newton, P. (1994) 'Analysing general practitioner referral decisions. II. Applying the analytical framework: do high and low referrers differ in factors influencing their referral decisions?', *Family Practice*, 11 (1): 9–14.

Burr, V. (1995) *An Introduction to Social Constructionism*. London: Routledge.

Cassell, C. and Symon, G. (eds) (1994) *Qualitative Methods in Organizational Research: A Practical Guide*. London: Sage.

Charmaz, K. (1995) 'Grounded theory', in J.A. Smith, R. Harré and L. Van Langenhove (eds), *Rethinking Methods in Psychology*. London: Sage.

Crabtree, B.F. and Miller, W.L. (1992) 'A template approach to text analysis: developing and using codebooks', in B.F. Crabtree and W.L. Miller (eds), *Doing Qualitative Research*. Newbury Park, CA: Sage.

Freeling, P. and Tylee, A. (1992) 'Depression in general practice', in E.S. Paykel (ed.), *Handbook of Affective Disorders*, 2nd edn. Edinburgh: Churchill Livingstone.

Glaser, B. and Strauss, A.L. (1967) *The Discovery of Grounded Theory*. New York: Aldine.

Goodwin, J.M., Goodwin, J.S. and Kellner, R. (1989) 'Psychiatric symptoms in disliked medical patients', *Journal of the American Medical Association*, 241: 1117–20.

Hycner, R.H. (1985) 'Some guidelines for the phenomenological analysis of interview data', *Human Studies*, 8: 279–303.

King, N. (1994) 'The qualitative research interview', in C. Cassell and G. Symon (eds), *Qualitative Methods in Organizational Research: A Practical Guide*. London: Sage.

King, N., Bailey, J. and Newton, P. (1994) 'Analysing general practitioner referral decisions. I. Developing an analytical framework', *Family Practice*, 11 (1): 3–8.

Kvale, S. (1983) 'The qualitative research interview: a phenomenological and a hermeneutical mode of understanding', *Journal of Phenomenological Psychology*, 14 (2): 171–97.

Miles, M.B. and Huberman, A.M. (1984) *Qualitative Data Analysis: A Sourcebook of New Methods*. Beverley Hills, CA: Sage.

Morgan, D.L. (ed.) (1993) *Successful Focus Groups: Advancing the State of the Art*. Newbury Park, CA: Sage.

Steyaert, C. and Bouwen, R. (1994) 'Group methods of organizational analysis', in C. Cassell and G. Symon (eds), *Qualitative Methods in Organizational Research: A Practical Guide*. London: Sage.

Strauss, A. (1987) *Qualitative Analysis for Social Scientists*. New York: Cambridge University Press.

Strauss, A. and Corbin, J. (1990) *Basics of Qualitative Research: Grounded Theory Procedures and Techniques*. Newbury Park, CA: Sage.

Weber, R.P. (1985) *Basic Content Analysis*. Beverley Hills, CA: Sage.

8   The Use of Stories

Yiannis Gabriel

'Now shall I, as an old man speaking to his juniors, put my explanation in the form of a story, or give it as a reasoned argument?'
  Many of the audience answered that he should relate it in whichever form he pleased.
  'Then I think,' he said, 'it will be pleasanter to tell you a story. Once upon a time . . .'

Plato, *Protagoras*

We all like stories. Stories entertain and good storytellers and raconteurs command power and esteem. But good stories also educate, inspire, indoctrinate and convince. Teachers, orators and demagogues have long recognized their value. In this chapter, I argue that stories also open valuable windows into the emotional and symbolic lives of organizations, offering researchers a powerful research instrument. I describe how field research on stories may be conducted and how the material generated may be classified and analysed.

Organizational theory has been late in taking an interest in stories that people tell in and about organizations. The functions of stories for group cohesion or for relieving tedium and tension have been noted, but it is only recently that the importance of stories in organizational research has started to be recognized. In the first place, there is a recognition that organizations are not story-free bureaucratic spaces; storytelling is an important organizational phenomenon in its own right, which merits research attention. 'If we listen carefully to the talk around, it is not difficult to think that storytelling goes on almost non-stop. People transform their lives and their experiences into stories with practised ease', argue Mangham and Overington (1987: 193). It is now becoming acceptable to talk of organizational lore which may be studied in ways similar to the study of folklore. As organizational theorists adopt the cultural 'paradigm' in their discipline, attention is turning to organizational stories, jokes and myths (Mitroff and Kilman, 1976; Pondy, 1983; Martin et al., 1983; Meek, 1988; Bowles, 1989), which have long been the stock-in-trade of ethnographers and folklorists.

The study of organizational storytelling, however, goes beyond the analysis of folklore, interesting as this is in its own right. By collecting stories in a particular organization, by listening and comparing different accounts, by investigating how narratives are constructed around specific events, by examining which events in an organization's history generate stories and which ones fail to do so, we gain access to deeper organizational realities, closely linked to their members' experiences. In this way, stories enable us to study organizational politics, culture and change in uniquely illuminating ways, revealing how wider organizational issues are viewed, commented upon and worked upon by their members.

In telling a story, the requirements of accuracy and veracity are relaxed in the interest of making a point. Poetic licence is the prerogative of story-telling. At the same time, by shrouding a point in symbolic terms, stories are able to evade censors, both internal and external, and express views and feelings which may be unacceptable in straight talk. Criticizing one's superior may be frowned upon in most organizations, but a joke at his/her expense is less so. A story or a tale is a way of 'testing the water' to see whether others feel like the storyteller, reading the same meaning into events. The teller of a joke or a story can always fall back on the defence 'It was only a joke/story!'

Stories are emotionally and symbolically charged narratives; they do not present information or facts about 'events', but they enrich, enhance and infuse facts with meaning. This is both their strength and a potential weakness. For stories will often compromise accuracy in the interest of pleasure; they may focus on the incidental details, remaining stubbornly silent about what a researcher may regard as vital clues; they may contain inconsistencies, imprecisions, lacunae, non sequiturs, illogicalities and am-biguities. Ultimately, the truth of a story lies not in its accuracy but in its meaning.

In this chapter, I shall argue that researchers who want to use stories as a research instrument must be prepared to sacrifice at least temporarily some of the core values of their trade and adopt instead a rather alien attitude towards their respondents and their texts. They must rid themselves of the assumption that quality data are objective, reliable, accurate etc. and must be prepared to engage with the emotions and the meanings which reside in the text. The very recognition that a narrative constitutes or is moving towards becoming a story rather than being a factual account depends on such an emotional engagement. Faced with distortions and ambiguities, researchers must resist the temptation of 'setting the record straight'; instead, they must learn to relish the text, seeking to establish the narrative needs, and through them the psychological and organizational needs, which distortions, am-biguities and inaccuracies serve. I shall argue that this is not merely a valid and useful way of doing research, but also a highly enjoyable one.

An illustration

Consider the following unedited story told by a senior clerk of a privatized utility about the visit of one of the company's own engineers to fix a problem at regional headquarters:

Lakeside is [our regional] head office; our engineer went out there, he thought it was an emergency call. The area is murder to park, he couldn't park anywhere and as far as he knew it's an emergency job, he's got to get there; he goes round the back of the building and there is the company's own car park, so he sees a vacant place and puts his van there. Goes into the main building, it wasn't an emergency job, just that they wanted priority treatment if you like, run of the mill job, he comes back out again and one of the senior managers had blocked him in with his car. And he wouldn't let him out . . . and that was one of the top cats in personnel department and he said to the car park attendant and he told him his name and he virtually refused to come down and shift his car. That's senior management and he just lost his rag because it is costing him money . . . and he threatened to smash his car with a hammer or get the police to tow it away for causing an obstruction, the engineer this was, he was raving and that's what they think of senior management. But by the same token that's what they think of them . . . You, you peasant you dare park there and blocks him in. There was a lot of sympathy for him here. (Narrative 674)

Faced with such narratives, researchers have certain choices. They may dismiss them as trifles of organizational life, which do not affect the basic organizational realities of structure, strategy, control etc. A second option would be to treat the story as a vignette, using it essentially in a journalistic manner to support, augment or spice up an argument. Alternatively, researchers may treat such a story as a clue or a sign leading to the 'facts' about the organization. They may then seek to elucidate what happened by asking questions such as 'Did the incident "really" take place? When? Where? How?', 'How typical is such an incident?' The researcher would then be treating the material as data in need of corroboration, which along with much else may eventually facilitate the formulation of a theory.

This chapter presents an alternative research strategy – one in which the researcher temporarily forgets his/her research role and becomes a *fellow traveller* on the narrative, engaging with it emotionally, displaying interest, empathy and pleasure in the storytelling process. In the example of the story above, the researcher may respond to the narrator's invitation to marvel at the arrogance of the senior manager, to berate the presumptuousness of headquarters staff, to sympathize with the engineer or even to admire his defiance. The researcher does not risk alienating the storyteller by seeming to doubt the narrative or by placing him under cross-examination, but conspires to detach the narrative from the narrowness of the discourse of facts, guiding it instead in the direction of free association, reverie and fantasy. Contradictions and ambiguities in the narrative are accepted with no embarrassment. Ambiguity lies at the heart of many stories, displaying an individual's ambivalent feelings or partial knowledge or understanding. While the researcher may ask for clarification of particular aspects of the story, the storyteller must feel that such clarification is asked in the interest of increased pleasure and empathy rather than in the form of pedantic inquiry.

The uses of stories in social research

Compared with research based on more conventional methods, research using stories is still in its infancy; yet it is clear that there is no one dominant way of using them. In fact, existing research indicates a bewildering variety of possibilities and a multiplicity of research agendas which may be pursued, based on stories. These include the following.

Stories as elements of organizational culture

Drawn from the ethnographic tradition, stories, along with myths, rituals, ceremonies and material artifacts, may be treated as manifestations of shared belief systems. This is an interpretivist approach, seeking to identify the meanings and symbolism of stories for organizational members (Allaire and Firsirotu, 1984; Mahler, 1988; Meek, 1988; Hansen and Kahnweiler, 1993).

Stories as expressions of unconscious wishes and desires

Alternatively, stories may be approached as manifest symptoms of unconscious processes. These processes may be unique to a single individual or shared by several and have both wish-fulfilling and consolatory qualities, which can be revealed using psychoanalytic interpretations (Bowles, 1989; 1990; Gabriel, 1991a; 1991c; Stein, 1994).

Stories as a vehicle for organizational communication and learning

Stories may also be approached as cognitive depositories in which important ideas are mapped and stored (Wilkins and Martin, 1979). Being memorable, they facilitate the transmission of knowledge among organizational participants (Martin, 1982; Barnett, 1988). They can determine action and strategy, by providing precedents for times of crisis or change (Boje, 1991; 1994).

Stories as an expression of political domination and opposition

Stories can be studied as an element of the political system of an organization, revealing the clash of different interests and offering a means both for enhanced management control (Wilkins, 1983; Deal and Kennedy, 1982; Martin and Powers, 1983) and for challenging, dodging or subverting management power (Rosen, 1984; 1985a; 1985b; Meek, 1988; Collinson, 1988; 1994; Trice and Beyer, 1984; Gabriel, 1995).

Stories as performances

Looking at how stories are performed in a dramaturgical context, it is possible to explore the relations between storyteller and listeners, the nature of shared assumptions, meanings and emotions and the quality of the performance (Boje, 1991; Mangham, 1986; 1995; Mangham and Over-ington, 1987; Case, 1995).

Stories as narrative constructions

Drawing on theories of mythology (like those of Lévi-Strauss, 1963; 1976; 1978; and Campbell 1986; 1988) and folklore (like Propp, 1984), another way of studying stories is by analysing their narrative structure and seeking to classify their plots, characters, dramatic and thematic qualities (Martin et al., 1983; Mahler, 1988). More recently deconstruction theory has been employed broadly to similar ends (Martin and Meyerson, 1988; Martin, 1990).

Some issues of methodology

Should the researcher elicit stories or not?

It is clear from the citations that each of these approaches is not exclusive of the others: researchers may be operating within two or more research agendas simultaneously, exploring different avenues using the same mate-rial. Nevertheless, certain important choices must be made at the outset of the research process. One of the first decisions is whether to elicit the stories by asking appropriate questions and explaining the point of the research or whether to collect them as and when they occur. Eliciting stories generates larger amounts of field material, the stories 'framed' for the benefit of the researcher. Different accounts of the same story may be compared, as can the story profiles of different organizations, in a relatively economical manner. The researcher knows when to switch his/her tape recorder on and off and may easily transcribe and process the material at his/her leisure later. This approach is favoured by many of the systematic researchers into stories (e.g. Mahler, 1988; Gabriel, 1992; 1995). The main disadvantage of eliciting stories is that the researcher risks imposing his/her definitions of what is important or enjoyable. The stories are not encountered in their natural state, i.e. as part of organizational talk, but are presented and performed for the benefit of an outsider. They are part of the dyadic research discourse rather than of organizational discourse proper.

The alternative of collecting stories when and as they occur is more time- and money-consuming and is part of a broader ethnographic approach. It has been used with notable success for studying humour (e.g. Coser, 1959; Collinson, 1988; Gabriel, 1991a; 1991b) and is especially important if the emphasis lies on approaching stories as performance rather than merely as text. Boje (1991), who has made a notable contribution using this approach, observed that, within their organizational settings, stories are fragmented, terse, discontinuous, polysemic and multi-authored: most renditions omit large amounts of information which is taken for granted. Observers who are not familiar with such taken-for-granted information may miss the point or the catch or may not be aware that a story is actually being performed at all. This is similar to the situation depicted in the joke about an outsider who overhears a conversation of friends in a train compartment. Each time one of the company shouts a number, the rest burst out in lively laughter. Eventually the outsider asks what the fun is all about and is told that each number corresponds to a previously agreed joke: the number evokes the joke which generates laughter. The outsider shouts a number, but generates no laughter. On inquiring why, he is told 'You didn't tell it right.'

The researcher who pursues storytelling as part of a broader ethnographic project, without specifically seeking to elicit stories, may be charged with pursuing research agendas hidden from his/her respondents. Besides ethical questions, this raises both practical and methodological questions. Does the researcher use a tape recorder? This risks intimidating or unnerving potential storytellers. The presence of a tape recorder may inhibit organizational participants from telling tales which may not be factually backed up or which may compromise them with colleagues, subordinates and superiors. The terseness and unimaginativeness of the stories reported by Boje (1991) on the basis of 100 hours of recorded material may reflect the inhibiting presence of the tape recorder rather than be features of organizational stories in general.

If no tape recorder is used, the researcher must rely on either hand-written notes or recollection. Written notes have a less disturbing effect than tape recorders but nevertheless slow down the storytelling and undermine the naturalness of the setting. It is often not possible to keep written notes if a story is told in a bar or a corridor. Recollection is not regarded as a very reliable method of recording research data. For the purposes of some types of research, recollection would be virtually useless. In the case, however, of stories, recollection is quite a legitimate method, especially if stories can be committed to paper, tape or electronic medium shortly after they were heard. Some stories may be remembered years after the researcher first heard them (e.g. Mangham, 1995) and occasionally their meaning becomes clearer after one has assumed a certain emotional and time distance from the narrative material (e.g. Gabriel, 1991a; 1991c). Like myths, some stories may be timeless and able to cross organizational and linguistic frontiers with minimal distortion (Lévi-Strauss, 1963; 1978). In spite of all these justifications, however, there is no denying that stories recorded, interpreted and analysed from recollection will bear the marks of the researcher's own conscious and unconscious elaboration and embellishment. Facets of the story which resonate with the researcher's desires, interests and research agendas are likely to be highlighted. Other features which the researcher finds uninteresting, incidental or distasteful may be omitted or repressed.

The unit of analysis

While collecting stories, researchers must reflect on the fundamental unit of analysis of their research. This may be the individual story, the individual storyteller, specific incidents in an organization's history (e.g. an accident or a crisis), specific story themes (e.g. the breaking of rules or meeting the organization's top leader) or types of story (comic, heroic, nostalgic etc.) Alternatively a particular organization may be the unit of analysis either as a space where stories happen (how many stories, what types of stories, etc.) or as the topic of stories (i.e. what kind of stories are told *about* IBM or McDonald's).

As with many types of qualitative research, the unit of analysis with story-based research tends to be frequently redefined in the course of the research; yet, it cannot be disregarded altogether. If the unit of analysis is the individual, the research must focus equally on individuals who are good raconteurs and those who are not; by contrast, if the unit of analysis is the individual story, the researcher will spend more time with those individuals who will supply many stories. If the researcher wishes to explore a specific incident, like for instance the one involving the engineer and the personnel manager above, he/she will seek to elicit accounts of the incident by direct or indirect means.

The role of the researcher and the practicalities of research

Granted that story researchers become fellow travellers in the narratives which they collect rather than collectors of facts, they must still decide how much of the researcher's role they are going to project. Will they prompt their respondents with questions on areas which interest them? Will they seek clarification when they do not understand something? Will they invite the tellers to give their interpretations of the meaning of their narrative? Will they ask questions regarding the feelings which the narratives evoke? The more interventionist researchers risk undermining the spontaneity of the storytelling, yet when they come to analyse their material they can speak with greater confidence and authority about the tellers' own sense-making processes.

Should the researchers join in the storytelling? This may increase the reciprocity of the research relation and may further encourage the respondent in his/her storytelling. The risks of this approach are numerous. The researcher's own stories may fall flat with the respondent, trivialize the research activity or generate a particular type of counter-narrative on the part of the respondent. The stories may then become specific to the research dyad and lose all organizational referent. So the same respondent may tell anti-management stories to a researcher who appears interested in them and anti-union stories to a different researcher. This may or may not be a serious drawback, depending on the research agenda being pursued.

A further set of questions which researchers must address concerns the locale, timing and context of the research. Such research can take place during working hours in a separate room, at a company restaurant over coffee or lunch, or after working hours. There are advantages and disadvantages to different arrangements, which must be weighed in the light of the specific concerns and agendas of the research at hand.

Access

The use of organizational stories as a research instrument is fairly time-consuming and researchers interested in this type of field research make considerable demands on the hosting organizations and on individual respondents. In my experience, few organizations are likely to provide access to researchers who are interested simply in exploring organizational stories. While those with the power of granting access may see the point of *using* stories to analyse some vital organizational issue, like the management of change, stress, departmental rivalry etc., they would not generally see much benefit in a researcher interested in collecting and analysing stories. In gaining access, therefore, researchers are faced with the issue of 'framing' their research agenda in ways likely to interest organizations. This is a difficulty but also a challenge. Researchers must resist the temptation of couching their research agendas in rhetorical forms acceptable to managers or using subtle deception and subterfuge in collecting their material. In gaining access, I believe that two strategies are viable; first, to hitch this research onto another piece of research which is of greater interest to the organization; and, second, to make research on organizational stories relevant to the interests or the requirements of the organization where access is requested. These strategies treat stories both as the vehicle of the research and as a topic of the research itself.

An application example

I shall now illustrate the earlier arguments by outlining the results of a six-month field project, entitled 'An exploration of organizational culture through the study of stories'.[1] Before this project, my interest in organizational stories had come from two directions. On the one hand, I had been struck by how often in field research in a particular organization I had been presented with the same story, for instance a worker's suicide in a London hospital or a catering employee's defiant outburst at a school kitchen (Gabriel, 1991a). Could such stories be seen as part of an organizational

Table 8.1 *Numbers of stories collected in different organizations*

Organization	Interviews	Number of stories collected
Research company	24	48
Manufacturing company	24	138
Privatized utility	47	112
Hospital	25	60
Consultancy unit	6	19
Total	126	377

folklore? On the other hand, I was curious to discover whether organizational stories may be interpreted by using a technique akin to psychoanalytic dream interpretation to reveal shared unconscious meanings and fantasies.

To obtain access, contacts were made with some organizations in which I had carried out research earlier. Responses ranged from indifference and hostility to mild interest. It was suggested to me by a colleague willing to introduce me to a company that access would be facilitated if I first focused on stories dealing with something of practical interest to managers, such as computers and information technology. The idea of collecting stories about computers (and machines in general) quite appealed to me; machines (especially mechanical breakdowns and magical devices) have always played important parts in stories, and as a relatively unthreatening topic of discussion they could provide a useful opening area of investigation before more 'delicate' stories could be elicited.

Letters were sent out to ten organizations requesting access and five of them responded positively. They represented a broad spectrum of organizations, including one of Britain's largest manufacturing companies, a research and publishing company, two district headquarters of a privatized utility, a hospital, and a consultancy unit attached to a university. Eventually, 126 individuals were interviewed by the author and one assistant, as described in Table 8.1. Four additional *ad hoc* interviews were conducted with computer analysts to obtain a sense of the type of stories favoured by computer experts. These yielded a further 27 stories.

The interviews

The interviews were loosely structured, seeking to evoke stories the respondents had recently heard, or memories of critical events which were then presented as stories. Initially the interviews explored information technology and especially computers as a feature of organizational stories. The findings suggest that these generate their own unique brand of folklore. Later other types of story were explored.

Following an explanation of the research purpose (which included an explanation of the idea that through stories we often express our real feelings), the researchers asked a small number of questions:

1   Do you see computers as your friends or as your enemies at the workplace?
2   Can you recall an incident which was widely discussed between yourself and your colleagues?
3   Are there any other incidents, not necessarily involving computers, that were widely discussed?
4   Can you recall an incident that made you laugh/concerned/sad/proud etc.?
5   Can you recall any practical jokes?

Respondents were also asked to try and describe their organization in terms of one of a list of metaphors (which included family, well-oiled or creaky machine, castle under siege, conveyor belt, dinosaur, football team etc.) and then asked to think of a critical incident which supported their preferred metaphor. The list of metaphors had been piloted with undergraduates being debriefed on their industrial placements and provided a light-hearted topic of conversation between the researchers and the respondents which naturally led to some stories.[2] Initially, the researchers did not prompt respondents to recall specific events or characters; however, in certain organizations where particular incidents or individuals were widely discussed, later respondents were asked on occasion if they had any recollections of them.

Most interviews lasted between 45 and 75 minutes. All but a handful of interviews were recorded. During the interviews, brief hand-written notes were kept to facilitate later transcriptions and analysis.

Processing

The interviews were then transcribed from tapes yielding 404 organizational stories, of which 159 involved computers. The stories were analysed with the help of a special version of a computer database package, Cardbox Plus.[3] Each story was entered on a separate record and the following information was recorded on a distinct field on the record:

serial number
author
organization
type of story
theme (a one-line summary of the events described)
emotions described in the story and the emotion generated by the delivery
moral of the story (if any)
main characters
keywords
subjective assessment of the story's quality.

Figure 8.1 is an example of a completed Cardbox Plus record. The software permits the selection of stories sharing specific qualities, or having particular

432	Authors: Emma Roberts (pseudonym)

Org: Utility, Division 2	Type: comic, black humour

Theme: Lorry killed cat; driver then kills wrong cat

Text: There was a chap driving a lorry and he hit a cat so he got out of the lorry and saw this cat on the side of the road and thought I'd better finish it off. . . . . smashed it over the head, got back in and drove off. A lady or a chap phoned the police and said I've just seen a lorry driver get out and kill my cat. So they chased after the van and found it and asked the driver whether he had killed the cat so he said he had ran over it and couldn't leave it like that. . . it's cruel so I finished it off.

  So they said can we examine your van and he said yes by all means so they examined the van and found a dead cat under the wheel arch. So it was the wrong cat [he had killed] sleeping at the side of the road.

Emotions: amusement, mild disparagement

Moral:
Similar stories 842, 917, 923

Characters: cat, lady, lorry driver, police	Quality: 10

Key words: cat, lorry, mistake, killed, black humour

Figure 8.1 **Completed Cardbox Plus record**

words in common. For example, it instantly retrieves all stories which involve a disparaging comment about one's supervisor, or all comic stories involving computers or animals.

Findings

Density of folklore

The number and quality of stories drawn from different organizations varies enormously. For example, 24 interviews at the manufacturing firm yielded 138 stories, whereas the same number of interviews at the research and publishing organization yielded a mere 48. I believe that this variation is not a product of the methodology but reflects, at least in part, the vitality and strength of folklore in different organizations. This appears to be linked to the length of service of those interviewed in their organization and the wider culture of the organization itself. The research and publishing organization had an ethos of factual precision and accountability which seemed to inhibit the making of unsubstantiated claims and the spinning of elaborate stories. The median length of service of those interviewed was less than 2 years. By contrast, the manufacturing company had many older participants who had known and worked with each other for a number of years; their median length of service was 5 years, with 10 having been with the company for more than 15 years.

Types of stories

The classification of stories into different types of narratives was the hardest part of the processing.[4] Some stories instantly fell into a well-established type, such as comic or epic, or were hybrids of two or more types (e.g. comic-tragic); yet, some were not easily classifiable in spite of several iterations. Several things eventually became clear. First, the same 'events' may feed different types of story. One particular event, involving the accidental explosion of a fire extinguisher, gave rise to an epic, a comic and a tragic narrative (Gabriel, 1995). Second, certain narratives described events purely as facts, devoid of emotional or symbolic content. These were often responses to the question regarding the most significant event an individual had witnessed during his/her service with an organization. Here is one such:

> I think the most important incident would have to be dealing with a particular incident that occurred on our system which I was personally involved in. A failure of a gas supply system and subsequent explosion . . . no injuries fortunately, nothing, that was the good . . . it was obviously a very unfortunate incident and fortunately no one was injured. We handled it very properly and obviously a certain amount of good fortune as well because it happened at unearthly hours of the morning. (Narrative 681)

Such an incident may have an element of pride in the manner the incident was handled, but could hardly qualify as 'epic', the category in which stories generating pride are usually placed. I decided therefore to classify such stories as either 'information' or 'historical' (in some cases specified 'personal history' or 'organizational history'). This follows the Aristotelean distinction between history as analytico-descriptive and poetry as emotional-symbolic.[5]

A third classification issue arose in connection with certain terse narratives with either a very thin plot or uncommitted emotional content; under certain conditions of repetition and embellishment these could yield fully fledged stories. I felt that I could not dispense with these narratives but chose to classify them as 'proto-stories'. Here are two examples:

> There is the gentleman across the corridor, I notice him because he's always working, he's such a nice gentleman, such a nice character, and I always say 'I just met him on the first floor, I think he's madly in love with me', silly things like that. We just laugh about them. (Narrative 92)

We have got a chap that lives on the streets, it is quite sad, he was a prisoner of war and he hates to be confined, and he comes in lots, he sort of lives in the centre. Occasionally he suffers from hypothermia and someone will call an ambulance and he will come in; he is quite a character and can be quite aggressive sometimes. (Narrative 857)

Both of these narratives focus on a character but the plot is rudimentary: hence they were classed as proto-stories, the former as proto-romance and the latter as proto-tragic. There were 119 proto-stories among the 404 narratives in the database, the commonest of any type.

What then are the main story types and what are their principal qualities? The following classification is not exhaustive, although it covers the great majority of stories collected.

Comic stories and jokes

A common quality of these stories, as identified by Aristotle, is 'deserved misfortune'. Their emotional qualities encompass amusement and mirth but also disparagement. The majority of these stories had a critical quality, i.e. were at the expense of an individual or group of individuals who appeared to deserve their misfortunes, for instance experts disparaging non-experts or vice versa. Specific groups in different organizations were targeted for special types of disparaging comic stories, e.g. lawyers at the manufacturing company or central management at the utility.

Epic stories

These stories focused either on achievement or on survival against the odds. Their chief emotional qualities were admiration, approval and especially pride. About one-quarter of epic stories had comic qualities as well. In many cases the central character of these stories is a hero or heroine, worthy of admiration.

Tragic stories

These stories focus on undeserved misfortune and tend to generate the classic mixture of horror and pity for the victim. These are variously mixed with bitterness, horror, guilt and anxiety. In the majority of these stories misfortune is not the result of accidental factors but the accomplishment of a villain.

Gripes

These are less sorrowful than tragic stories and usually focus on personal injustices and injuries experienced. A few of them have a jocular quality. They were generally associated with feelings of self-pity, disapproval, sadness and resentment.

Traumas

These involve much deeper psychic injuries than gripes and are associated with feelings of anger, outrage and despair. In many cases, these stories were

Table 8.2   *Story types*

Type	Total number	Total number excluding proto-stories
Comic	108	89
Epic	82	59
Tragic	53	42
Gripe	40	25
History	38	32
Joke	38	36
Practical joke	23	23
Traumas	22	19
Romantic	20	13
Romance	12	8

so powerful that they coloured the storyteller's total emotional outlook towards his/her organization.

Practical jokes

These accounts of events were organized and conceived as practical jokes. They generally generated amusement although they often expressed hostility or disparagement. Owing to the nature of the research, 12 of the 23 practical jokes involved tampering with other people's computers.

Romantic

These are stories which express gratitude, appreciation and love. Many of these stories involve gifts and acts of unsolicited kindness. These were often associated with feelings of affection but also nostalgia or self-pity.

Romance

These are stories which focus on love affairs or love fantasies at the workplace, without turning romantic attachments into an occasion for disparagement or ridicule.

The 404 stories in the database were divided up as shown in Table 8.2. In the table, mixed types such as tragic-comic have been entered as both tragic and comic. Fewer than five stories fall into other categories, such as morality tales, horror stories, ironic tales etc.

Distribution of stories across organizations

The distribution of story types varied in the five organizations surveyed. Clearly, the methodology of the research was not geared at establishing the 'story profile' of each organization, conditions not having been standardized. Moreover, 'sad' stories are under-represented, as they have been sub-classified into three types (tragic, gripe and trauma). Nevertheless, Table 8.3 suggests that exploring such profiles may be a fruitful line of inquiry.

The value of such quantitative tables for research based on subtle gradations of meaning and interpretation is limited. They do, however,

Table 8.3   *Distribution of stories across organizations*

	Research company	Manufacturing company	Privatized utility: distribution		Hospital	Consultancy unit
			A	B		
Comic	12	49	13		10	2
Epic	9	36	14	5	12	3
History	8	18				
Tragic	7	18	11	5	9	2
Gripe			10	5	12	
Romantic				6	7	
Practical jokes						8
Ironic						2

indicate possible uses of stories in comparing the folklore and even the
culture of different organizations.

Thematic distribution of stories

In each organization, a small number of events generated a large number of
the stories; for instance, the imbroglio over the introduction of a new
information system, the disturbance during a Christmas party, an office
romance leading to marriage, the death of a colleague, a practical joke
involving a horse, were recounted by more than three interviewees in each
case, with a minimum of prompting. Comparison of the different accounts
reveals wide variations in matters of fact, substance and meaning. If one
were to try and reconstruct 'what actually happened' from these accounts it
would be very difficult. The retired chief executive officer of the manufacturing company, a man of considerable public profile, had generated
many stories within the company. With little prompting 11 such stories were
collected, most of which present him as a 'hero' or at least as a leader
admired by his 'troops'.
   Favourite themes of stories were as follows:

computer	90 (prompted)
leader or director	40
personal trauma or emotional injury	32
accident	30
special characters in the organization	26
crisis	23
practical jokes	23 (prompted)
cock-up	21
nostalgia	20
sex and love	17
sackings and redundancies	14
death	10

Raconteurs

The narrative ability of different individuals differed greatly, as did their willingness to share a story with a stranger. There were some respondents who turned the thinnest material into meaningful stories through embellishment, timing and suspense; others who failed to bring to life vivid scenes which they had experienced; yet others who reported events in a highly factual, 'objective' way, seemingly unwilling to sacrifice accuracy for effect. For example, one respondent provided 14 high quality stories (with virtually no prompting) while several others provided no stories at all, in spite of considerable prompting.[6]

Most of those who related several stories seemed to have one or two preferred types of stories, e.g jocular gripes, personal traumas, cynical jokes, romance, which accorded with their personality and their experience at work.

Narrative complexity and emotional richness

Very few of the stories collected combine the emotional, symbolic and narrative complexities and wide dissemination to be properly described as myths. Only 12 of the 404 stories exceeded 300 words when transcribed and only 30 had more than three distinct characters or groups of characters. Yet, the emotions generated and communicated by these stories were quite powerful, and go some way towards reinforcing the view of organizations as emotional arenas (see Fineman, 1993). In fact, the stories provide a fascinating window into a wide range of emotions which one may not normally associate with organizations.

It is not possible to analyse and bring to light every emotional nuance present in a story: the same story may evoke different emotions in different individuals, and the narrator him/herself may have ambiguous or confused feelings about his/her material. The emotional content of a story comprises the emotions recollected by the narrator, the emotions which the story seeks to communicate to the listener, the emotions which the listener experiences while hearing the story, and the emotions which he/she later feels on recollecting it. Thus, a comic story which generates mirth and amusement to the teller may be based on events which at the time generated horror and panic, and are received with disgust by the listener. The complications resulting from any attempt to classify stories solely in terms of their emotional content are, therefore, formidable. Nevertheless, a preliminary exploration of the emotional tone of the stories in my database identified the following as the most frequent emotions: the number of stories in which each was resident is shown.

amusement	114
disparagement	82
pride	70

disapproval	57
relief	20
anger	19
pity	19
reproach	17
sadness	17
satisfaction	15
affection	14
approval	14
frustration	14
nostalgia	14
derision	13
worry	13
bitterness	12
horror	11
admiration	10
disappointment	9
diversion	9
panic	9
irony	8
mockery	7
anxiety	6
fun	6
guilt	6
scorn	6
self-disparagement	6

It will be noted that certain important emotions, such as embarrassment, happiness and hate, are conspicuous by their absence from the list. Doubtless, by scrutinizing the stories in the database, one could discover numerous stories in which such emotions are present. This illustrates the shortcomings of using quantitative techniques in analysing *en masse* what is highly subjective, delicate material. Different readers, reading the same story, will read different emotional nuances in the text; a person not sensitized to hate or embarrassment may pass by several stories in which someone else would immediately identify these emotions. In my own research, I have used this database as the starting point of an exploration of organizational nostalgia, an emotion infrequently encountered in organizational literature but not in organizational stories. Initially, nostalgia had been recognized as an emotion present in six stories, though on closer reading a further eight nostalgic stories were identified (Gabriel, 1993).

Story interpretation

Perhaps the most promising use of organizational stories lies in their interpretation. Only the rudiments of story interpretation can be offered in this chapter (for details, see Gabriel 1991a; 1991b; 1995) but I hope to demonstrate some of the possibilities available. Here is a relatively straightforward story:

> I used to work for a company where we had regular bomb practice. The security chief would hide a package with a sign saying 'BOMB', to see how quickly people got out of the building and how quickly his boys would locate the 'bomb'. They carried out this exercise many times and were pleased with their response times. Until eventually the bomb was hidden under the mainframe, where it proved impossible to locate; for hours they searched all over the building, but nobody thought of looking under the machine! (Narrative 213)

This story, recounted light-heartedly over lunch by a computer executive (and recalled by the author from memory later), generated much amusement. The storyteller invites the listener to speculate why the security staff failed to check under the mainframe. Was the machine seen as being above suspicion or was it a taboo object? Did the men perhaps fail to see the computer altogether, regarding it as a fixed part of the building, in the same way that our untrained eyes fail to distinguish the dozens of types of snow apparent to an Eskimo? What made this a good story? Does the story try to tell us something more general about computers and organizations?

The meaning of the story (at least as far as the storyteller was concerned) is unlocked when we learn that it was recounted in response to a casual comment to the effect that to the non-expert, computers are mystifying and threatening. The story came as an amplification and embellishment of this rather trivial point, as if to say that even security men, hardened men who will go after bombs, share in the general malaise when confronted with computers. They didn't dare touch the computer or even get close to it, as if *that* was the real bomb. And given that the teller was a man working constantly with computers, is the implication of the story not that computer experts are the real hard men of the organization, dealing with the truly dangerous objects? Such an interpretation may find some support in a subsequent story related by the same individual:

> I had been doing consultancy for the launch of a US software product, called Soft-tool. With a name like this, you don't stand a chance, I told the manufacturers, you have to change the brand name. No luck, it was company policy to use the same name in all its geographic divisions. My job was to come up with a logo for this product, imagine now, 'Buy Soft-tool to increase your performance.' When they realized their gaffe, they changed the name to . . . Hard-tool! (Narrative 215)

This storyteller appears to equate masculinity with hardness and hardness with computers. (For more extensive interpretations of this story, see Gabriel, 1992.)

Is it possible to codify interpretive rules or techniques? Martin (1990) has proposed nine specific techniques to enhance deconstruction (her term for what amounts essentially to depth interpretation) of organizational stories. These include:

1 dismantling a dichotomy, exposing it as a false distinction;
2 examining silences or absences in the text;
3 examining disruptions or collapses in the text;
4 focusing on the most alien feature of the text;
5 interpreting metaphors;
6 analysing *double ententes*;
7 iterative substitution of key features of the discourse;
8 reconstructions – unexpected ramifications of small changes;
9 identifying the limitations of reconstruction.

Thus, for example, using technique 7 on the two stories above we may substitute a Xerox machine for the computer and explore what happens to the meaning of the story. Hard-tool and Soft-tool may be deconstructed as a false dichotomy. Martin's techniques facilitate interpretation, though interpretation can never be reduced to the application of uniform rules and techniques. As Ginsburg (1980) has noted, interpretation relies as much on 'rule of thumb', makeshift and *ad hoc* inferences as on systematic generalizations. In the last resort what makes interpretations valid is their ability to suddenly shed light on what seemed opaque, to make sense of what seemed senseless, to explain the unusual and unexpected.

Some stories may be interpreted very extensively, like dreams, revealing rich combinations of meanings in many different layers. Like works of art, some stories permit of different and even contradictory interpretations. How can we distinguish between valid and spurious interpretations? What corroborations may be offered to strengthen specific interpretations? Since the work of Barthes (1973) and postmodernist theorists, we have learned that we read meanings not only in stories but in virtually any cultural artifact, from particular advertisements to blue jeans and from businessmen's grey suits to AIDS. Are all interpretations equally valid? I do not believe so. As Ginsburg (1980) has shown, interpretation lies at the heart of semiotic processes like forensic investigations, medical diagnoses, authentication of works of art as well as psychoanalysis. In all of these areas, one seeks to paint a general picture from individual signs or clues, like the primitive huntsman who pursues traces left by his prey, observing and interpreting every broken branch, every footmark and every disturbed bit of terrain as something leading to his prey. Interpretation is an art and a skill owing as much to tacit skills and know-how as to scientific method. Specific interpretations may not be proved or disproved by conventional scientific criteria. Yet, this does not make every interpretation equally meaningful or valid. An interpretation may be original, clever, perceptive, incomplete, misleading or even plain wrong.

I would argue briefly that there are four corroborating techniques which may be used to strengthen interpretations in virtually any field. First, the interpretation should demonstrate internal consistency. In a successful interpretation, the interpretation of parts is consistent with the interpretation of the whole, different signs or clues pointing in the same direction. Second, in strong interpretations specific outcomes are over-determined, i.e. not only do different signs point in the same direction, but different mechanisms can be established leading to the same outcome. Third, strong interpretations, although not falsifiable on the grounds of individual pieces of evidence, do, nevertheless, make clear what evidence would lead to their refutation. Fourth, strong interpretations will generally address, account for and supersede weaker ones.

The quality of the stories

Rating the quality of stories makes the selection of stories for use in research and teaching materials easier. An attempt was made to assess the quality of each story on a scale of 1 to 10. This is a highly subjective measure of how interesting, memorable, repeatable, meaningful and telling each story seemed to me. The measure is evidently inadequate as an analytic device but permits the easy selection of 'the best' stories of each genre for the purposes of analysis, discussion and illustration. To this end, 11 stories were given a 10 rating, 24 were given 9, 79 were given 8, 71 were given 7, 59 were given 6 and the rest were given 5 or less. A preliminary attempt has been made to identify what constitutes 'a good story'. Happy endings, comeuppance, coincidence, and above all unpredictability, the ability to hold the listener in suspense, featured in many of the best of these stories. Another feature noticed is the seemingly insignificant detail which forms part of the story's backcloth and adds to its credibility and vividness. The following is an example of a story rated 10:

> I had an office next to the girls in the legal department, and they were talking about the sexiest man in the building and came up with all these I'd never heard of before, so I said, 'Sorry about this ladies, I thought that I was the real myo-star, the hulk' and they cracked up laughing and said 'We had a vote and you were voted the most boring old fart in here.' So, I'd say definitely not, they do not wolf-whistle as I walk down the corridor. (Narrative 132)

Stories, myths and folklore

Some of the stories in the database have quite complex symbolic qualities, revealing strong emotions, expressing powerful unconscious fantasies (see Gabriel, 1992; 1995). Yet, there are numerous reasons why I am disinclined to see organizational stories as being part of a 'mythology'. The stories lack the sweeping grandeur, narrative complexity or overwhelming emotional charge of ancient Greek, native American and other myths. Their characters can be interesting, unusual or even brilliant but they lack the towering presence of true heroes. Within their locale, such characters may generate admiration, pity, anger, fear or enthusiasm – but these emotions hardly cross organizational boundaries. The comic or humorous qualities which feature in many of the stories undermine any mythical pretences; as Campbell (1988) has noted, comedy and myth do not inhabit the same narrative or psychological space. The stories we encounter in organizations lack the sacral qualities of myths. They hardly even address the great universals of myths: good and evil, human and divine, wild and tame, agency and fate, heroism and victimhood. Expressing a widely held view, Barthes argues that 'myth is constituted by the loss of the historical quality of things: in it, things lose the memory that they once were made' (1973: 142). By contrast, organizational stories remain bound to the mundane realities of everyday experience, the provincial, parochial concerns of life in most organizations; they are tied to the concrete, the fact, the historical rather than the mythological past. Even a cursory reading of serious mythological texts (Campbell, 1986; 1988; Lévi-Strauss, 1963; 1976; 1978; Calasso, 1993) enables one to understand the impatience of anthropologists or ethnographers when management and organizational theorists use the idea of myth to denote any symbolically charged organizational narrative (see Helmers, 1993).

Looking at organizational stories as mythology inevitably leads to the conclusion that organizational mythology is emasculated, lifeless, and unimaginative. Looking at them as folklore, on the other hand, highlights their vitality and invention. Folklore, unlike mythology, is the lore of ordinary people. Slang, jokes, traditions, proverbs and idiosyncrasies, which are so alien to myth, all lie at the very heart of folklore (Dundes, 1965; 1980). It is perfectly possible and meaningful to talk of Xerox or Internet lore or the folklore of computers or, indeed, the folklore of surfers and network surfers without debasing the concept of folklore. The story of the lorry-driver who killed the cat (see Figure 8.1) would be a rather impoverished example of myth but is a fine example of lorry-driver folklore, capable of yielding telling and fruitful interpretations. Likewise, the myo-star story outlined above (Narrative 132) can tell much about gender relations at the organization concerned as well as about the storyteller's own fantasy life, without being elevated to the state of a myth.

The researcher who looks for mythology in organizations is likely to be disappointed or may end up with a trivial view of mythology. By contrast, the researcher with an interest in folklore will find much fascinating material in organizations. As folkloric elements, rather than as mythological structures, organizational stories present many interesting possibilities. They offer a way of making comparisons between organizations, opening many windows into the idiosyncrasies of each rather than providing access into human universals. Individual narratives also offer access to the specific wishes and dreams of each storyteller, their fantasies and their emotions, their symbolic and cognitive constructions.

Limitations of story-based research

The most evident danger of story-based research is the selective use of organizational narratives to amplify or reinforce the researcher's preconceived ideas or assumptions. Organizational narratives then become ingredients in the researcher's own agendas. They are especially pernicious because of their memorable qualities. As every journalist knows, through selective presentation, editing, headlining and framing, a narrative may be put to work within virtually any overall story. This danger is ever present in ethnographic research and does not imply any conscious malfeasance on the part of the researcher. Researchers who are pursuing a particular line of investigation may focus on those stories or story interpretations which support their ideas and disregard or underestimate the importance of others.

A second danger of story-based research is the risk of regarding stories as facts, especially if a storyteller insists that the events described in the story 'actually happened' or were actually witnessed by him/her. In many stories, the idea that something 'actually happened' or that it was 'witnessed with one's own eyes' is itself part of the poetic elaboration, or what I have referred to, in analogy to dream-work, as story-work. Philosophers of science, especially Kuhn (1962) and Feyerabend (1975), have established very persuasively that even scientists talking about 'facts' are actually making use of inferences, assumptions and frames of reference, presenting plausible stories rather than describing 'objective' observations.

The opposite danger, however, is to regard everything as narrative and to lose sight of the importance of actual events in organizations. Some postmodern approaches have tended to reduce everything, including organizations, to discourse and narrative: this tendency, which denies any difference between text and context, narrative and meta-narrative, fact and fantasy, views all social reality as mediated by language and existing through language. Numerous writers have challenged this approach, which has nevertheless acquired something of a *succès de scandale* (see e.g. Parker, 1992; 1995; Thompson, 1993). It seems to me that postmodern approaches have made considerable contributions to elucidating the role of language in organizing, structuring and occluding our understandings, without for one moment convincing us that everything *is* language. Between the Scylla of objectivism and the Charybdis of pantextuality, this chapter advocates the use of organizational stories as poetic elaborations on actual events, as wish-fulfilling fantasies built on everyday experience and as expressions of deeper organizational and personal realities. From this point, different researchers may make use of organizational stories to pursue different lines of inquiry – into organizational politics and resistance, into psychological injuries and discontents at work, into the dissemination of organizational knowledge or lore, into culture and symbolism, into interpretation or into the process of storytelling itself.

Notes

1 This was undertaken with the aid of a grant from the Economic and Social Research Council (R 000232 627).
2 A different list of opening questions can be constructed, adapted to other research agendas. 'Are there any special characters in this place?' would be a suitable question if research interest lay more specifically in story characters.
3 Cardbox Plus (Version 4) is supplied by Business Simulations Limited, 30 St James's Street, London SW1A 1HB.
4 I have discussed the different types of organizational story in Gabriel (1995). Each of the main story types constructs a different type of subject, as follows: the epic story constructs the subject as hero or heroic survivor, the tragic story as victim, the comic story as trickster or fool, and the romantic story as love object.
5 Aristotle must be credited with the first clear statement of the difference between stories and other narratives. He viewed stories as emotional-symbolic texts and used the term 'poetics' to describe the type of work that is involved in transforming facts into stories. By contrast, he viewed history as analytico-descriptive. While poetry is a discourse of meanings, history is a discourse of facts, causes and effects. He is also credited with the first convincing statement of the distinction between comedy and tragedy, in terms of the emotions they generate. Both comedy and tragedy are poetic forms. See Aristotle's *Poetics*.
6 When asked what stories they had heard or what incident had been discussed at the workplace, such individuals would say 'Nothing interesting ever happens here' or 'People only talk about work in this place.'

References

Allaire, Y. and Firsirotu, M.E. (1984) 'Theories of organizational culture', *Organization Studies*, 5 (3): 193–226.

Barnett, G.A. (1988) 'Communication and organizational culture', in G.A. Barnett and G.M. Goldhaber (eds), *Handbook of Organizational Communication*. Norwood, NJ: Ablex. pp. 101–26.

Barthes, Roland (1973) *Mythologies*. London: Paladin.

Boje, D.M. (1991) 'The storytelling organization: a study of story performance in an office-supply firm', *Administrative Sciences Quaterly*, 36: 106–26.

Boje, David M. (1994) 'Organizational storytelling: the struggles of pre-modern, modern and postmodern organizational learning discourses', *Management Learning*, 25 (3): 433–62.

Bowles, M.L. (1989) 'Myth, meaning and work organization', *Organization Studies*, 10 (3): 405–21.

Bowles, M.L. (1990) 'Recognizing deep structures in organizations', *Organization Studies*, 11 (3): 395–412.

Calasso, Roberto (1993) *The Marriage of Cadmus and Harmony*. London: Jonathan Cape.

Campbell, Joseph (1986) *Occidental Mythology*. Harmondsworth: Penguin.

Campbell, Joseph (1988) *The Hero with a Thousand Faces* (1949). London: Paladin.

Case, Peter (1995) 'Representations of talk at work: performatives and "Perform-ability" ', *Management Learning*, 26 (4): 423–44.

Collinson, D.L. (1988). ' "Engineering humour": masculinity, joking and conflict in shop-floor relations', *Organizational Studies*, 9 (2): 181–99.

Collinson, D.L. (1994) 'Strategies of resistance: power, knowledge and subjectivity in the workplace', in J. Jermier, W. Nord and D. Knights (eds), *Resistance and Power in Organizations*. London: Routledge. pp. 25–68.

Coser, R.L. (1959) 'Some social functions of laughter', *Human Relations*, 12: 171–82.

Deal, T.E. and Kennedy, A.A. (1982) *Corporate Cultures: The Rites and Rituals of Corporate Life*. Reading, MA: Addison-Wesley.

Dundes, Alan (1965) *The Study of Folklore*. Englewood Cliffs, NJ.: Prentice-Hall.

Dundes, Alan (1980) *Interpreting Folklore*. Bloomington, IN: Indiana University Press.

Feyerabend, Paul (1975) *Against Method*. London: New Left Books.

Fineman, S. (ed.) (1993) *Emotion in Organizations*. London: Sage.

Gabriel, Yiannis (1991a) 'Turning facts into stories and stories into facts', *Human Relations*, 44 (8): 857–75.

Gabriel, Yiannis (1991b) 'On organizational stories and myths: why it is easier to slay a dragon than to kill a myth', *International Sociology*, 6 (4): 427–42.

Gabriel, Yiannis (1991c) 'Organizations and their discontents: a psychoanalytic contribution to the study of corporate culture', *Journal of Applied Behavioral Science*, 27: 318–36.

Gabriel, Yiannis (1992) 'Heroes, villains, fools and magic wands: computers in organizational folklore', *International Journal of Information Resource Management*, 3 (1): 3–12.

Gabriel, Yiannis (1993) 'Organizational nostalgia: reflections on "the golden age" ', in Stephen Fineman (ed.), *Emotion in Organizations*. London: Sage. pp. 118–41.

Gabriel, Yiannis (1995) 'The unmanaged organization: stories, fantasies, sub-jectivity', *Organization Studies*, 16 (3): 477–501.

Ginsburg, C. (1980). 'Morelli, Freud and Sherlock Holmes: clues and scientific method', *History Workshop*, 9: 5–36.

Hansen, C.D. and Kahnweiler, W.M. (1993) 'Storytelling: an instrument for under-standing the dynamics of corporate relationships', *Human Relations*, 46 (12): 1391–409.

Helmers, Sabine (1993) 'The occurrence of exoticism in organizational literature', paper presented at the EGOS Conference, Paris, 6–8 July.

Kuhn, Thomas S. (1962) *The Structure of Scientific Revolutions*. Chicago: University of Chicago Press.

Lévi-Strauss, Claude (1963) 'The structural study of myth', in Claude Lévi-Strauss (ed.), *Structural Anthropology* (1968). Harmondsworth: Penguin.

Lévi-Strauss, Claude (1976) 'The Story of Asdiwal' (1958), in Claude Lévi-Strauss (ed.), *Structural Anthropology*, Vol. 2. Harmondsworth: Penguin.

Lévi-Strauss, Claude (1978). *Myth and Meaning: The 1977 Massey Lectures*. London: Routledge.

Mahler, Julianne (1988) 'The quest for organizational meaning: identifying and interpreting the symbolism in organizational stories', *Administration and Society*, 20: 344–68.

Mangham, I.L. (1986) *Power and Performance in Organizations.* Oxford: Black-well.

Mangham, I.L. (1995) 'Scripts, talk and double talk', *Management Learning*, 26 (4): 493–511.

Mangham, I.L. and Overington, M.A. (1987) *Organizations as Theatre: A Social Psychology of Dramatic Appearances.* Chichester: Wiley.

Martin, Joanne (1982) 'Stories and scripts in organizational settings', in A. Hastorf and A. Isen (eds), *Cognitive and Social Psychology.* New York: Elsevier–North Holland. pp. 225–305.

Martin, Joanne (1990) 'Deconstructing organizational taboos: the suppression of gender conflict in organizations', *Organization Science*, 1 (4): 339–359.

Martin, Joanne, Feldman, Martha S., Hatch, Mary Jo and Sitkin, Sim B. (1983) 'The uniqueness paradox in organizational stories', *Administrative Science Quarterly*, 28: 438–53.

Martin, Joanne and Meyerson, Debra (1988) 'Organizational cultures and the denial, channeling and acknowledgement of ambiguity', in Louis R. Pondy, Richard J. Boland Jr and Howard Thomas (eds), *Managing Ambiguity and Change.* New York: Wiley. pp. 93–125.

Martin, Joanne and Powers, Melanie E. (1983) 'Truth or corporate propaganda: the value of a good war story', in L.R. Pondy, P.J. Frost, G. Morgan and T.C. Dandridge (eds), *Organizational Symbolism.* Greenwich, CT: JAI Press.

Meek, V.L. (1988) 'Organizational culture: origins and weaknesses', *Organization Studies*, 9 (4): 453–73.

Mitroff, I.I. and Kilman, R.H. (1976) 'On organizational stories: an approach to the design and analysis of organizations through myths and stories', in R.H. Kilman, L.R. Pondy and D. Slevin (eds), *The Management of Organizational Design.* New York: North Holland.

Parker, Martin (1992) 'Post-modern organizations or postmodern theory?' *Organization Studies*, 13 (1): 1–17.

Parker, Martin (1995) 'Critique in the name of what? Postmodernism and critical approaches to organization', *Organization Studies*, 16 (4): 553–64.

Pondy L.R. (1983) 'The role of metaphors and myths in organization and in the facilitation of change', in L.R. Pondy, P.J. Frost, G. Morgan and T.C. Dandridge (eds), *Organizational Symbolism.* Greenwich, CT: JAI Press.

Propp, Vladimir (1984) *Theory and History of Folklore.* Manchester: Manchester University Press.

Rosen, M. (1984) 'Myth and reproduction: the conceptualization of management theory, method and practice', *Journal of Management*, 21 (3): 303–22.

Rosen, M. (1985a) 'Breakfast at Spiro's: dramaturgy and dominance', *Journal of Management Studies*, 11 (2): 31–48.

Rosen, M. (1985b) 'The reproduction of hegemony: an analysis of bureaucratic control', *Research in Political Economy*, 8: 257–89.

Stein, Howard F. (1994) 'Workplace organizations and culture theory: a psycho-analytic approach', paper presented at the Symposium of The International Society for the Psychoanalytic Study of Organizations, Chicago, 2–4 June 1994.

Thompson, P. (1993) 'Postmodernism: fatal distraction', in J. Hassard and M. Parker (eds), *Postmodernism and Organizations.* London: Sage. pp. 183–203.

Trice, H.M. and Beyer, J.M. (1984) 'Studying organizational cultures through rites and ceremonials', *American Management Review*, 9: 653–69.

Wilkins, A.L. (1983) 'Organizational stories as symbols which control the organization', in L.R. Pondy, P.J. Frost, G. Morgan and T.C. Dandridge (eds), *Organizational Symbolism*. Greenwich, CT: JAI Press.

Wilkins, A. and Martin, J. (1979) 'Organizational legends', Research Paper No. 521, Graduate School of Business, Stanford University, Stanford, CA.

9 Conversation Analysis

Dalvir Samra-Fredericks

> Talk is at the heart of all organizations. Through it, the everyday business of organizations is accomplished. People in organizations talk all day, every day.
>
> Boden, *The Business of Talk*

In the general literature on organization theory and organizational behaviour, the talk of 'people' is largely absent or is reduced to the broad term 'communication skill'. In addition, it is rare for this notion of communication skill to be developed from detailed studies of *naturally occurring talk* in organizations (e.g. Margerison, 1987; Wright and Taylor, 1994). One possible reason for the absence of studies of naturally occurring talk may be that of access and this is discussed later. Another reason may be unfamiliarity with the various systematic approaches for analysing recorded talk. This chapter will introduce conversation analysis (CA) as one approach for the analysis and description of naturally occurring talk and will illustrate the approach from my research into boardroom talk. Given the constraints on length here, readers are urged to read the seminal texts (e.g. Sacks et al., 1974; Sacks, 1992; Schegloff, 1972; Schegloff and Sacks, 1973) to appreciate CA's original aims and methods, as well as more recent studies (e.g. Boden and Zimmerman, 1991; Drew and Heritage, 1992; Heritage, 1997). Without doubt, ongoing developments in the CA field (see for example Drew, 1990 and the collection of papers introduced by Pomerantz, 1993 in *Text*) are extending our understanding of human interaction and continue to address a wide range of issues and concerns in sociology. In 1976, Giddens contended that

> social theory must incorporate a treatment of action as rationalized conduct ordered reflexively by human agents, and must grasp the *significance of language as the practical medium* whereby this is made possible. (1976: 8, emphasis added)

To this end, the dynamic processes of structuration which Giddens (1984) has proposed in theoretical terms are explored in Boden's (1994) work which employed the CA method (see also Boden and Zimmerman, 1991; Heritage, 1997). However, it is important to note here that, like Drew, I feel 'I cannot claim to speak in any sense "on behalf of" conversation analysts, some of whom may demur at points I've made, or may have different priorities' (1990: 34). CA is a diverse area of study and, as Heritage notes, there are 'two kinds' of CA research today. One 'examines the social institution *of* interaction . . . The second studies the management of social institutions *in* interaction' (1997: 162). What can be stated with some confidence though is that those who seek to work within this tradition 'share a common assumptive base'. They

> believe that talk should be studied in context, that interaction is best studied as an on-going accomplishment of the participants and that discourse is both responsive to and produces/reproduces features of social life. (Pomerantz, 1993: 155)

The relatively recent 'intellectual turn' in the social sciences has led to greater interest in the 'discursive nature of social life' and 'communal' meaning-making for the ongoing construction/reproduction of reality (1993: 155). CA is an approach and a systematic method for examining *social interaction* (rather than language *per se*). The founder of CA, Harvey Sacks (1984: 26), asserted that it was because social organization must be apparent at the level of mundane face-to-face interactions that he turned to conversation (also Schegloff, 1987). CA, based upon naturally occurring talk, explores 'social phenomena' to discover the form, structure, machinery and methodical procedures (Psathas, 1995) of social actions. I broadly adhere to the approach forwarded by Boden (1994). Boden's analysis of talk draws upon ethnomethodology, conversation analysis *and* organization and social theory.

In this chapter, I will *only* refer to that part of my study into boardroom talk which illustrates the CA approach and hence I do not refer to the additional analyses of this talk employing Habermas's (1979; 1984) theory of communicative action or begin to discuss the nature of role enactment against Turner's (1988) theory of social interaction. To begin to grasp the complex nature of human interaction in the boardroom, a multi-level, multi-disciplinary approach was deemed necessary (Samra-Fredericks, 1994; 1996a; 1996b). In particular, given my interests, I explore the range of conversational resources for developing strategy in the boardroom; the *real time* exercise of power to influence and resist definitions of the prevailing context; and what constitutes professionalism (Table 9.1 is discussed shortly and depicts the overall research process).

In ethnomethodological terms, the members (directors and senior managers, also referred to as 'actors' here) have basic procedures for making sense, the 'ethnomethods' (Garfinkel, 1967; Turner, 1988; also Heritage, 1984) or 'culturally based methods' (Feldman, 1995) which comprise verbal behaviours. Within an ethnomethodological programme, members' ongoing use of norms during the course of their interaction is examined and from this a key issue for social science is 'not whether social facts are objectively grounded' but how such 'grounding is accomplished' (Suchman, 1987: 57 in Feldman, 1995: 8; also Heritage, 1984). This aspect has been examined in my research into boardroom talk but, as noted above, the focus here is limited to that of introducing CA.

Recently there has been the suggestion that CA as a term is a *misnomer* (Psathas, 1995: 2). This is primarily because it is 'talk-in-interaction that is the broader and more inclusive characterization of the phenomena of study' (1995: 2; Boden, 1994; Schegloff, 1987). Psathas suggests that an even better term would be *interaction analysis* or even *ethnomethodological interaction analysis* (1995: 2). This chapter adopts the term 'talk' as a shorthand version of talk-in-interaction. What will become apparent from the discussion here is that ethnostudies such as CA are characterized by a particular disposition to social phenomena (see, in particular on CA and institutional talk, Heritage, 1997: 162–4). Consequently, to offer here 'instructable features' (Psathas, 1995) for discovery, analysis and description of talk presumes a range of 'beliefs' or assumptions carried by the researcher about the nature of the social world, the role of talk and the scope for agency. The epistemological and ontological issues cannot be easily divorced from the CA approach which then raises problems concerning a neutral 'stand-alone' rendering of 'the methods' of CA in this chapter. Yet, there is a constraint on space here. All that can be said is that to reduce CA to a series of 'stand-alone' techniques is problematic and goes against what the founders of CA proposed (see Psathas, 1995). In a simple but quite profound move, what both Garfinkel's ethnomethodology and Sacks's CA sought to do was to turn the 'problem of order' upside down (Boden, 1994). Boden elaborates by stating that CA seeks to 'answer' an overriding

> question [which] is not one of how people respond to normative constraints, but rather how it is that order is produced as a situated social matter . . . To understand the profound orderliness of social life requires not aggregation and abstraction but attention to the finegrained details of moment-to-moment exist-ence, and to their temporal, spatial and profoundly sequential organization. (1994: 65)

In this chapter, *one* aspect of the 'moment-to-moment existence' of directors and senior managers will illustrate the 'hallmark of all CA', namely, sequential organization in terms of turn-taking. It is the basic 'method' or procedure used for organizing conversation as a social activity. From this basis, an introductory understanding of CA can be offered and, very briefly, 'what else I did to understand boardroom talk' will conclude the chapter.

Since ethnomethodology asserts that members employ a series of implicit 'folk' practices or 'ethnomethods' to create a 'presumption' that they share a common world (Garfinkel, 1967; see also Boden, 1994; Heritage, 1984; Psathas, 1995; Turner, 1988), my *overall* goal was (and still is) to examine directors' and senior managers' 'folk' practices and, from that, discern the nature of their *skilled* accomplishments. Garfinkel (1967) asserted that members/actors are not 'dopes' following the rules of conversation but are knowledgeable and reflexively employ a myriad of 'procedures'. Procedures are conceived as *resources* that enable hearers/ speakers to achieve order for each other *and*, if recorded, for the analyst. This also alerts those working with talk that although the tapes and transcripts exhibit general examples of procedures-in-use, they also exhibit 'circumstantial variation' (see Jefferson, 1980). For example, in terms of boardroom talk, although the localized turn-taking system at various junctures conformed to the general system first noted by Sacks et al. (1974, see below; and Boden, 1994), there was also notable systematic variation, which studies of institutional talk have documented (see below and Heritage, 1997).

Basic assumptions of CA

A focal point of Garfinkel's (1967) original ethnomethodological studies was members' accomplishments, and his colleague Sacks began to system-atically document in more detail the nature of members' *methods*. The implicit procedures by which talk is performed – pauses, turn-taking, interruptions etc. – were subjected to detailed study. The first CA studies conducted by Sacks and colleagues analysed basic methods such as turn-taking (Sacks et al., 1974) and adjacency pairs such as questions/answers and procedures for opening and closing conversations (Schegloff and Sacks, 1973). These studies have provided a foundation for ongoing CA research (see, for example, Boden, 1994; Boden and Zimmerman, 1991; Drew and Heritage, 1992) and for the continuing *emphasis upon sequential organiza-tion and its orderliness*.

The analyst's role will become apparent shortly but at this stage we can summarize the basic assumptions of CA as follows:

1   Order is a produced orderliness and is repeatable and recurrent.
2   Order is produced by the members *in situ*.
3   Members orient to that order themselves (order is not an analyst's preformulated theoretical conception).
4   Discovery, description and analysis of produced orderliness are the analyst's task.
5   Frequency or how often particular phenomena occur is to be set aside (adapted from Psathas, 1995: 2–3; see also Boden, 1994).

It is asserted by CA scholars that through the turn-by-turn analysis and description of talk, a sense of *how* social order is a members' accomplish-ment can be discerned. Equally, locational matters in CA are appreciated in the context of 'other sequential details' (see Wieder, 1988: 451). Given this, preserving the sequential nature of the talk is important.

A fundamental theory about how actors 'orient to interaction' is summa-rized well by Heritage (1997: 162–3). Heritage states that CA are 'analyses of action, context management and intersubjectivity' (1997: 163). Moreover, Wieder (1988: 453) has suggested that the process of *actual analysis* can be seen as one of continually making the *'tacit explicit'*. The issue of the analyst's tacit knowledge informing (or disinforming) analyses is considered by Zimmerman (1988; also discussed in the two subsequent 'commentaries' by Jacobs, 1988; Wieder, 1988). Zimmerman (1988: 449), for instance, notes that the 'initial purchase on some phenomena may be gained on intuitive grounds, but this is merely the beginning'. From this beginning, the phenomena is 'worked up' through a process of searching across a number of conversations. This was the process adopted in my research into board-room talk (discerned in Table 9.1).

The research

My interest in talk and *how* accomplished actors go about their daily tasks began in the early 1980s whilst I was still an undergraduate. This interest continues today, widening to understand *how* actors go about socially constructing world(s) and making sense of what is happening and can happen as well as the basic ethnomethods or conversational resources for 'doing social life' as we know it. Since 1986 I have focused upon organizational arenas, and thereafter on groups of senior managers.

This chapter will refer to the specific research conducted into director and senior manager routines and their resources for *doing* (ethnomethodo-logically speaking: see Garfinkel, 1967 and Heritage, 1984) strategy in *real time* which was deemed to be a neglected area in management literatures (Samra-Fredericks, 1994; 1996a; 1996b).[1] The audio and video recording of manager interactions *as they happen* has been termed *real time* research (Samra-Fredericks, 1995; 1996a) as opposed to interviewing and observation (arguably observations are *real time* but also limited because of human capabilities in terms of recall and coding at that time). However, I also did interview, observe, work shadow some of the directors and senior managers and collect any available written documentation. This was part of a move to understand the tasks being *done* therein along a broader dimension which recent CA studies appear to address in various ways (Drew and Heritage, 1992; Boden, 1994; also Drew, 1990: 28 on CA's neglect of contexts of discourse, but also see Heritage, 1984; 1997). The reference above to interactions *as they happen* is drawn from Boden's (1994) insistence that there is a need to study organizations *as they happen* rather than continue with the usual practice of conducting studies after the event. In other words, rather than study the development of strategy and the management of change *as reported* by the actors during formal and informal interviews, or from administering questionnaires or from collecting company documents, I audio and video recorded events (such as board-level meetings, departmental meetings, audit review sessions). They were *happening* 'then and there' in the actors' *real time* and constituted a ' "reasonable record" of what happened during a particular strip of social life' (1994: 65). From this basis it became possible to discern *how* it happened and, for me, which conversational resources had pragmatic utility for the directors and senior managers as they sought to determine a strategic direction for their company. The recordings, then, enabled me to listen to quite complex talk-based interactive routines again and again as if they were happening 'then and there' (as far as this is possible with such technology).

The biggest problem I faced was that of gaining access to senior management teams. As far back as 1986 initial attempts were made to negotiate such access. However, the companies who were willing to discuss the research 'brief' expressed reservations since the 'method' (recording in *real time*) was perceived to be too invasive. Consequently, I was confined to the more traditional methods of interviews and limited observations in these companies. (Clearly, it must also be stated that personal circumstances as well as the assumptions, skills and qualities of the researcher must impact upon the process of doing research generally.) Finally, after a series of protracted negotiations with another set of companies over several months, high-level access was granted to two organizations. Armed with a camcorder, tripod and tape recorder I finally entered the 'field' in the way I had envisaged many years earlier. This chapter will illustrate the CA approach from one of these two organizations – a manufacturing company based on two sites employing approximately 700 people. The organization had instigated a move to cellular manufacturing (financed by the parent company in Europe) and clearly this had immense implications for the employees in terms of reorganization and retraining efforts. Talk in the boardroom was dominated by such matters as well as the need to secure quality standards. Indeed, talk about outdated practices and belief systems were communicated in complex but subtle ways, as the micro-analysis was to reveal.

Initially, I conducted a series of formal and informal interviews as well as observing work processes and work shadowing a small group of senior managers. During this initial period, information about the espoused change programme and the issues that appeared to face 'the organization' as stated by the actors was 'gathered'. Equally, from just 'being there', knowledge about the core group of actors, their current interests and goals, their likes and dislikes and how they talked and presented themselves generally was also being noted. The tape recordings themselves were collected over a period of time with numerous reassurances of confidentiality and minimal disruption. During the monthly board-level meetings I soon discovered that, for the actors, the significance of the 'task' – the management of the general change programme as well as a sudden product failure in the market place mid-way through the research – was greater than any interest in me. Consequently, the need to monitor their talk because of my presence was overridden by a need to track the conversation as a participant and to determine the implications (for them and their functions) of what was being 'done' as they talked.

In *content* terms the talk was about (a) 'delayering' (stripping out levels of management), (b) the introduction of cellular manufacturing (building a new factory), (c) a process of 'empowering' line managers to take responsibilities and establish accountability (training and development), (d) developing human resource capability in R&D and IT functions (to realize the espoused 'vision'), and (e) ascribing negligence (product failure). All of this talk was set against the immediate goal of securing various general and industry specific quality standards. When I entered the organization the actors were approximately nine months into their espoused five year 'plan' of change. As a collective, they appeared to have a general (espoused) 'vision' of what the organization would be like in five years' time. As individuals, responsible for specific functional areas, there were ongoing differences of opinion and inevitably conflict surfaced when face met face across the boardroom table. In terms of managing strategic change, the work of Pettigrew and a team of Warwick researchers was of particular interest to me (Pettigrew, 1985; 1987; 1990; Pettigrew and Whipp, 1991; Pettigrew et al., 1992). Yet, in terms of recording and analysing the actual 'sayings' to discover *how* senior management teams may *realize* strategic change, there was silence in the literature. For a relatively young woman, whose ethnic origins were 'unclear', entering the boardroom and recording the talk posed some problems, but these were overcome as time progressed (Samra-Fredericks, 1995).

A major issue of *when* to record the talk was resolved on a practical level over a 12 month period and was initially informed by Glaser and Strauss's (1967) suggestion of theoretical sampling. Since the general interest was in '*how* do senior managers *do* strategy when face meets face?', taking 'do' in its ethnomethodological sense (see Garfinkel, 1967; Heritage, 1984), talk recorded during the monthly day-long board meetings was *selected* for detailed analysis but after that there was no attempt to *select* as such.[2] It is accepted that the talk during the more informal meetings between the directors, as well as in corridors, car parks and the men's toilets (all were men), impacted upon the development of a 'strategy'. Yet, this talk, if it was significant *for the actors* (their goals and interests), found its way into the boardroom through 'reported' speech, and here the pragmatic function of metalingual expressions was examined (not reproduced here: Samra-Fredericks, 1996b). As the research progressed and my theoretical and conceptual focus crystallized, it was also deemed to be consistent with Forester's (1987; 1992) notion of a 'critical ethnography' since the enactment of social and political relations has also been explored, enabling a grounded appreciation of the way power is 'exercised' in the boardroom.

During the initial series of monthly board meetings in the manufacturing company, I sat in a corner and took notes and more notes. Later, the camcorder and tape recorder were introduced and set up in a corner of the boardroom and I sat on the floor, out of sight (long skirts or trousers were essential!). The only thing in view was a microphone on the table and the video camera in a corner. I could change the audio tapes without any disruption to the flow of talk. In addition to recording these meetings, I also recorded the routine meetings that took place between the sales and marketing director and his senior management team (for example, during the budget-setting period) and the operations director's meetings with his senior management team (for example, when reviewing the move to cellular manufacturing and progress regarding quality control procedures). Any other events, such as a day-long internal audit review session attended by *all* the senior managers across the organization, were also captured on audio and video tapes.

For their part, the organization/actors expected 'feedback' sessions to comprise a *general* analysis of the interactive routines and comment on the actual change programme and its management. Clearly, it was important for me to state that confidentiality and anonymity would characterize the feedback and that no one actor was to glean 'information' (my interpretations) about any other actor. However, if any director or senior manager wanted to listen to my interpretation of *their* 'performance', then I would have provided that. It was felt that this stance was important in order to build trust and to establish a clear and honest mode of operation since I would be 'in and out' of the organization over many months to come. To achieve this, the MD was clearly important. He was a man of great integrity who respected this 'contract'. However, given the invasive nature of the research, the organization/actors expected to be consulted if and when the 'findings' were to be made public (published). Indeed, in 1994 prior to presenting at an international conference, I arranged a meeting with the operations director (who emerged as my first point of contact about any matters arising from my presence in the company) to show him what the transcribed talk would 'look/read like' in a conference paper. He was satisfied that the organization, the actors and the products could not be identified. This is an ongoing concern and I feel that only through building a relationship based upon trust and understanding each other's needs can research of this nature continue. Without doubt, exposing oneself to such a microscopic and potentially critical analysis engenders anxiety. All tapes have been coded and whilst I have played parts of the tapes to fellow academics/researchers in various settings, they are carefully selected so that references to names, the company and the products are not voiced at that time.

Transcription

Transcribing any spoken text is a time-consuming activity and this was multiplied many times since I was dealing with multi-party talk as opposed to two-person interviews. Equally, in terms of CA, the level of detail and the need for 'accuracy' are crucial.[3] It is the intricacies of interaction and *not* just the 'content' of what is said that must be transcribed. In addition, both Fairclough (1992) and Psathas (1995) have observed that it is the objectives of the research which guide the employment of particular symbols or system of notations. A key point made by Psathas and Anderson (1990) is that transcription *is* analysis since interpretations are being made and decisions are being taken about what to leave out. For example, the issue of silence may require a decision as 'to whom does it belong?' (Fairclough, 1992;

Jefferson, 1989). Fairclough adds that depending upon the system of transcription it may 'take anything from six to twenty hours or more to transcribe *one* hour of recorded speech' (1992: 229, emphasis added). In addition, recording clarity and the passion with which the actors in the boardroom spoke all impacted upon the hours invested to transcribe the talk. Difficulties in identifying who was talking were resolved by playing the video recordings of the meetings alongside the audio tapes. A foot and headset transcriber also assisted the transformation of the talk into the written format as the tapes could be slowed down so that inaudible speech could be discerned. Yet, even then there were occasions where there were difficulties in discerning utterances (Psathas, 1995; Psathas and Anderson, 1990).

Transcription is then a 'selection process' where variation in transcribers' 'practices introduce directly and specifically the analyst's interests and theories' (Psathas and Anderson, 1990). The transcripts generated from the boardroom talk recorded false starts, hesitations and interruptions. However, and this is an important point which does *not* conform to CA, pauses were *not* recorded as tenths of seconds but were divided into two types: first, a short pause (less than a second) was marked by '(.)' in the transcript; and secondly, a longer pause (more than a second) was represented as '[brief pause]'. This level of transcription detail varies from CA studies where pauses are timed in a split-second fashion (Jefferson, 1989; Psathas, 1995; Psathas and Anderson, 1990) and from those studies which include organizational talk (e.g. Forester, 1992; Knights and Willmott, 1992; Mangham, 1986; 1988) where pauses appear to be not noted systematically and/or are not timed at all. Details of the various transcription systems in use and for noting features such as laughter, coughs, tempo and intonation are to be found in the CA studies referred to in this chapter. Psathas and Anderson (1990) in particular offer a short but informed introduction to transcription generally. The key features to facilitate the reading of the transcripts below are to be found in the Appendix.

Representing the overall research process visually

Over the course of two years in terms of the boardroom study, I listened to the tape recordings, generated transcripts and sought to understand *how* social order is produced so that decisions are *made*, meetings are *realized*, role identities are enacted and 'organization' is (re-)created. It is, as Boden (1994) notes, a 'laminated effect' of talk over time/space dimensions. Boden employs this specific term to convey the essence of a process where the talk works to 'frame succeeding interactions' and builds towards 'decisions' or objects that 'retrospectively, will look like decisions' (1994: 91). This clearly has a specific theoretical and methodological orientation. During these two years, the actual 'task' of developing a strategy and managing the

change programme in the manufacturing company became almost periph-
eral, reduced only to a 'theme' or thread connecting me and the actors to the
management literature and business school orthodoxy whilst the 'problem of
order' was prioritized. To attempt to represent this process visually I include
Table 9.1 and stress that *each* series of listenings included *many* occasions
where the tapes were listened to. In addition, analysts working with talk
acknowledge that there is a need to continually refer back to the original tape
recordings since the 'status of the transcript remains that of "merely" being
a representation of the actual interaction' and that 'it is not the interaction
and it is not the "data"' (Psathas and Anderson, 1990: 77; Zimmerman,
1988). Initial repeated listenings of both the audio and the video tapes have
been termed 'methodical listenings' by Psathas and Anderson (1990). It is
during this overall process that a transcript is produced which 'captures/
displays those features of the interaction that are of analytic interest' (1990:
76). The table also depicts in part the *grounded* nature of the research
(Glaser and Strauss, 1967).

Table 9.1   *Series of methodical listenings and viewings*

Listenings	Objectives of listenings: intended and emergent
1st series of listenings/viewings of complete 'capta' set[1]	To determine overall issues, understand cultural 'context': was *content* focused
2nd series of listenings of complete 'capta' set	To determine and understand 'where' strategy is being developed, and 'how' change management is 'materializing'
3rd series of listenings/viewings of complete 'capta' set	To identify the verbal features for the interpersonal development of strategy and changing; to identify the significant features for *process* management
4th series of listenings	To theoretically sample a series of meetings: three consecutive meetings selected
5th series of listenings/viewings	To transcribe selected core meetings
6th series of listenings	To analyse *together* with the transcriptions of the meetings: identify the verbal features and consider the turn-taking system
7th series of listenings	To continue analysis (and embark upon validity claim analysis and role enactment); to select 'moments'[2] to illustrate theory development in the area of change management and strategy development
8th series of listenings/viewings	To confirm confidence in the interpretation/analysis
9th series of listenings of the complete 'capta' set	As above *and* to ensure representativeness

[1] The term 'capta' set is used since it conveys the sense that information is captured from
rather than given by a social setting (Gherardi and Turner, 1987: 13).
[2] Moments where the actors struggled to 'have a say' and where there was rapid 'turnover' in
speakers were compared and contrasted against those where the interaction proceeded
'smoothly'. There was still an element of interruption during these latter 'moments' but they
were opportunities for the actors to sense-make as opposed to challenge another's
perspective.

I entered the manufacturing company with no hypothesis or specific framework apart from a general interest in capturing talk for *doing* strategy and to detail the nature of the actors' accomplishments as they 'do' social life. During the fifth and sixth series of listenings, CA was undertaken where the turn-taking system and adjacency pairs were examined. *As noted earlier, this chapter refers to these two series of listenings only.* Consequently, in terms of the overall theoretical and conceptual framework for understanding boardroom talk, the discussion and illustrations (four brief extracts representing under two minutes of talk!) presented here are indeed a *partial* account.

From the seventh series of listenings the issue of displaying or illustrating the 'findings' also emerged. Theory was generated to understand the nature of the interactive routines and conversational resources for *doing* strategy and *realizing* change when face meets face. In particular, what began to interest me was the way competing rationalities were articulated and interpersonally managed through basic conversational resources such as metalingual expressions. From this initial micro-analysis of talk through the CA method, what transpired as the analysis proceeded was that a range of conversational resources which had pragmatic utility for the actors *at that time* could be identified.

On the issue of theory development and the CA method, Heritage (1989: 36) observes that the 'pure' CA orientation towards systematic description may be 'criticized as resulting in an atheoretical taxonomy'. He adds that such an approach requires 'no apology' and clearly one consequence of this is that the move from systematic description to theory development (evident in my own research) may be problematic for (some) 'pure' CA scholars. To partly overcome this, it is suggested that detailed transcripts are offered so that researchers who adopt an alternative stance or have different interests and theoretical orientations can confirm, add to, critique and challenge *both* the description and the subsequent theoretical elaboration (the need to listen to the original recordings given the nature of transcription as analysis is acknowledged).

The next section will now very briefly illustrate the hallmarks of CA from boardroom talk: the taking of turns. To offer the analysis of the actors' use of other conversational resources such as questions (which posed problems for the recipients and were found to be critical for legitimating one's perspective or vision over another's) necessitates protracted discussion which cannot be entered into here.

Illustrating conversation analysis

Given that turn-taking is 'the central focus for all researchers in CA' (Boden, 1994: 66), the analysis of boardroom talk could not avoid this 'most fundamental unit of social action'. Turns, as a basic unit of social action, 'provide a simple, economic and extraordinarily efficient way of allocating activities' (1994: 66). Taking a turn at talk is so taken for granted that its close study may at first appear trivial and mundane. Indeed, where is the study of turn-taking in the ever-growing organization behaviour, organization theory and strategic management literatures?!

The major principle of sequential organization, a simple turn-taking system, was initially forwarded by Sacks et al. (1974). The discovery of this 'deep structure' of turn-taking led to a process of identifying the following essential features (Boden, 1994: 67):

1   One speaker speaks at a time.
2   Number and order of speakers vary freely.
3   Turn size varies.
4   Turns are not allocated in advance but vary.
5   Turn transition is frequent and quick.
6   There are few gaps and few overlaps in turn transition.

(See also Boden and Zimmerman, 1991: 9; Sacks et al., 1974; and Levinson, 1983; Nofsinger, 1991 and especially Heritage, 1997: 163–73.) Equally, the system provides for another basic 'premise', that of local determination (Zimmerman, 1988: 423). Subsequent research has noted variants to the system above, e.g. in courtrooms, doctor/patient and teacher/pupil interactions (Atkinson and Drew, 1979; Atkinson, 1982; Greatbatch, 1992; Heritage, 1989; Mehan, 1979). In terms of meeting talk, Boden's (1994) study also provides an account of variation and one which the formal setting of a boardroom meeting also confirmed. However, it is important to stress that, like Drew (1992: 517), my concern was 'not with the management of turn-taking itself' but with 'the interactional management of activities in the turns' which the actors take.

Turns in the boardroom were 'valued' and 'shared' amongst the actors and, as Boden (1994) notes in meetings, were found to 'pace topics' and 'space speakers'. During the monthly board meetings this notion of pacing and spacing was found to be critical for conveying and legitimating perspectives (visioning) so that the formal strategy that was eventually adopted reflected the particular interests and goals of the various actors. But, in contrast to earlier studies within an institutional context – courts, classrooms and the medical consultations – boardroom meetings did not yield an easy 'identification' of the rights and obligations of the actors for the use of the turn-taking system. Consequently, institutional identities (see Greatbatch, 1992) were not so easily assembled from the types of turns taken *and* the scope of the activities that could be legitimately produced therein. Given this, once the general parameters of the localized turn-taking system and the nature of question use were examined, the process of making validity claims as proposed by Habermas (1979; 1984; see also Forester, 1992) was also explored. This analysis enabled further understanding of the complex nature of social and political relations as *instantiated* through mundane talk in the boardroom as well as that of 'institutional role identities'. Heritage (1997) does however provide an excellent account of the CA approach to this complex, elusive issue, that is, institutional identities and talk. He notes three features which create a 'unique finger-print' for different kinds of institutional interaction and 'six basic places to probe the "institutionality" of interaction'. These are: turn taking; overall structural organization; sequence organization; turn design; lexical choice; epistemological and other forms of asymmetry (Heritage, 1997: 164). The research summarized in Table 9.1 does encompass elements of these 'six basic places'.

The following extracts are brief illustrations of the broad parameters of the turn-taking 'system' which typically characterized the boardroom meetings. The speakers are: managing director (MD), finance director (FD), sales and marketing director (SMD), quality manager (QM), purchasing manager (PM) and operations director (OD). Our focus will remain with the MD for analytical purposes whilst *remembering* that others are vital for 'organization'.

Extract 1

1	MD	OK [name of FD] do you want to take us through=
2	FD	=yes ok well the April results urm (.) UK operations . . . [cont.]

Extract 2

1	MD	right [name of QM]
2	SMD	ok[?]=
3	MD	=you are on (.)
4	QM	right=
5	MD	=BS5750

Extract 3

1	MD	so (.) bit of a culture shock that I think [quietly spoken] err
2		are we missing somebody?
		[brief pause]
3	SMD	{no [name of QM]
4	PM	{no er [name of QM] was [er
5	MD	[oh OK yeah fine 'Attendu'
6	FD	yeah=
7	MD	=you all got it
8	FD	um=
9	OD	=yep
		[pause as actors locate their copy amongst their papers and find appropriate pages]
10	MD	err what we tried to do in that document is really to say . . . [cont.]

In extracts 1 and 2 the MD selects the next speaker *given* the next item on the formal agenda. Overall, the agenda (circulated prior to the meeting) dictated the sequence of the topics or items discussed but transgression occurred *if* relevance could be *made*. This emphasis on *made* is to highlight the fact that these are strategic, reflexive actors who employed a range of verbal strategies to make their views known. Returning to extract 1, the 'well' uttered by the FD in response to the MD's invitation to talk is an example of a 'pause marker' (Fraser, 1990; Schiffrin, 1987). This function has been differentiated from the use of 'well' as a turn-initial marker signalling dissonance which became apparent during the conflictual encounters (Samra-Fredericks, 1996b).

In extract 2, the SMD's inserted 'ok' concludes a preceding extended turn by him and acknowledges the MD's *right* to move onto the next item/topic (at line 1 by naming the next speaker). In extract 3, after 'so' (line 1), the MD signals his move as concluding the preceding 'presentation' on securing quality standards.[4] The MD continues by 'self-selecting' since it is his item that is next on the agenda (line 5), but he still needs to 'tie' his talk to this agenda, announced through 'Attendu' (line 5, the budget). In this way, he 'marks' his talk as that of being a participant/presenter of an item. In other words he moves from one who regulates others' turns, to one who is a participant and whose forthcoming talk was characterized by 'information dissemination' (not reproduced here). Equally, it is noteworthy that for the formal status of the meeting to continue, particular actors did *need* to be present. Here for example, at line 2 in extract 3, the MD asks who is missing. The absence of the QM is accounted for, here implicitly (it is shared knowledge demonstrated by the need for it not to be voiced: that is, once an item has been presented and discussed by a *senior manager*, he may leave if there is other 'business'). The QM's presence is *not* required to give the subsequent talk legitimacy. Boden (1994: 89) has proposed that 'the essence of membership is marked by some kind of listing display' or the 'presence of a quorum' and that this is important if the meeting is to be organizationally and interactionally meaningful.

Extract 3 also illustrates another feature of meeting talk generally. Whilst documents were circulated beforehand (here, the Attendu, lines 5 and 7), the actors still *spoke* about them and through this talk conveyed *how* they should be interpreted. This was a sensitive and political issue on many occasions and the process was subjected to detailed analysis in order to establish the resources the actors deployed in this setting to *persuade and influence*. In terms of the Attendu, at line 10, the MD begins by stating 'what we tried to do in that document is really to say . . .'. He refers to prior talk-based events which led to the written document before them. In this way he ties that prior talk to the present and, from the overall analysis conducted so far, it can be suggested that this is an important recurring feature for 'organizing' (Weick, 1979). Whilst he infers that there was joint agreement through the collective 'we', it was *still* a sensitive issue since there had been some dispute over the finer details of the budget and the actual process of putting it together. It is being suggested in effect that they as a board had already agreed to what was said and then documented in writing. Through this utterance at line 10, the MD secured an extended turn (not reproduced here) to *select and reformulate* the important parts of the budget. The listeners then tracked the 'multiplicity of conversational objects' (assessments, invitations to agree/disagree, to confirm and so on; see Boden, 1994) that followed such an opening. It is this taken-for-granted way of talking 'meeting talk' which, as each face-to-face encounter unfolded over time, eventually 'laminated' into well-known 'organizational objects' (Boden, 1994) such as the budget and strategy documents which were handed to me on entry to and during my 12 months in and out of this organization. Yet, these artefacts were being continually reinterpreted and *made* relevant or irrelevant during the actors' ongoing *real time*. From the stance adopted (Samra-Fredericks, 1995; 1996a; 1996b) and alluded to in this chapter, it can be suggested that given the complexity with which we are dealing when researching organizations and management, to study strategy documents in isolation as a record of the process or progress of strategy development is indeed limited. Equally, to take reported speech in isolation during interviews is also a partial understanding of what actually happened and the skills for making it happen when it did. Capturing the routines and the skills and competencies to accomplish this 'activity' (doing strategy) continues to evade many researchers since they do not capture it *happening as it happens*. Seeing and hearing *how* actors *use* such artefacts and what they *mean* to them during their efforts to influence and resist in the boardroom begins to allow a deeper understanding of workplace interactions and, for me, the range of resources that actors deploy to manage each other and (re)construct 'organization'. It is accepted that the three extracts above are too brief to illustrate the multitude ways that orderliness is achieved and to allow the complexity of boardroom interaction to be rendered transparent to the reader. It can only be tentatively stated here.

Returning to the nature of turn-taking, it is possible to suggest that through the localized management of pre-allocations and the types of turns permissible (expected), a 'shared attentiveness' was sustained *and* the 'institutional role' of the MD as chair was *instantiated*. The issue of 'expectation' also refers us to the notion of 'stocks of knowledge' and typified schemes that actors hold (see Berger and Luckmann, 1967). The other actors seated around the boardroom table did not challenge the types of turns *taken* by the MD (or by each other for that matter) and thus they demonstrated their shared knowledge of the type of interaction they were 'doing' and, through this, *realized* the 'context/setting' – boardroom meeting. Clearly, the nature of discourse identities and institutional roles needs to be substantiated from extended analyses and descriptions, which have been conducted but would detract from the objective of this chapter – introducing CA (a brief comment to illustrate more recent developments in CA regarding this particular area concludes this chapter).

In the boardroom, then, it was found that there was adjustment to the basic model of conversational turn-taking proposed by Sacks et al. (1974) since there was the *initial allocation of turns* where the current speaker (MD) selected the next speaker (director or senior manager) leading to extended monologues. However, there were also occasions where the basic model *appeared* to be adhered to, characterized by short economical turns secured through self-selection. The former (MD selects next speaker) occurred at junctures where talk about a specific item had been exhausted (decision made, information/opinion shared). These occasions contrasted with those where turns were *not* allocated in advance and *needed* to be secured by the 'community of speakers', primarily through self-selection. This was most evident during the 'discussion phase' (Bargiela, 1993; see also Bargiela-Chiappini and Harris, 1997) which was marked as such either by the MD or through self-selection by an actor whilst another was 'presenting' an item (their monologue). It was the nature and goal of the interaction that modified the mechanism of turn-taking. On only one occasion did an actor attempt to formally 'go through' the chair (the MD) although turns did regularly revolve back to him. The monologues were also expected and, as a technical departure from the system proposed by Sacks et al. (1974), were 'warranted' as actors made reports, statements and assessments about the state of the company. Interestingly, what Boden (1994) noted, and was confirmed in my analysis of boardroom talk, was that during the routine long turns, like in the courts or plea-bargaining settings (Maynard, 1984), the actors also accomplished 'stories' and used them to 'construct positions and realize agendas'.

A point also noted by Sacks et al. (1974) was that as each speaker takes a turn they do have recipients in mind, and indeed listeners are 'motivated to "hear" a turn that is for them'. Boden has suggested that this aspect also gives 'talk its rather syncopated and agreeably collaborative quality' (1994: 71). To illustrate this and the nature of interruption and 'latching on' where there were repeated instances of self-selection as well as the embedded use of adjacency pairs, extract 4 is presented below. Short, economical turns pervade this extract. The 'board' here are evaluating bar coding products as a way of ensuring that quantities are correct before dispatch. Is this a strategic issue or not? This is a question the researcher asked herself many times whilst analysing boardroom talk. It may indeed seem trivial. However, the *realized* (in the double sense proposed by Knights and Willmott, 1992) implications, and more importantly the immediate investments in effort on the part of the actors during the exchange, warranted further examination and evaluation of its status as strategic or not. It was found that talk in the boardroom about apparently trivial issues *did* influence the development of a strategy and hence the talk had strategic implications which were *realized* by the actors. The overall analysis of the meeting from which extract 4 is taken suggested that the bar coding issue fell into that bracket. Subsequent boardroom meetings and their analysis confirmed such interpretations for the analyst later *but were demonstrated at that time* by the actors for each other:

they knew what could transpire and this warranted the effort invested on their part.

The bar coding issue was important to the SMD who needed to minimize customer complaints and the subsequent increased manual intervention to raise credit notes. The attention given to it by these actors was 'framed' by the discourse of 'customer care' (not reproduced here). The discussion below cannot detail the actual implications for the 'company' or the simultaneous implications for the actors' role-making efforts (extracts have been analysed in some depth to understand and then further substantiate this intricate and fragile process as well as the resources deployed by the actors). The primary objective here is to illustrate the nature of collaborative turn-taking, the sequential nature of talk and the embedded use of adjacency pairs – here, questions (in bold) and their paired answers. Speakers are as before, with the addition of the production controller (PC).

Extract 4
```
 1   PC        the bar code (.)
 2   MD        yeah that's why I'm saying [they
 3   PC                                    [and then key in the quantities
 4             don't [they?
 5   MD              [yeah=
 6   FD        =and the price is already in the machine
 7   SMD       yeah=
 8   PC        =oh yeah that's all [central
 9   SMD                            [the I mean then then the supermarkets
10             run the stock (.)
11   FD        it's the [same stock er that's right
12   SMD               [programme
13   SMD       so the supermarket system is a count? (.)
14   OD        no the supermarket the girl on the checkout is the [count
15   FD                                                            [puts the
16             number in
17   OD        she [puts the number in
18   PC            [inaudible word]
19   FD        you think about when [we we've arrived with four
20   OD                             [you take
21   FD        bottles of [wine and got them [dated]
22   OD                   [if you take six [she can take six packs of those
23   SMD                                    [she wipes every bottle of wine
24             through
25   OD        [if you put six packs of those and they're identical=
26   SMD       [yeah
27   SMD       =yes
28   OD        what [if I buy six packs?
29   SMD            [she puts one through and presses [six
30   OD                                               [and presses six=
31   FD        =yeah [yeah
32   SMD             [she has that option=
33   OD        =yep
```

34   *SMD*   or she can wipe [all six
35   *FD*   [yeah yeah yeah=
            [cont.]

We can see that the answers to the questions here are provided in the next response, although this was not always the case (that is, insertion sequences were also evident). Primarily three directors compare the possibility that a particular type of system will solve a long-running operational problem with an *already known* everyday 'world' – the supermarket checkout system. The possible occurrence of error in the system at supermarket checkouts provides a basis from which to assess the value of a similar type of system in the company. The collaborative nature of the talk, which is over in a matter of seconds, has interruption and latching-on as the norm. As each actor takes their turn they *elaborate* upon the prior talk *and* both convey and confirm their mundane, *shared* 'stocks of knowledge'. One trivial example here is the invoking of the typification of 'supermarket checkout girl' (Lines 14, 17, 22, 23, 29, 32, 34). If one of the actors were to employ 'he' instead of 'she' it is possible to say with some confidence that the flow of talk would be disrupted. The other actors would perhaps overtly question the gender composition at that actor's local supermarket. As it is, they confirm a shared world and the interaction proceeds smoothly. They note that given human intervention, error cannot be discounted (the checkout person could still count up 'how many' and swipe 'one' item through).

Stock replenishment and dispatch to customers was discussed inter-mittently in the boardroom and a conflictual encounter (as opposed to this more collaborative one) surfaced later. It was a problem that affected both the SMD (customer complaints and staff time sorting them out) and the OD (production scheduling) *but* was under the jurisdiction of the FD (a historical situation). Two directors felt that this needed to change, and the apparently trivial talk captured in extract 4 *led* to talk about reorganizing various departments set against the issue of accountability and the failure of some senior managers in the past to address operational problems with strategic foresight. All this was *achieved* through recourse to the discourse of customer care and the need for formal procedures given the ongoing introduction of quality systems. All this *transpired* through the strategic and reflexive use by the actors of the localized management of turns combined with other crucial but basic conversational resources (not reproduced here).

Extract 4 also illustrates on a simple level a point made by Boden (1994). It is where, as each turn is taken up, it constrains and projects the talk along a particular path. The importance of this of course depends upon the issues that are being discussed and the interactional activities which are being 'done'. The trajectory of the talk during the *conflictual* moments was found to have greater implications for the task (developing strategy) and the actors' role-making efforts. Other features of the turn-taking system which are not illustrated here were that departures from the established procedures were marked in some way. Interestingly, the MD also marked his interruptions and waited to be granted a turn. He said 'hang on, hang on' as a turn-entry device. In employing this function *consistently* throughout the more conflictual interactions to slow down the turnover in speakers, the MD's role as chair was being enacted and was found to be 'fine-tuned' on many occasions to signal neutrality. Through the consistent employment of such basic 'methods' or procedures (and being uncontested by the community of listeners) the MD was *enabled* to *assemble* his role identity as chair, as MD and strategist. The MD's role identity was further fine-tuned as one who was neutral and the term 'arbitrator' crystallized to convey this (Samra-Fredericks, 1996b).

Whilst the analysis here has not provided an account of this elaborate and intricate process, or the range of conversational resources deployed by these actors as the dynamic spirals of interaction unfolded, an introduction to CA and its central hallmark, namely turn-taking, has been offered. The extracts above have many features which are of interest but could not be discussed here. The next section will briefly elaborate upon how the solid foundations offered by this rigorous and systematic approach are being developed and extended.

Taking a turn to talk and instantiating institutional identities

The comment above on the MD's 'role' as it emerges from the routine interactions is another potentially problematic issue given the 'pure' CA perspective. The analysis of boardroom talk has examined and tracked the process of taking a turn, and the type of turn therein, and moved on to explore the implications for the actors' apparent role-making and role-taking efforts (Turner, 1988) which was termed role enactment (Samra-Fredericks, 1996b). Heritage observes that recent studies of institutional talk recognize that the 'creation and maintenance of institutional roles is *ultimately realized through specific sequences of conversational actions*' (1989: 36, emphasis added; Drew, 1990: 32; Drew and Heritage, 1992; Heritage, 1997). But there are critics. Psathas (1995) has strongly warned against formulations that employ the 'vocabularies and theoretical perspectives' of organizational sociology. Here he refers to concepts such as roles, status, authority and so on and stresses continuing adherence to the 'problem of order' posed by the early ethnomethodologists and which subsequent CA studies sought to document. This appears inconsistent with my own study where the analysis of talk is eventually elaborated against the more traditional sociological and organizational concepts. *But*, and this is an important *but*, as Boden (1994: 77) asserts, the *status* of speakers is *not* assumed to 'dictate the talk', although 'discourse identities and institutional roles . . . [were] surely instantiated *through* talk.' It is from this fundamental basis that the study of boardroom talk encompassed the vocabularies of organizational sociology. Indeed, following Zimmerman (1988: 408) 'the nature of the setting or social identities of the participants [was] suspended' as far as this was possible (see Schegloff, 1987: 214–20; Heritage and Greatbatch, 1991).

Adhering to the original CA approach, 'interpretations' have to be *demonstrated* first by the participants for each other. As Boden and Zimmerman (1991: 13) note, analysing 'institutional interaction' necessitates careful attention and 'care' to 'demonstrate in the details of conduct, the "normatively oriented-to" (Heritage, 1984) or interactionally relevant identities' (see also Heritage, 1997). This principle guides my analysis (not illustrated here) and without doubt it continues to occupy researchers working with talk, since intuition and inference pose potentially insurmountable problems. Moreover, there is the suggestion for the need to 'warrant' the analysts' inferences since one is potentially faced with an 'indefinitely large set of "contextual" information that could be relevant' (Zimmerman, 1988). Again, what is critical though is to demonstrate how 'contextual facts' are 'connected to a particular conversation' (1988: 418). Secondly, it is possible through 'empirical control over inference' for the analyst to support the claim that the actors actually display particular understandings of a conversational event by presenting collections of conversational materials which can be compared (a very general picture of how this process unravelled is indicated in Table 9.1 and illustrated more recently in Heritage, 1997).

Greatbatch (1992) does examine the issue of types of turns taken and 'institutional identity'. In his research the institutional talk allowed some clear statements to be made concerning the types of turns available to particular actors in that setting. He examined the organization of disagreement in news interviews through focusing on the taking of turns and suggested that the institutional identities of interviewer and interviewee placed constraints on the types of turns the 'incumbents of these roles' could produce (see also Heritage and Greatbatch, 1991). Here, as roles were prescribed, actors confined themselves to asking and responding to questions respectively (Greatbatch, 1992: 269). Yet in so doing, they enact roles (assembling institutional identities). This dynamic can also be discerned from analyses of courtroom questioning where, because of the types of turns available to professionals and witnesses (see Drew, 1992; Dillon, 1990), particular roles are *instantiated*, or in Greatbatch's (1992) terms, institutional identity is constructed and ascribed. In contrast, the institutional role identities of the senior managers and directors in the boardroom are not *constrained* by the types of turns which allocate clear 'positions' to questioner or to answerer so that particular 'roles' or institutional identities crystallize. The only role that appeared to necessitate 'occasioned obligation' (Goffman, 1983: 7) in any clear way was that of the 'chair', the MD.

To *construct*, ascribe and confirm director and senior manager 'roles' as they were locally *realized* by the actors *was* more fluid and was based upon turns where the complex articulation of statements, assessments and information disseminating 'turns' either in response to a question or not were locally *made*. Self-selection to perform any function was permissible in the boardroom meetings providing it appeared to contribute to the prior talk. This contribution varied from confirming, adding to or modifying, challenging or contesting the prior talk. Consequently, and without doubt, the actors in these meetings *took* the general framework of the turn-taking system and *made* it work for them, 'for their immediate needs, topics and tasks' (Boden, 1994). Whilst it could not be illustrated here, through such a basic, taken-for-granted 'method' combined with a number of other identified resources (not discussed here), differentials in power were *realized* over time/space and the institutional role identity of director, senior manager or strategist was simultaneously *instantiated* (Samra-Fredericks, 1996a; 1996b). Asymmetrical power differentials were realized then as the interaction unfolded and it *eventually* encompassed all four types of asymmetry noted by Heritage (1997), namely: participation; 'know-how' about the interaction and the institution; knowledge; rights to knowledge (1997: 175–9).

Studies of talk in news interviews then, as well as in courts, schools and surgeries, note the restricted pattern of conduct as being primarily the product of the localized turn-taking systems where there is the pre-allocation of specific types of turns to the participants. In particular there are speakers (interviewer, lawyer, teacher and doctor) asking questions and those that provide answers (interviewee, witness, pupil, patient). In the study of boardroom talk the way in which the institutional context is recursively evoked and maintained through the talk of the directors and the senior managers was more fluid and difficult to categorize into neat communication formats. Equally identifying a simple, direct relationship between roles (and tasks) and discursive rights and obligations was not possible in this setting (apart from 'the chair'). However, this should not result in neglecting this pervasive and arguably critical arena of human interaction, that is, the boardroom and 'business/commercial' organizations generally.

Displaying competent membership in the boardroom meetings entailed what Zimmerman (1971, quoted in Boden, 1994) called the 'competent use of a given rule or set of rules'. They are 'founded upon members' practiced grasp of what particular actions' would achieve. Knowing when to take a turn or when to question ('ethnomethods') ascribed competent membership both as a *social* actor and as a more specific 'role' *enactor* (Samra-Fredericks, 1996b).

Clearly, the turn-*taking* system in the research briefly referred to here did not operate 'behind the backs' of its users. It was though:

> *structural* in the sense that it provides a stable, patterned and predictable scaffolding for talk, but it is also *interactional* in that anyone can create any variety of conversational collaborations through it, *all* of which are locally managed, that is, from within the interaction. (Boden, 1994: 73)

Boden does note that the traditional CA focus has been upon turn-*taking* where there is an insistence upon examining 'immediate adjacent ordering' of the talk. However, in work settings such as the boardroom meetings, 'variation in turn-*taking* reflexively embeds a variety of sustained aspects of turn-*making*' (1994: 18; Heritage, 1989). This required the close micro-analysis of many segments of boardroom talk.

Concluding comment

Research into *how* (through which conversational resources) organizational actors *do* strategy and realize social and political relations of one sort or another, whilst simultaneously witnessing the crystallization of a 'strategy document', necessitated repeated listenings and detailed analysis. Part of that analysis into boardroom talk employed CA. Whilst it could not be demonstrated here, power differentials between the directors and senior managers were *realized* over time/space and competence was confirmed or questioned. This was one 'outcome' of a series of complex interactive routines where through the strategic and pragmatic use of particular conversational resources (and drawing upon the wider prevailing discourses of strategy, quality and customer care), the actors sustained that construct, 'organization'. Management/organization scholars have rightly sought to document the political nature of organizational behaviour and the conditions where certain functions (e.g. finance or marketing) have a more dominant 'position' in 'dictating' the allocation of resources. To understand and appreciate this complexity further necessitates getting close and listening to talk-in-interaction. The basic procedures or conversational resources for 'doing' organization need to be systematically subjected to analysis. For example, the 'well-anchored' turn-taking system that was deemed fair and allowed the actors to have their say was a basic shared resource – otherwise 'business' would not have been done *legitimately* in the boardroom. The system is so taken for granted that it becomes almost invisible and eludes the naked eye (ear).

The illustrations above, whilst limited, focused upon the MD and his *role* as chair, yet it was undoubtedly an *achieved phenomenon*. Through the process of allocating specific turns and the types of turns the MD *takes* and *makes* available for others, the organizational hierarchy as an abstract concept is materially made evident. In other words, the research did not take the role of MD and strategist as well as the chair for the monthly board meetings as given. Equally, through an analysis of *when* the turn was taken and the *type* of turns, the MD's *role* was fine-tuned as 'arbitrator' during the conflictual encounters. It is through such mundane talk, employing basic ethnomethods as glimpsed in this chapter, that the actors accomplished role identities, the meeting and 'organization' in ways that defy simplistic analysis and prescriptions.

Moving beyond the early CA studies, where the relationship 'between a particular institutional setting and the talk that occurs within it' (Zimmerman, 1988: 406) was not the focus, boardroom meetings have been subjected to an analysis (not produced here) displaying how they 'internally create both discourse identities and emerging work tasks' (Boden, 1994: 102) through their sequential structure. Whilst the limitations of the 'pure' CA approach were considered during my analysis of talk employing CA, they were not insurmountable (see Drew and Heritage, 1992; Heritage, 1997). What continues to be preserved in my research is the strong reaction against the notion that complex empirical data can be reduced to 'aggregations and abstractions', losing the 'agents' and their interactive routines. CA has made and continues to make a significant contribution to understanding the organization of social interaction *as it happens* and, from this basis, to widen its net. Indeed, the recent discussion by Heritage (1997) offers a coherent and insightful commentary on CA today and on institutional talk and ways to analyse it systematically. It is an ongoing endeavour which raises important issues in both the methodological and substantive fields. Equally, as Maynard and Clayman (1991) observe, as more and more studies are conducted under the ethnomethodological umbrella it widens and challenges prevailing orthodoxies (Boden, 1994; Boden and Zimmerman, 1991). There were a number of reasons why my own study into boardroom talk embraced CA and then broadened to critically assess both Habermas's (1979; 1984) notion of validity claims as proposed in his theory of communicative action (see also Forester, 1987; 1992) and Turner's (1988) theory of social inter-action. Nevertheless, the insistence that social phenomena must be observable and reportable from the conversational materials has been maintained (Schegl-off, 1987). Even the quite broad notion of cultural capital (Collins, 1987) must in its most foundational sense comprise stores of ethnomethods, basic con-versational resources, and then the more general stocks of knowledge. Together, they ascribe competent membership of the social world and enable the (re)production of that same world in an orderly fashion.

To understand *how* taking a turn at talk both embeds and enacts organizations and institutions there is a clear need to capture that talk *as it happens* and then to subject that talk to rigorous and systematic analysis. CA offered a means for beginning to do that and one which has a credible lineage. The conversational 'materials' as noted by Boden (1994), such as the extracts of talk reproduced here, are a way of capturing the fleeting quality of this mundane social life. Indeed, to examine the interface between talk and social structure, the systematic methodology of CA is a key analytical 'tool'. To use Boden's own words: 'by observing people talking their way through the business day, we can locate, quite specifically, the *structuring* of organizations' (1994: 1).

In the organization theory literature, Weick's (1979) term 'organizing' is well known. Meetings are places where the practical activity of organizing is maintained (Boden, 1994; Schwartzman, 1986; 1989). Rules and routines are conceived as being enacted by actors and subject to interpretation *then and there*. For ethnomethodologists and CA, social structure is something organizational actors do (see Psathas, 1995 and also Boden, 1994; Boden and Zimmerman, 1991; Giddens's 1976, 1984 concept of the duality of structure is also relevant here). The theoretical orientation of the study into boardroom talk adheres to the perspective where 'social order is organized *from within* and social structure is thus endogenous to action' (Boden, 1994: 46). Consequently, the agency/structure debate is recast as 'structure-in-action' since social structure is conceived as the 'practical accomplishment' of members/actors (Boden and Zimmerman, 1991: 19). This is not to suggest that there is no 'larger social order' but to state that the focus of ethnomethodologically informed studies is '*how, with whom,* and even *why* particular aspects of social structure' or 'historical conditions are *made relevant* in concrete situations'. CA, then, is concerned with the detailed analysis and description of a number of basic methods for *doing* social life. Perhaps, more significantly in widening its net, as Heritage (1997) observes, CA 'may end up with an affinity with a rather Foucauldian conception of power' (1997: 179).

A study of the methods or conversational resources of director and senior managers was deemed to be long overdue. Getting past the gloss and vagueness of what is meant by terms and concepts such as 'experience', influence, judgement and so on, required capturing managers managing (*talking*) in *real time* and painstakingly subjecting the talk to close analysis. In so doing, one cannot help but be dazzled by human accomplishment in mundane settings. As far back as 1979, Mintzberg commented that rather than have 100 researchers conduct a survey of 100 organizations, it would perhaps be better to have 100 researchers each study one organization *in depth* and in this way throw light on management and organization (1979: 583–4). I would add that by taking talk-in-interaction as a topic of analysis we are better able to extend our current understanding of what has interested so many researchers of 'management', namely, what it is that managers do and *how* do they do it.

Appendix: transcription conventions

[	indicate overlapping/interrupted [speech 　　　　　　　　　　　　　　　　　　　[speech
{ {	indicates {simultaneous speech 　　　　　　{simultaneous speech
=	continuous speech where actor's utterance latches onto= =previous actor's speech
::	elon::gated pronunciation of that word
italics	indicate emphasis
[word(s)]	indicate transcriptionist doubt and will say [inaudible] or state that the speech referred to: either the actual names of actors; or the organization; or the products; or to financial figures [to ensure confidentiality]

Notes

1   Notwithstanding the pervasive output of research into leadership (see reviews by Bryman, 1986; 1992; Smith and Peterson, 1988; Yukl, 1994; and especially Knights and Willmott, 1992), as well as literature on strategy development and change management (for example, Dawson, 1994; Hendry et al., 1993; Petti-grew, 1985), arguably we still don't know *how* leaders or senior managers lead in *real time* and what they say to 'do it' or the resources for developing strategies for organizational renewal when face meets face.

2   Zimmerman (1988: 413) notes that tapes of conversation are 'not usually collected for specific purposes', enabling the means for 'encountering otherwise unnoticed features of talk'.

3   The various notation symbols to assist the transcription of different features of speech such as intonation, stress, pauses, tempo, overlap and so on have been added to since the original system developed by Jefferson (see Sacks et al., 1974; and also Atkinson and Heritage, 1984; Drew and Heritage, 1992; Boden, 1994; Psathas and Anderson, 1990; Zimmerman, 1988: 413–15). The symbols seek to capture numerous phenomena that organize conversation such as beginnings of speech, overlap of speech, silences and turn-taking.

4   *So* has been identified as signalling 'of result' (Fraser, 1990) and which Boden (1994: 96) noted was a standard topic transition marker.

References

Atkinson, J.M. (1982) 'Understanding formality: notes on the categorization and production of "formal" interaction', *British Journal of Sociology*, 33: 86–117.

Atkinson, J.M. and Drew, P. (1979) *Order in Court: The Organization of Verbal Interaction in Judicial Settings*. London: Macmillan.

Atkinson, J.M. and Heritage, J. (eds) (1984) *Structures of Social Action: Studies in Conversation Analysis*. Cambridge: Cambridge University Press.

Bargiela, F. (1993) 'The language of business: discourse patterns in British and Italian meetings'. PhD thesis, Nottingham Trent University.

Bargiela-Chiappini, F. and Harris, S. (1997) *Managing Language: The Discourse of Corporate Meetings*. Amsterdam and Philadelphia: Benjamin.

Berger, P. and Luckmann, T. (1967) *The Social Construction of Reality*. Harmonds-worth: Penguin.

Boden, D. (1994) *The Business of Talk*. Cambridge: Polity.

Boden, D. and Zimmerman, D.H. (eds) (1991) *Talk and Social Structure: Studies in Ethnomethodology and Conversation Analysis*. Cambridge: Polity.

Bryman, A. (1986) *Leadership and Organisations*. London: Routledge and Kegan Paul.

Bryman, A. (1992) *Charisma and Leadership in Organizations*. London: Sage.

Collins, R. (1987) 'Interaction ritual chains, power, and property', in J. Alexander, R. Munch, N.J. Smelser and B. Giessen (eds), *The Micro–Macro Link*. Berkeley, CA: University of California Press.

Dawson, P. (1994) *Organizational Change: A Processual Approach*. London: Paul Chapman.

Dillon, J.T. (1990) *The Practice of Questioning*. London: Routledge.

Drew, P. (1990) 'Conversation analysis: who needs it?', *Text*, 10: 27–35.

Drew, P. (1992) 'Contested evidence in courtroom cross examination: the case of a trial for rape', in P. Drew and J. Heritage (eds), *Talk at Work: Interaction in Institutional Settings*. Cambridge: Cambridge University Press.

Drew, P. and Heritage, J. (eds) (1992) *Talk at Work: Interaction in Institutional Settings*. Cambridge: Cambridge University Press.

Fairclough, N. (1992) *Discourse and Social Change*. Oxford and Cambridge: Polity and Basil Blackwell.

Feldman, M.S. (1995) *Strategies for Interpreting Qualitative Data*. London: Sage.

Fisher, S. and Todd, A.D. (eds) (1986) *Discourse and Institutional Authority: Medicine, Education and Law*. Norwood, NJ: Ablex.

Forester, J. (1987) 'Critical theory and planning practice', in J. Forester (ed.), *Critical Theory and Public Life*. Cambridge, MA: MIT Press.

Forester, J. (1992) 'Critical ethnography: on field work in a Habermasian way', in M. Alvesson and H. Willmott (eds), *Critical Management Studies*. London: Sage.

Fraser, B. (1990) 'An approach to discourse markers', *Journal of Pragmatics*, 14: 383–95.

Garfinkel, H. (1967) *Studies in Ethnomethodology*. Englewood Cliffs, NJ: Prentice-Hall. Paperback (1984) Cambridge: Polity.

Gherardi, S. and Turner, B.A. (1987) *Real Men Don't Collect Soft Data*. Dipartimento di Politica Sociale, Universita di Trento and Organizational Research Unit of the Department of Sociology, University of Exeter.

Giddens, A. (1976) *New Rules of Sociological Method*. London: Hutchinson.

Giddens, A. (1984) *The Constitution of Society*. Oxford: Polity and Basil Blackwell.

Glaser, B.G. and Strauss, A.L. (1967) *The Discovery of Grounded Theory: Strategies for Qualitative Research*. Chicago: Aldine.

Goffman, E. (1967) *Interaction Ritual: Essays on Face-to-Face Behaviour*. Harmondsworth: Penguin.

Goffman, E. (1983) 'The interaction order', *American Sociological Review*, 48: 1–17.

Greatbatch, D. (1992) 'On the management of disagreement between news interviewees', in P. Drew and J. Heritage (eds), *Talk at Work: Interaction in Institutional Settings*. Cambridge: Cambridge University Press.

Habermas, J. (1979) *Communication and the Evolution of Society*. Boston: Beacon Press.

Habermas, J. (1984) *The Theory of Communicative Action: Reason and the Rationalization of Society*, Vol. 1. Cambridge: Polity.

Hendry, J., Johnson, G. and Newton, J. (eds) (1993) *Strategic Thinking: Leadership and the Management of Strategic Change*. Chichester: Wiley.

Heritage, J. (1984) *Garfinkel and Ethnomethodology*. Cambridge: Polity.

Heritage, J. (1989) 'Current developments in conversation analysis', in D. Roger and P. Bull (eds), *Conversation: An Interdisciplinary Perspective*. Clevedon: Multilingual Matters.

Heritage, J. (1997) 'Conversational analysis and institutional talk: analysing data', in D. Silverman (ed.), *Qualitative Research: Theory, Method and Practice*. London: Sage.

Heritage, J. and Greatbatch, D. (1991) 'On the institutional character of institutional talk: the case of news interviews', in D. Boden and D.H. Zimmerman (eds), *Talk and Social Structure: Studies in Ethnomethodology and Conversation Analysis*. Cambridge: Polity Press.

Jacobs, C. (1988) 'Evidence and inference in conversation analysis', in J.A. Anderson (ed.), *Communication Yearbook II*. Beverley Hills, CA: Sage.

Jefferson, G. (1980) 'On "trouble premonitory" response to inquiry', *Sociological Inquiry*, 50: 153–85.

Jefferson, G. (1989) 'Preliminary notes on a possible metric which provides for a "standard maximum" silence of approximately one second in conversation', in D. Roger and P. Bull (eds), *Conversation: An Interdisciplinary Perspective*. Clevedon: Multilingual Matters.

Knights, D. and Willmott, H. (1992) 'Conceptualising leadership processes: a study of senior managers in a financial services company', *Journal of Management Studies*, 29 (6): 761–82.

Levinson, S. (1983) *Pragmatics*. Cambridge: Cambridge University Press.

Mangham, I.L. (1986) *Power and Performance in Organisations: An Exploration of Executive Process*. Oxford: Basil Blackwell.

Mangham, I.L. (1988) *Effecting Organisational Change: Further Explorations of the Executive Process*. Oxford: Basil Blackwell.

Margerison, C.J. (1987) *Conversation Control Skills for Managers*. London: Mercury.

Maynard, D.W. (1984) *Inside Plea Bargaining: The Language of Negotiation*. New York: Plenum.

Maynard, D.W. and Clayman, S.E. (1991) 'The diversity of ethnomethodology', *Annual Review of Sociology*, 17: 385–418.

Mehan, H. (1979) *Learning Lessons: Social Organization in the Classroom*. Cambridge, MA: Harvard University Press.

Mintzberg, H. (1979) 'An emerging strategy of "direct" research', *Administrative Science Quarterly*, 24 (4): 582–9.

Nofsinger, R.E. (1991) *Everyday Conversation*. Beverley Hills, CA: Sage.

Pettigrew, A. (1985) *The Awaking Giant: Continuity and Change in ICI*. Oxford: Basil Blackwell.

Pettigrew, A. (1987) 'Context and action in the transformation of the firm', *Journal of Management Studies*, 24 (6): 649–70.

Pettigrew, A. (1990) 'Longitudinal field research on change: theory and practice', *Organization Science*, 1 (3): 267–91.

Pettigrew, A., Ferlie, E. and Mckee, L. (1992) *Shaping Strategic Change: Making Change in Large Organisations: The Case of the NHS*. London: Sage.

Pettigrew, A. and Whipp, R. (1991) *Managing for Competitive Success*. Oxford: Blackwell.

Pomerantz, A. (1984) 'Agreeing and disagreeing with assessments: some features of preferred/dispreferred turn shapes', in M. Atkinson and J. Heritage (eds), *Structures of Social Action: Studies in Conversation Analysis*. Cambridge: Cambridge University Press.

Pomerantz, A. (1993) 'Introduction', *Text*, 13: 151–5.

Psathas, G. (1995) *Conversation Analysis: The Study of Talk-in-Interaction*. Newbury Park, CA: Sage.

Psathas, G. and Anderson, T. (1990) 'The "practices" of transcription in conversation analysis', *Semiotica*, 78: 75–99.

Sacks, H. (1984) 'Methodological remarks', in J.M. Atkinson and J. Heritage (eds), *Structures of Social Action: Studies in Conversation Analysis*. Cambridge: Cambridge University Press.

Sacks, H. (1992) *Lectures on Conversation*, ed. G. Jefferson, 2 vols. Oxford: Blackwell.

Sacks, H., Schegloff, E. and Jefferson, G. (1974) 'A simplest systematics for the organisations of turn-taking for conversation', *Language*, 50 (4): 696–735.

Samra-Fredericks, D. (1994) 'Organising the past in the present as a way of beginning to construct tomorrow – talking change and changing talk', paper presented to the Standing Conference on Organizational Symbolism, Calgary University, Canada.

Samra-Fredericks, D. (1995) 'The experience of being a "single-case" woman (in a multi-case world)', paper presented at the British Academy of Management, Sheffield.

Samra-Fredericks, D. (1996a) 'Talking of emotion for the development of strategy in the boardroom', paper presented to the Organizational Discourse Conference at King's College, London. Synopsis in C. Combes, D. Grant, T. Keenoy and C. Oswick (eds), *Organizational Discourse: Talk, Text and Tropes*. London: KMCP.

Samra-Fredericks, D. (1996b) 'The interpersonal management of competing rationalities: a critical ethnography of board-level competence for "doing" strategy as spoken in the "face" of change'. PhD thesis (access restricted until after 1999), Henley Management College and Brunel University.

Schegloff, E.A. (1972) 'Notes on a conversational practice: formulating place', in D. Sudnow (ed.), *Studies in Social Interaction*. New York: Free Press.

Schegloff, E.A. (1987) 'Between macro and micro: contexts and other connections', in J. Alexander, B. Giesen, R. Munch and N. Smelser (eds), *The Micro–Macro Link*. Berkeley, CA: University of California Press.

Schegloff, E.A. and Sacks, H. (1973) 'Opening up closings', *Semiotica*, 8 (4): 289–327.

Schiffrin, D. (1987) *Discourse Markers*. Cambridge: Cambridge University Press.

Schwartzman, H.B. (1986) 'The meeting as a neglected social form in organisational studies', *Research in Organisational Behaviour*, 8: 233–58.

Schwartzman, H.B. (1989) *The Meeting: Gatherings in Organizations and Communities*. New York: Plenum.

Shotter, J. (1993) *Conversational Realities: Constructing Life through Language*. London: Sage.

Smith, P.B. and Peterson, M.F. (1988) *Leadership, Organisations and Culture*. London: Sage.

Suchman, L.A. (1987) *Plans and Situated Actions*. Cambridge: Cambridge University Press.

Turner, J.H. (1988) *A Theory of Social Interaction*. California: Polity.

Weick, K.E. (1979) *The Social Psychology of Organizing*, 2nd edn. New York: Newbery Award Records.

Wieder, D.L. (1988) 'From resource to topic: some aims of conversation analysis', in J.A. Anderson (ed.), *Communication Yearbook II*. Beverley Hills, CA: Sage.

Wright, P.L. and Taylor D.S. (1994) *Improving Leadership Performance: Interpersonal Skills for Effective Leadership*, 2nd edn. Hemel Hempstead: Prentice-Hall.

Yukl, G. (1994) *Leadership in Organizations*, 3rd edn. Englewood Cliffs, NJ: Prentice-Hall.

Zimmerman, D.H. (1971) 'The practicalities of role use', in J. Douglas (ed.), *Understanding Everyday Life*. London: Routledge and Kegan Paul.

Zimmerman, D.H. (1988) 'On conversation: the conversation analytic perspective', in J.A. Anderson (ed.), *Communication Yearbook II*. Beverley Hills, CA: Sage.

10   Pictorial Representation

David Stiles

Numbers, words and pictures

As we near the end of the millennium, an image revolution is taking place. We are becoming not just passive recipients of pictures but also active users of them. No longer is the creation and use of complex images the unchallenged domain of the professional artist or designer. As technology has developed, graphics software and telecommunications have allowed anyone with access to a personal computer to produce, manipulate and distribute sophisticated images. In these multi-media days, exploring the Internet, reading a CD-ROM encyclopaedia, or playing a computer game would certainly be less pleasurable if images did not enhance text.

Academics use illustrations, charts and diagrams to summarize, clarify and enrich verbal arguments. So, why not go one step further and use images in the research process itself? As management researchers seek ever more lucid means of analysing organizations, image might begin to challenge the supremacy of the written word and the number. Yet, despite 15,000 years of art history (Gombrich, 1967), the use of image as a scientific instrument is still in its embryonic stages.

This chapter explores the origins and use of pictorial representation as an innovative research technique for the exploration of organizational con-structs. The next section paints a background to the use of image, a brief but necessary note on the philosophical roots of pictorial representation. This helps to provide a firmer theoretical foundation for using image in qual-itative research. Pictorial representation methods developed by the author are detailed in the third section, giving the reader some methodological insight into the use of image in research.

The methodology is then applied in a 'live' situation, with glimpses provided of the strategic use of pictorial representation in two real organiza-tions. Data from the project are presented to illustrate how image can be used for strategy formulation and implementation. The chapter concludes with a discussion of the advantages and disadvantages of the methods used, and proffers advice to anyone considering experimenting with image in their research.

Overall, it is felt that images can be as valuable as words or numbers in exploring people's organizational constructs. Although written text or numerical measures may still be the most favoured means of organizational analysis, in the quest for a richer understanding of organizations, images should certainly not be ignored.

The use of image in qualitative research

As their users quickly recognized, as well as a mystical quality, pictures often have the ability to communicate rapidly and universally, with or without verbal interaction; to record and summarize ideas; and, as marketing research shows, to influence the perceptions and even the behaviour of actors (Kotler, 1986). Yet the use of image in management research has, until recently, been very limited. Subjectivity in interpretation is one explanation for this, as are extreme variations in drawing ability, and – before the advent of electronic scanning devices – technical publishing difficulties. Perhaps a more fundamental reason in a largely positivistic academic domain, however, is the unfashionability of using a medium which is not only non-numerical, but also non-verbal.

Lately, an embryonic research area has begun to emerge in the use of image, synthesizing elements of social and psychological sciences and recent developments in the organizational disciplines. Such visual techniques are often developed to stimulate creative thinking and problem solving (Maddox et al., 1987; Rickards, 1988; Morgan, 1989; Russell and Evans, 1989; Checkland and Scholes, 1990; Henry, 1991; Majaro, 1991). Such developments point towards a burgeoning interest in the use of image as a research instrument in the 1990s and beyond. However, many of these forms of pictorial representation are based upon management theories categorized by Burrell and Morgan (1979) as being essentially functionalist. In other words, they represent the dominant orthodoxy in sociological approaches to research because they emphasize *realist* ontologies (assumptions about the social world we inhabit) and *positivist* epistemologies (assumptions about knowledge, or the way we understand that world). Simply put, realism argues that there are hard, tangible, empirically 'real' and reasonably unchanging structures that exist in the social world. These structures can be identified and measured because such knowledge is verifiable and testable by using hypotheses and other positivist scientific approaches.

So, Maddox et al., Majaro and Kotler try to solve marketing problems through image by generating and measuring responses to pictorial data. Maddox and colleagues, for example, use a 'guided imagery process' to help group participants imagine their organization is a museum. Participants are encouraged to 'visit' the imaginary museum in their minds and relate which exhibits change and why; what critics would say about the museum; and what the key activities, people and resources are in that building. The idea is to generate new insights into their organizations by using the museum metaphor as a substitute for their normal view of the places they work in.

However, one problem with this approach is its epistemological stance. Although more original than conventional approaches, the technique is used as only one part of a larger traditional planning process, involving sequential and objective attention to organizational mission (the desired purposes, philosophy, values and critical factors in the success of the organization), objectives, customer analysis, and analysis of the internal and external environments facing the organization. As such it is a long way from more 'interpretivist' approaches which explore subjective data, such as feelings, emotions and values, in order to 'understand the subjective experience of individuals' (Burrell and Morgan, 1979: 253). Such subjective insights, it is argued, add greatly to our knowledge of how organizations work because they help explain more fully what underlies people's perceptions and actions.

Ultimately, despite an overt research agenda aimed at 'meeting customer needs', Maddox et al.'s aim is really to regulate or control organizations and consumers. Similarly, Checkland's soft systems methodology, as described by Clegg and Walsh (Chapter 11 in this volume), is based upon viewing the organization as a social system interdependent with or open to other social systems and the wider environment. As such, there is an assumption of the organization as a bounded entity capable of being adjusted mechanistically to generate greater technical efficiency or effectiveness. The whole point of systems approaches is to maintain the existing system whilst permitting incremental adjustments and avoiding radical change if possible. Human beings are seen as fairly passive participants in organizations, lacking agency and self-will. Their perceptions, emotions and values are largely ignored as unimportant to the effective functioning of the organization.

The sort of pictorial representation described in this chapter is based upon attempts to avoid a realist, positivist approach (Stiles, 1995). It takes a 'social constructionist' view, as embodied in the work of Berger and Luckmann (1965) and Weick (1979). These authors argue that individuals and groups can experience the same reality in different ways. People form their own 'social constructions' (constructs) or 'enactments' – shared perceptions that serve to reconstruct the reality they have experienced or can contemplate. As such, constructs constitute the basic building-blocks of meaning. Implicit here is the understanding that an organization contains a 'deeper' level of latent, embedded phenomena, such as human assumptions, values and perceptions. If these constructs can be examined in an integrated way, we might come closer to understanding organizations. We might then be able to suggest which organizational change strategies are most likely to succeed.

It is argued here that such constructs can be articulated mentally as verbal concepts and/or as images. Extending Wittgenstein's (1964) reasoning implies studying human ideas and expressions not only as verbal constructs, but also as visual images. The argument is that if data capture is limited to verbal *forms* of expression only, an equally valuable source of data might be overlooked.

According to the dictionary, an *image* is 'A representation of the external form of an object', a 'figurative illustration' or a 'likeness' of something real or imaginary (Hawkins and Allen, 1991). As such, it can be regarded as a particular form of construct that can be either a spatial mental representation or a more tangible visual representation of an object. Langer (1957: 145) distinguishes between an 'inner picture' and a 'fabrication'. The former is a subjective, projected record of a sense experience mainly created for someone's own sake; the latter is an impression communicated by a sender to an audience. Alvesson (1990) uses the term 'corporate image' in a way that integrates Langer's concepts, by referring to 'A holistic and vivid impression held by a particular group towards a corporation', partly because of the group's own sense-making processes and partly because of the communication of the corporation itself. Such an impression can be held by external audiences or by internal members of the organization (1990: 376–8).

This chapter follows in this tradition, but makes an important distinction between images and words as being different *forms of expression*. Sometimes one can think of definite words that capture a particular construct. For example, words associated with a relaxing seaside day could include 'sand', 'beach' and 'hot'. At other times, one might actually *picture* oneself on that hot sandy beach lazily sipping a long, cool drink! Such words and pictures are conceptually linked: words often conjure up associated images, and vice versa. They are also used in tandem to represent common ideas or constructs. However, they can be regarded as different forms in the expression of that idea. They can exist as elements of mental processes (inner pictures) or be captured by different media as more concrete representations (fabrications), such as drawings, paintings, movies or photographs. At one time, pictures were a society's sole means of recorded expression – such as in ancient Chinese pictograms. More recently, as human expression has become more sophisticated, words and pictures have developed as alternative, if complementary, systems of meaning.

The difference between words and images is not in the degree of abstraction, since art can itself be abstract in the extreme. Indeed, non-representational images form an important constituent of modern art. Rather, the difference is one of form. Images can use words as a complementary or contrasting element, but not as the sole functional means of expression.

It is also necessary to distinguish between the terms 'image' and 'symbol'. Words, images and actions can be described as *symbols* where they are an indirect, abstract representation conventionally seen as typifying, representing or recalling something else to an audience (Hawkins and Allen, 1991). They are a type of fabrication rather than an inner picture. A symbol could be a company logo representing a desired corporate impression; a gold watch representing loyal service; a verbal expression of praise or admonish-ment for something; or an action such as the placement of an employee's desk in a corridor to signify that person's redundancy!

Concern with symbols has led to the emergence of a school of thought known as 'organizational symbolism' – represented in strategic management by writers such as Green (1988). Green is primarily interested in how managers' symbolic actions and words communicate messages intentionally or unintentionally to others within their organizations: for example, an organizational leader giving new wristwatches to his staff in an effort to improve punctuality (1988: 127).

However, this chapter does not restrict its definition of image to com-municated fabrications only, but concerns itself with inner pictures as well. For this reason, drawings are generated which capture deep-set internal visual constructs about particular organizations. These are subsequently translated by respondents into verbal constructs as a double-check on respondents' intentions, but the exercise is led by the physical drawing of an organizational picture. In this way, both pictures and words are used complementarily to explore ideas, but the pictorial form is given greater emphasis in the generation of ideas.

The images produced here are based on the use of a *metaphor*. This involves 'The application of a name or descriptive term or phrase to an object or action to which it is imaginatively but not literally applicable' (Hawkins and Allen, 1991). In other words, one is invited to think of an object or action as though it *is* something quite different. So, for example, one might say that the sea *is* a dragon, clawing away at the rocky coast; or that this book *is* a pot of gold. Thinking about an object or action in such a way that one imagines it *is* something else can lead to important insights. For example, to a child unaware of the dangers of ocean currents, thinking of the sea as a dragon rather than as a paddling pool might teach him to be more careful when bathing. Thinking of this book as a precious resource might mean you dip into it from time to time, rather than try to memorize its entire contents at once.

The emphasis on imaginative knowledge rather than literality is import-ant, because metaphor helps one to break away from seeking the kind of literal truth about something that positivism stresses. Seeing things in new ways can help solve seemingly intractable problems, by challenging tradi-tional ways of confronting issues.

For example, Morgan (1993) introduces novel views of organizations as cartons of yoghurt, sailboats and even spider plants in an attempt to help managers beyond restrictive, customary ways of managing them. You might be more familiar with thinking of organizations as 'cash cows', 'stars', 'dogs' and 'question marks' when deciding whether to invest in them or not. 'Cash cows' are usually those generating money; 'stars' might provide ample future returns on your investment. Conversely, 'question marks' are uncertain cash-making prospects; and 'dogs' are perhaps best avoided for investment altogether (Johnson and Scholes, 1993: 144).

Pictorial representation techniques: personality images

The techniques used here depict the organization as a human personality. The next main section shows how this metaphor has been used to generate strategy in two real organizations. This is done by using two techniques: a *free-drawn personality image* and a *pre-constructed personality image*. In the first stage organizational members are interviewed individually. In stage two focus groups of members are held to aggregate data and to check and explore themes appearing in the first stage.

Individual interviews

The free-drawn personality image is used firstly in a face-to-face interview setting. This is the least structured of the two techniques, and follows on from more orthodox verbal questioning. To begin with, respondents are asked to complete two 'warm-up' exercises following Edwards's (1981) suggestions. These allow participants to become more used to the idea of drawing and to think in visual terms. The objective of promoting greater creativity is the major reason given to the interviewee for the use of pictures. The warm-ups involve respondents first drawing a profile of an imaginary human face, then inverting the image. They are then encouraged to be more creative by drawing a profile of a more unusual humanoid. The actual *free-drawn personality metaphor image* is then completed by the respondent with no prompting beyond a request to represent the 'personality' of the organization:

> Imagine that you're trying to communicate with someone who can't read or write. Some people say that each place you work in has its own personality. I want you to imagine that the organization has its own personality and do a rough sketch to try to explain to this person who can't read or write what that personality looks like.

The imaginary communicatee is described as being illiterate to encourage the respondent not to use words when drawing the image. Interpretation of the resulting drawing is made by the respondent, not by the interviewer. This limits the researcher's structuring to mostly innocuous probes and non-verbal cues, themselves transcribed in full to allow complete analysis.

Interpretation of the verbal explanations of the pictures is based upon Potter and Wetherell's (1987) discourse analysis approach. Patterns are sought in the verbal data relating to (i) variability and (ii) consistency between the answers given by respondents to the same question. Variability relates to differences in either the form or the content of answers across respondents. Consistencies are similarities in either. In simple terms, the researcher is looking for patterns across the transcribed data of all those interviewed, where more than one respondent mentions the same thing (a consistency); or where a unique perception (a variability) appears in the text. An attempt is also made to analyse the possible functions and effects of verbal and visual responses and perceptions. For example, do hesitancies denote the respondent is unsure about an answer, or reluctant to articulate a construct? Discourse analysis merely provides suggestions as to how these phenomena might be interpreted, rather than stating categorically that a response means a certain thing. The text itself, and visual observations, are presented in full in any final project report to allow the reader to make up his or her own mind.

Note that consistent themes emerging across the drawings are as important as the individual pictures themselves, since these are designed to reveal common organizational characteristics.

Focus groups

Before a final report is prepared, and following Schall's (1983) suggestions, initial data are presented to focus groups consisting of members of the organization. Representative groups are selected to (a) review and validate initial interview data; (b) determine, again by drawing pictures, both 'realistic' and 'ideal' views of their organizations; and (c) filter previously emerging suggestions on possible strategies, and generate alternatives. The use of focus groups also serves to ensure that members continue to be involved in the change process beyond initial interviews. Such participation helps build greater acceptance of resulting changes amongst organizational members.

A selection of individual drawings is fed back into focus groups to determine whether one image best captures the organization's culture and whether common themes prevail. These *pre-constructed personality images* allow the aggregation of personal constructs into common group constructs, by building on individuals' constructs to ensure the continuity and grounding of data. Using focus groups also allows a time dynamic to be incorporated into the data collection process, if groups are established months or even years after the original interviews take place. Further focus group iterations are also possible. For example, focus groups were replicated two years later for the Canadian case detailed in the next section, because it was felt that a change of leader might have created substantial organizational change.

Each pre-constructed image is by definition multi-dimensional, because it is intended by its original drawer to reflect several organizational characteristics. However, if the images are carefully selected by the researcher to show a variety of points of view, the device can be quite powerful. This means choosing five pictures to represent views ranging from a very unfavourable depiction of the organization through a neutral view to a very favourable one. Participants are thus presented with what is almost a 'pictorial Likert scale' from which to choose a consensus image.

A summary of the discourse explaining each image is read to focus group members, as each picture is revealed in turn. Participants are then asked, as a group, whether any of the five images reflect the character of the organization. A group consensus is sought on which image is most appropriate. Votes for each are recorded to assist in obtaining a majority view. Where no majority occurs, a split vote is recorded. In any case, the full discourse is recorded and analysed, including rationales for consensus and dissensus images. Because of the difficulty in identifying separate speakers in a group format, sessions can also be video-taped to assist in later transcription.

As a second group exercise, a composite *free-drawn personality image* is then produced similar to the face-to-face pictures. These summary personality metaphor drawings are facilitated to encompass the perceptions of all group members, so that no one individual's input dominates. Verbal explanations are again discourse analysed.

Of course, the organizational researcher does not have to have strategy generation in mind when using this technique. Even if the analysis stops here, it provides a powerful way of producing rich insights into the organization that are difficult to generate by verbal means alone. Organizational psychologists, behavioural analysts, and marketers amongst others will discover that pictures enhance their understanding of their subject matter more than using words alone. There is, for example, a substantial literature on the use of images in social-psychological projective techniques (see Semeonoff, 1976; Branthwaite and Lunn, 1985). Identifying an 'organizational personality' could be useful in surfacing latent tensions, to help a deal with shared psychological problems. In marketing, Ziff (1990) shows how image can be used to explore people's emotional reactions to advertising images. Using the personality technique to define a common internal or external organizational image might help the marketer develop a campaign to promote a more desirable corporate image inside or outside the company.

Pictures in action

This section illustrates the use of pictorial representation by presenting interview data relating to two 'live' case studies. These happen to be university business schools in the UK and Canada, but the personality metaphor is sufficiently flexible and simple to use in any organizational setting. In fact, the author has also applied it to private financial services organizations.

The aim of the study was to generate organizational strategies for the two schools by examining images of the organization held by internal members (academics, secretaries and students) and external actors (representatives of the business community). Data are from 76 initial face-to-face interviews with Canadian and British academics, as the main internal decision-makers; and 18 focus groups containing representatives from all interested parties.

So, separate groups were held of academics, secretarial staff, undergraduate students, postgraduates and business people in each location.

The discourse indicates that the interviewer successfully adopted a pacifying role, easing any creative 'blocks' and calming any apprehensions about drawing that began to surface. Only three respondents refused to participate in the free drawing part of the interview. They did so because of a verbalized inability to draw or discomfort with the technique. However, the vast majority were willing to attempt a free drawing. In fact, respondents generally appeared relaxed during this exercise. To minimize potential anxiety and interviewer effect, the researcher left the room whilst drawing took place. Recording devices remained running, however, to record any data emerging. A verbal explanation of the drawing was then sought and recorded on the interviewer's return. Drawings were not allowed to be amended by respondents at this stage, since it was important that *post hoc* verbal justification was minimized. Rather, explanation was limited to the image already drawn.

Video-taping did not appear intrusive enough to significantly affect focus group discussions. Any potential concerns were addressed by the facilitator at the beginning of each session, when the need to use video to assist transcription was explained. Careful placing of the video camera on the other side of the room, using a telephoto lens, helped reduce any overt intrusion. In fact, transcribed evidence seems to suggest that the camera was not visually or verbally referred to after this point. Indeed, several respondents expressed surprise at having forgotten about it.

Initial examination of the drawings themselves indicates varying degrees of drawing ability. However, this does not matter, since the true value of the exercise lies in revealing insights into the organization. Although respondents were given a free rein to represent the 'personality of the organization', virtually all chose to do so by drawing a whole humanoid body. Only one decided to retain the facial profiles used in the preceding 'warm-up' exercises, which appeared to indicate that the warm-ups did not significantly influence respondents during the free drawing itself.

Transcription of the postgraduate students' focus group at the UK school proved especially problematic, because the mix of diverse nationalities created difficulties in interpreting accents. This meant reviewing the audio tapes several times more than normal; but video tape was extremely useful in this process, allowing individuals to be identified and lip and other bodily movements examined.

As indicated earlier, a voting system was used to determine the pattern of preferences for the pre-constructed images in each group. In fact, discourse analysis showed that in all groups respondents did not choose one image without some debate. Yet, a clear favourite emerged in all groups except the second academic group at the UK school.

For UK respondents, the image in Figure 10.1 was most popular across the groups. This was because of the perceived facelessness of the school, resulting in feelings of anonymity amongst internal stakeholders. It was also

Figure 10.1 **Most popular pre-constructed personality image, UK school**

Figure 10.2 **Most popular pre-constructed personality image, Canadian school**

thought to represent the role conflict within the school between business and academic demands. A perceptual gulf between old and young academics was depicted through wearing a business suit jacket at the same time as jeans, and with a mug of coffee casually carried.

For all Canadian focus groups, the image in Figure 10.2 was selected as favourite. This was because of a sense of lack of strategic direction, represented by a crossroads resulting from a change in leader. Inherent academic–business role conflict was seen in a split academic robe and business suit. Cautious optimism was embodied in a half-smile; and fragmentation and lack of interaction within the academic body was shown by feet facing in opposite directions.

Focus group participants were then asked to draw their own composite image. Selected individual and focus group drawings for the UK organization are reproduced in the accompanying figures as examples of data generated. Space unfortunately precludes anything more than a limited number of illustrations and supporting quotes, but it is hoped they will bring further methodological insight to the reader. Remember, in a full report, all images and a large number of verbatim quotes provide full richness and enhance understanding of the organization. Rather than being placed in appendices, the drawings themselves should appear as an integral part of the final report. Quotes allow the reader the opportunity of deciding whether the researcher's observations seem justifiable. Editing is avoided, beyond the minimum necessary to ensure readability. The interviewer's interaction is also presented (shown here as text related to 'DS'), to reproduce as closely as possible the dialogue that takes place. The removal of any text at all is represented by two or more full stops in succession and appears only because of space requirements in this chapter. Individuals are not identified and focus group participants are allocated a designatory group letter and number (for example, F1 for the first member of the academic faculty group; A4 for the fourth administrative staff member; S3 for the third student member; and B2 for the second business community representative).

The strongest theme to emerge from both interviews and focus groups is that the two institutions were regarded as unhappy or neutral in character, the result of different frustrations. Both organizational leaders seemed to have generated a significant degree of negative feeling owing to their management styles. One might think this inevitable in universities where, protective of their self-autonomy, academics might resent any attempts to lead or manage them. However, at the UK school, hostility towards the leader seemed particularly strong. The leader was believed to be overly dominant in terms of both strategic and operational decision-making, abrasive in style and uncommunicative with internal members – creating unnecessary 'social distance' between himself and others. Representing this belief amongst academic interviewees (Figure 10.3):

> [Er, a big face, (DS: Yes) with the unhappy (DS: Yes) er look, I think, was the centralized er administrative leadership role within that. (DS: Right.) And a sort of the purveyor of unhappiness lowering morale and things like that. (DS: Right.) But very big. (DS: Right.) A long, thin, narrow neck, (DS: Right) because er emphasizing the distance between him and the rest of the organization in many ways it creates.]

This facet also appeared strongly in the focus groups. In the second academic and postgraduate groups' pictures, social distance is symbolized by a long neck separating the head and body. In the second academic group picture (Figure 10.4), a mask of Janus from Roman mythology signifies the dominance of the leader, superimposed upon an otherwise faceless

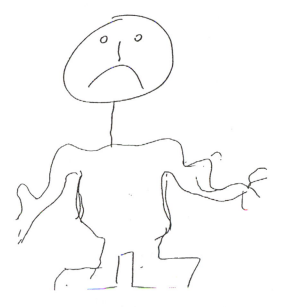

Figure 10.3   **Face-to-face interview image, UK school**

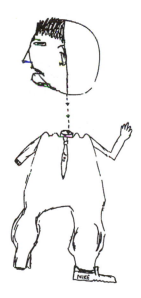

Figure 10.4   **Academic focus group image, UK school**

entity. The figure's neck is also dotted to represent extreme thinness, with downward-pointing arrows to show a one-way flow of information, influence and communication. The powerlessness of the subject-group section heads in relation to the leader is depicted by four carbuncles on the figure's shoulders; with the majority of academics at the bottom providing the research and teaching work to sustain the school, but missing a shoe to show lack of movement/change, clenching one fist in frustration and waving 'goodbye' to symbolize the lack of loyalty amongst academics resulting from top-down management:

> [F4: I mean we as individual lecturers and researchers and what have you, have no real power. We cannot within sections decide who is head of section. That comes from <names leader>, as devolved, sending it down through his system. OK, once it gets to <names leader>, he is the decider when it comes to this department.] [F3: To all the stuff . . . [names F2] is talking about hierarchy.] [F2: Yeah.] [F3: And I thought if we are going to draw it in terms of hierarchy coming down, then you have got what we call the er the weak little spots of the place. Four little heads. Thin shoulders and big fat thighs, big muscularly thighs that keep it going.]

Undergraduate and postgraduate students also emphasized this distance. The latter mentioned the lack of effect they believed they had through the Staff–Student Panel, particularly on the actions of the leader. This was a point that had not been made before, and was underlined by a long neck, and by folded arms signifying lack of approachability. At the UK school, a feeling of disenfranchisement and restricted personal autonomy prevailed.

Lack of direction and fragmentation of academics were sensed more strongly in the Canadian organization, in this case because of the perceived outgoing leader's inconsistent management style rather than the perceived communication problems and decision-making supremacy characterizing the UK school leader. For example, hostility towards the leader appeared especially intense amongst contractual academics, who felt poorly treated in relation to permanent colleagues over teaching and research opportunities and contract renewal (Figure 10.5):

> [That's me! (DS: A small figure?) Yes. (DS: Why?) Because I feel so small. Powerless. (DS: Right.) And that's <names head of school>. [both laugh] He

Figure 10.5   **Face-to-face interview image, Canadian school**

constantly says 'No'. (DS: Are you holding your hands up to your head?) Yes. (DS: Why, why's that?) 'Cos I'm losing my mind. I really am, I'm going insane. (DS: Why's that?) [interrupts] Because I'm totally frustrated. (DS: Right.) [nervous laughter] (DS: And he he personifies what you feel about your situation, does he?) Oh, yes. Definitely. (DS: Right. And and the organization in general?) Well, I [more assertive] I think that the situations differ so much, depending on who you are. (DS: Right.) You know, but this is *me*, and that's him. There's no question about it. (DS: Right. Right.) And I'm getting smaller. (DS: You're getting smaller?) Oh, yes. Yeh. And he's getting bigger.]

However, a year later a new organizational leader had generated a sense of 'cautious optimism' within the school. The organization was now believed to be at a critical juncture in terms of its strategic direction: a very strong theme in all focus groups. According to the postgraduate students' image (Figure 10.6), the choice is between the roads of mediocracy and success, with cautious optimism represented by a simultaneous frown and smile. Positive factors are seen to be students' talents and enthusiasm and support for the new leader from most internal stakeholders. Rock-like obstacles on the road to success are the wider university bureaucracy, the deteriorating economy, overcompetitive students, diverse academic personalities and the outgoing leader:

[S1: Yeah, well I think it's at a crossroads, getting another dean.] [S2: Yep a new system, dean.] . . . [S3: Hazy vision. [laughs]] . . . [S4: I think it's the blind leading the blind] . . . [S2: Uh, don't know which way we are going and which

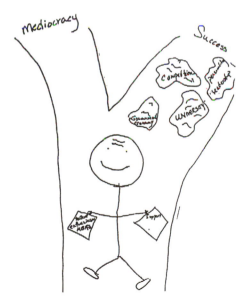

Figure 10.6 **Postgraduate students' focus group image, Canadian school**

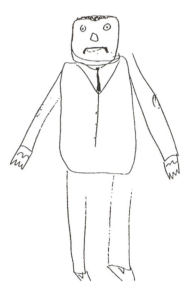

Figure 10.7   **Face-to-face interview image, UK school**

way they are going.] . . . [S1: I think it's the road meets resistance in a certain way, but if we want to make it what we want, then it's got to get over a lot of obstacles.]

The concept of an image mismatch was shared, to some extent, in both case study organizations. Suits, ties and other aspects of a male business uniform created a degree of perceived respectability in both places – but also a degree of formality, conservatism and hierarchy. Canadian academics saw an image mismatch more as a conflict between business and academic roles, represented by figures clad half in business suits and half in academic regalia. However, the UK school's academics also viewed the image mismatch as a clash between internal and external perceptions of the professional or business-like nature of the organization. In other words, the UK school academics believed that their projected professionalism was illusory (Figure 10.7):

[(DS: Why's he wearing a suit?) Oh, conventional. A grey suit. (DS: A grey suit?) It's done up as well – all three buttons. (DS: Why's that?) 'Cos that's what repressed, tight-arsed people do. (DS: Right.) . . . Very besuited, very wants to be seen as a a manager, an accountant, or er someone of that sort. Greasy, yeh – Brylcreem. (DS: Right.) That sort of thing. (DS: It it it's not a high-flying sort-of executive-type?) Oh, no, no, no! It's more like a glorified clerk. (DS: Right.) Possibly slightly shiny bits on the suit. (DS: Right.) Sort of a bit tatty.]

Certainly, both case study institutions were depicted as male in academic numbers, although this characteristic was less strongly expressed at the UK school than in the Canadian organization. This could be a simple description of the sheer number of male academics in relation to their female counterparts, but there also appeared an important articulation of 'male' values, such as competitiveness and lack of emotional support for organizational members. Both organizations were also seen as young/middle-aged. However, the UK organization was seen as large/tall in size terms, whereas the Canadian organization was seen as medium in stature. Finally, Canadian academics appeared to view each other as being more intellectual than the UK academics did their own colleagues.

Several pictorial characteristics were wholly unique to each institution. In the UK organization, perceived preoccupation with money and research, a lack of business world links and a feeling of size-based anonymity were mentioned frequently. In addition, high power relative to other faculties, a feigned hi-tech orientation and a competitive environment were each referred to. The Canadian organization was seen to have particular problems of recruitment and retention owing to its geographical location. Also emerging were an extreme lack of financial resources, a perceived degree of intellectualism and the wider university bureaucracy representing a barrier to change. Remaining Canadian themes included lack of strategic direction, a watershed resulting from a recent change of leaders and cautious future optimism.

Overall findings

A summary of the pictorial exercises revealed organizational elements not previously identified using verbal research instruments. For the organizational researcher, the generation of new insights is the acid test of using image. The top five newly emerging constructs for each school are shown in Table 10.1 as an example of how the researcher could present study results. These are given in order of descending frequency of mention, in terms of how many focus groups and interviews contained each characteristic. This helps to show how intensely and widely held is each of these constructs. The number of focus groups referring to the construct is given first, because each represents at least five people and because groups served as a double-check on original face-to-face interviews.

If strategy development is not the research objective, one could stop here with an insightful analysis of each organization's culture. If, however, one is required to make strategic recommendations, one could then identify which of the organization's more problematic characteristics could be addressed and which would be more difficult to change. For example, slow organizational response might be inevitable, given the nature of decision-making in academic committees. Conversely, a lack of direction could be tackled with the development of a well-defined strategic plan. One outcome from the study was the formulation of written strategic objectives for each institution, designed to help alleviate some of the major organizational difficulties

Table 10.1   *Example organizational characteristics, generated by*
pictorial exercises

Organizational characteristic	Frequency of mention	
	Focus groups	Interviews
UK school		
Unhappy/frustrating nature of organization	5	21
Respectability/business orientation	5	9
Maleness in faculty numbers and attitudes	4	28
Mismatch in appearance/role conflict	4	15
Research orientation/preoccupation	3	7
Canadian school		
Watershed of cautious optimism	6	29
Lack of direction	6	8
Reasonably intellectual academics' nature	3	4
Slowness in response to external stimuli	1	11
Maleness in faculty numbers and attitudes	1	10

identified. These are confidential, but are geared around such areas as research, teaching, external target markets and human resource management.

In addition, data on the existing image of each school enabled guidelines to be drawn up concerning internal and external image management. For the UK school, emphasizing and accentuating the organization's respectability, its business orientation and its research orientation might help mould a more positive impression of the institution. Challenging the perceived role mismatch in projected professionalism might boost the school's image further. Such factors, it was concluded, needed to be addressed in a continuous external and internal organizational image campaign, communicable to all stakeholders. Yet, it was also felt that only *real* changes in strategy would be likely to alter perceptions in the long term.

For the Canadian organization, a general feeling of cautious optimism upon the arrival of a new dean emphasized that the new leader was in a good position to make positive changes with the support of internal and external stakeholders. Anxieties concerning financial resources, salary inequities, economic instability, role conflict and the overall university bureaucracy were still prevalent. However, if the new leader was able to deal with these matters, further fragmentation, academic turnover and internal organizational conflict would be reduced.

Conclusions: the power of image

Certainly, the 'live' research presented here has revealed several potential problems the unwary researcher might experience when trying to operationalize pictorial techniques. Some of the more important of these are discussed below, together with suggestions on how they might be overcome.

Firstly, some people decline the invitation to draw pictures. Sometimes individuals claim they are more verbally or numerically literate than they are image literate. However, experience has shown that this is more often because of a reticence to make public one's creations, rather than because of a total lack of drawing ability. Using *warm-up exercises* prior to asking for a final image does improve the chance of someone completing the exercise. After this, as in all interview situations, the respondent can normally be put at ease with a few words of encouragement. Such persuasive skills can be learned relatively quickly with a little thought and perseverance. Try giving reassurance to reluctant drawers, rather than rebuking or pressurizing them. If it helps, leave the room during drawing to minimize anxiety. You might even like to offer a cup of coffee to those more difficult to tempt into drawing!

Once people are persuaded to draw, the results are often insightful. Of course, a tiny minority cannot be convinced of this. However, these numbers can be minimized by using an appropriate metaphor. For example, pilot work showed that most people identify more readily with a familiar metaphor such as personality than with some other possibilities. Using cloud formations or motorbike metaphors to represent their organization will probably have most people scratching their heads. So, it is important to choose metaphors that are widely understood and can involve all organizational members.

On occasion, respondents might incorporate words into their drawings, contrary to instructions. Some discretion must be exercised by the facilitator in these instances. As long as the major impact of the representation is conveyed through its pictorial content, it is perhaps better to accept such minor verbal encroachments rather than risk interrupting the creative process unduly. In Figure 10.6, words are simply used as labels to clarify what particular items in each picture show. In Figure 10.5, the word 'no' increases the power of the drawing, although its removal would not alter the overall impression of the piece. In such cases, image is still the main means of communicating the idea.

A third set of problems is centred around the issue of interpretation. The researcher should not rely purely on her or his own judgement of what the drawer intended to convey. Any second-hand account might be wrong. For this reason, one should not attempt to interpret the picture directly, but should rely on the drawer's own explanation. In doing so, remember that one is trying to identify themes generated across pictures, in order to avoid accusations of reification – that one is treating the personality drawing itself as real.

This leads to a related interpretive issue, endemic to many forms of qualitative research. Transcribing and examining transcripts using discourse analysis is very time consuming, because one is interested in interpreting all recorded interaction between interviewer and interviewee. One might prefer to use a simpler approach, such as content analysis or cognitive mapping (see Jones, 1985), although richness in discourse will be traded off against speed of analysis.

A fundamental question also arises as to whether such methods reveal truly latent or just manifest organizational constructs. What counts as 'latent' is a very difficult issue. Just because pictorially stimulated constructs had not emerged in other verbal dimensions, does this mean they are really latent? It might be that respondents had merely overlooked items they would in other circumstances have articulated earlier in interviews or group discussions. To counter this argument, constructs undoubtedly appeared during the case studies that had not been articulated earlier. Participants even said they had not thought of such things before. Ultimately, perhaps, it is impossible to prove beyond doubt that what is being surfaced here is truly 'latent'. However, this assertion is more likely to gain support if pictorial techniques are used *after* more orthodox verbal cultural and political descriptions have exhausted respondents' articulated data about the organization.

A fifth problem is that of aggregating individuals' constructs into common constructs. If individuals' face-to-face drawings had been solely relied upon, the methodology would have run the risk of not surfacing constructs that are shared by a number of people within the organization. Even if several people had eventually articulated the same construct, others might simply not have thought of it. Since people are not used to surfacing and questioning their own assumptions, such data might be more difficult to uncover. One solution is to use focus groups to aggregate constructs, building on individuals' pictorial output by using these as input into group processes. Such focus groups serve as a 'double-check' on individuals' perceptions by seeing how widely shared they are throughout the organization. If focus groups are repeated after a significant period of time has elapsed, the extent to which such constructs have changed can also be examined. Of course, what is a 'significant' period depends upon the rapidity and intensity of change within the particular organization and its context.

Pictorial representation, then, is not without its problems. However, it can be a very illuminating alternative to more orthodox research techniques. This is particularly so in strategy-making, where tools such as SWOT (strengths, weaknesses, opportunities and threats) analysis are often too familiar to participants and too lacking in flexibility to generate truly creative thinking. Images can be a novel, ice-breaking and insightful way of surfacing people's latent constructs. They can reveal what words alone cannot, since they place participants in an unfamiliar situation, thereby breaking down mindsets and circumventing the reluctance to verbalize.

Ultimately, the true test of pictorial representation is in the field. Certainly, the technique has proven useful in this study as a means of exploring latent perceptions, and as a bridge to more creative strategy formulation and implementation. Whilst it is unlikely that this cursory exploration of image will change the minds of ardent positivists, it is hoped that some eager researchers will be tempted to explore less orthodox alternatives to the written word.

References

Alvesson, M. (1990) 'Organisation: from substance to image?', *Organization Studies*, 11 (3): 373–94.

Berger, P.L. and Luckmann, T. (1965) *The Social Construction of Reality: A Treatise in the Sociology of Knowledge*. Harmondsworth: Pelican.

Branthwaite, A. and Lunn, T. (1985) 'Projective techniques in social and market research', in Robert Walker (ed.), *Applied Qualitative Research*. Aldershot: Gower.

Burrell, G. and Morgan, G. (1979) *Sociological Paradigms and Organisational Analysis*. London: Heinemann.

Checkland, P.B. and Scholes, J. (1990) *Soft Systems Methodology in Action*. London: Wiley.

Edwards, B.R. (1981) *Drawing on the Right Side of the Brain: How to Unlock Your Hidden Artistic Talent*. London: Souvenir.

Gombrich, E.H. (1967) *The Story of Art*, 11th edn. London: Phaidon.

Green, S. (1988) 'Strategy, organizational culture and symbolism', *Long Range Planning*, 21 (4): 121–9.

Hawkins, J.M. and Allen, R. (eds) (1991) *The Oxford Encyclopedic English Dictionary*. Oxford: Clarendon Press.

Henry, J. (ed.) (1991) *Creative Management*. London: Open University/ Sage.

Johnson, G. and Scholes, K. (1993) *Exploring Corporate Strategy*, 3rd edn. Hemel Hempstead: Prentice-Hall.

Jones, S. (1985) 'The analysis of depth interviews', in Robert Walker (ed.), *Applied Qualitative Research*. Aldershot: Gower.

Kotler, P. (1986) *Principles of Marketing*, 3rd edn. Englewood Cliffs, NJ: Prentice-Hall.

Langer, S. (1957) *Philosophy in a New Key*. Cambridge, MA: Harvard University Press.

Maddox, N., Anthony, W.P. and Wheatley, W. Jr (1987) 'Creative strategic planning using imagery', *Long Range Planning*, 20 (5): 118–24.

Majaro, S. (1991) *The Creative Marketer*. Oxford: Butterworth Heinemann and Chartered Institute of Marketing.

Morgan, G. (1989) *Creative Organization Theory: A Resourcebook*. Newbury Park, CA: Sage.

Morgan, G. (1993) *Imaginization: The Art of Creative Management*. Newbury Park, CA: Sage.

Potter, J. and Wetherell, M. (1987) *Discourse and Social Psychology: Beyond Attitudes and Behaviour*. London: Sage.

Rickards, T. (1988) *Creativity at Work*. Aldershot: Gower.

Russell, P. and Evans, R. (1989) *The Creative Manager*. London: Unwin.

Schall, M.S. (1983) 'A communication-rules approach to organizational culture', *Administrative Science Quarterly*, 28: 557–81.

Semeonoff, B. (1976) *Projective Techniques*. London: Wiley.

Stiles, David R. (1995) 'The art of organisations: picturing UK and North America business school strategies in four dimensions'. PhD thesis, University of Cardiff.

Weick, K.E. (1979) *The Social Psychology of Organising*, 2nd edn. Reading, MA: Addison-Wesley.

Wittgenstein, L. (1964) *Preliminary Studies for the 'Philosophical Investigations': The Blue and Brown Books*. Oxford: Basil Blackwell.

Ziff, K. (1990) 'Focus group "art" reveals in-depth information', *Marketing News*, 3 September: 7, 20.

11 Soft Systems Analysis

Chris Clegg and Susan Walsh

Soft systems analysis (SSA) is primarily a method for investigating problems located within a system. The method is used to plan and implement change, although it can also be used to design new systems. Typically, the focus of the method is on rather complex systems involving human activity. Our general aim in this chapter is to introduce some of the key ideas in soft systems thinking. More specifically, our objectives are to:

1 describe soft systems analysis;
2 give some examples of its application; and
3 comment on some of the strengths and weaknesses of the method.

To these ends we have organized the chapter into six sections. First we provide a brief outline of the method and its underlying rationale. We then describe how it actually works, providing an introduction to each of its stages. Next, we present two instances of its application, selecting examples from our own experience to try to illustrate ways in which the method can be used. Finally, we identify some of the strengths and weaknesses of the method based on our own experiences, and then draw brief conclusions. We stress that this chapter provides an introduction to the method; in places we have simplified our descriptions for the sake of clarity and to ease understanding.

What the method is

Soft systems analysis has been developed since 1969 by Peter Checkland of Lancaster University (Checkland, 1981; Checkland and Scholes, 1990). It has been used in several hundred instances. The core idea is that people work through the method to analyse complex systems in order to plan and manage change. The method has a strong pragmatic focus and can be seen as a practical working tool. However, it can also be used in applied research; indeed the examples described later in this chapter incorporate both a practical emphasis on change and a research focus involving analysis of an applied problem.

As we will describe below, the method is organized in a series of relatively formal and well structured stages through which its users work. In practice, considerable iteration can take place, and, as we will demonstrate in our examples, parts of the method can be used in isolation.

Systems thinking represents an overarching meta-theory for examining and understanding the behaviour of complex entities. Systems thinking was imported into the study of organizations and the people in them from the physical and biological sciences. The underlying notion is that a system is composed of parts or elements which are themselves interrelated and interconnected to form some whole. A system transforms inputs into outputs, has transactions with its environment, has to adapt to changing circumstances, and attempts to regulate its behaviour (see for example Cummings, 1995; Morgan, 1986).

To try to convey what 'soft systems' thinking is about, it is easiest first to discuss the meaning of 'hard systems'. Hard systems logic embraces the assumption that one can develop a model of the system under analysis, and that this is non-problematic. The system has a definable set of objectives or goals, there are some identifiable alternatives to reach the goals, and it is logically possible to identify optimal solutions. Implicit in hard systems thinking is the idea that there are objective truths about the system, that reality is independent of the actors (i.e. not subject to separate and independent interpretation). Hard systems abound in everyday life: consider, for example, lighting, heating and plumbing systems. Engineering disciplines typically study hard systems of this kind. One of Checkland's central arguments is that thinking about systems in this 'hard' and rationalistic way is dominant, and that this reflects prevailing values and epistemologies within our education and training. This is not to argue that hard systems thinking is wrong, but rather to suggest that it may not always be appropriate.

So what is meant by 'soft systems'? A central assumption is that people see and interpret the world differently. Discrepancies in the views held by individuals are not sources of invalidity or 'noise' in the data; rather, differentiation reflects the nature of reality. People hold different interpretations; pluralism is the norm. Especially in complex systems, individuals or groups are likely to construct quite different views on how the system works, what may be wrong with it, and how it should be improved. Table 11.1 is a somewhat playful attempt at demonstrating some differences in perspective held by people working in a variety of roles in a company. In this fictional example, they have been asked an apparently simple question; however, their answers and quotes reflect their professional roles and orientations.

Checkland argues that change in complex human activity systems is best achieved by debate and the pursuit of agreement, rather than by edict and the use of power. He argues for analysis in an open, public and participative manner. As such SSA emphasizes participation in the method by the actors working in the system under consideration.

Furthermore, the (soft systems) analyst is part of the situation. S/he is not a domain expert, but acts more as a therapist working with clients, helping

Table 11.1 *Different views*

In answer to the (apparently straightforward) question '2 + 2 = ?', people working in different roles gave the following answers.

Role	Quotation	Answer
Manufacturing manager	'We're doing the best that we can. I can't get blood out of a stone.'	3.5
Purchasing manager	'If we are buying that much, I'd want a discount.'	3.6
Engineering manager	'The computer's down and it's ages since I used logs.'	40.00
Marketing manager	'Our mission is synergy.'	5.0
Data processing manager	'You don't mind it in base 2 do you?'	100
Industrial relations manager	'In the current economic climate, we can't afford any more.'	3.8
Trade union convener	'I'll be advising my members.'	4.2

them analyse and address their problems. The role is similar to that of the change agent in the tradition of action research, where the researcher is a participant in the process (as opposed to a disinterested 'scientific' observer) with a dual commitment to improvements in practice and advances in theory (see for example Foster, 1972). Using Burrell and Morgan's (1979) distinctions, soft systems analysis can be located within an interpretive perspective, assuming an ontological commitment to order and an epistemological concern for the subjective nature of reality.

Checkland stresses that hard and soft modes of thinking are complementary and their appropriateness is dependent on the situation and the questions being asked. In his view soft systems thinking is especially relevant to human activity systems. Otherwise, the method has generic applicability; it is not limited to particular kinds of problem domains.

How it works

Whilst recognizing that SSA can be used in a variety of ways, it is easiest to describe in the first instance in its most straightforward format. In essence SSA is very simple. The analyst initially gathers data about the problem situation, and this is represented in pictorial form. The users of the method, i.e. the analyst and the system participants, then explicitly try looking at the system in a number of different ways, searching for views which add some new light. They select a new perspective on the problem situation, and develop a model of what the system would logically have to do to meet the requirements of this new view. This model is then compared with the existing problem situation to see if there are any lessons for change. These

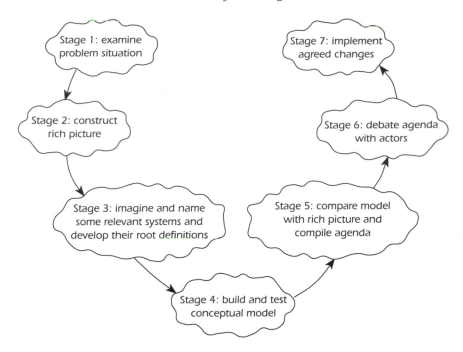

Figure 11.1   **Stages of soft systems analysis: stages 1, 2, 5, 6 and 7 are real world activities, stages 3 and 4 are conceptual activities**

are then discussed by the participants to decide which should be implemented. If the new view does not appear to offer help to the participants, another perspective is tried.

SSA has a number of essential characteristics. Thus, in its various stages, the method incorporates:

1   participation by the actors in the system;
2   structure and organization of the process;
3   imagination and innovation; and
4   analysis and logic.

In more detail, the method can be most easily visualized in seven stages as represented in Figure 11.1.

Stage 1

This stage involves a preliminary examination of the problem situation under analysis. The situation is typically a complex human activity system. It can be large scale, as in the case of a multinational company or a government department, or quite small scale, for example involving a small working group. At this point, the analyst resists the temptation to impose (or indeed accept) a premature understanding about the situation or its charac-terization as a problem of a particular type with an identified set of causes. This is more easily said than done, given the predilection for 'experts' to view the world in a particular way and to have fairly specialized sets of interests. Furthermore, there is a strong likelihood that actors in the system will themselves describe the situation as a problem of a particular kind. It may well be that the actors have been working in this situation for some considerable time. It would be most unusual for them not to have made their own interpretations of what is happening and what is going wrong. Of course, there may be several alternative and conflicting versions.

During this stage the analyst begins to identify the scope of the system under review, and also negotiates arrangements for collecting data, along with 'contracts' about anonymity and confidentiality. The analyst should identify key roles at this time, especially regarding who is the client of the study (who caused the study to happen?), the problem-solver (who hopes to do something about the problem situation?), and the problem-owner (who 'owns' the problems under investigation?). These roles are important since these people need to be involved in agreeing the terms of reference and methods of working for the study, but also later in debating what changes are appropriate.

Stage 2

This stage entails gathering a wide range of relevant data which are represented in a 'rich picture' and presented to the study participants. Data gathering at this stage can take a variety of forms, including, for example, interviews, participant observation and questionnaires. The data should be broad-based, encompassing all those individuals (or an appropriate subset of them) who have inputs to, and interactions with, the system under study. This stage will normally incorporate the collection of 'hard' data (for example, regarding outputs and performance of the system) as well as the 'soft' data (for example, including attitudes and emotions).

The rich picture is a cartoon-like representation of the problem situation and includes a wide range of information, of both qualitative and quantitat-ive kinds. The picture includes information on the tasks that the system must perform and also data on the issues that people raise, i.e. topics of concern or dispute. Also included may be elements of structure, process and climate, i.e. important aspects of the system. But this picture is not a systemic representation of the problem domain, and nor is it a characterization of a problem type. Thus the analyst still refrains at this stage from constructing an explanatory model of the problem situation, either in the form of a systems diagram or by describing it in a particular way (e.g. that this is a problem of employee morale caused by an inappropriate reward system). The output of stage 2 is a rich picture which includes tasks and issues which are relevant to the system under study.

Both the first two stages are concerned with present day reality: Check-land labels them as 'real world' activities. In contrast, the stages 3 and 4 are predominantly intellectual and conceptual.

Stage 3

In this stage the analyst and participants search for new ways of looking on the existing problem situation. These new ways of looking on these complex interrelationships are called 'relevant systems'. In essence, the analyst says 'let's try looking on this situation like this.' This is the imaginative part of the method. For example, a pub can be visualized in a number of alternative ways (based on Naughton, 1984). Thus, it can be seen as a system for:

1   providing drinks;
2   initiating adolescents into adulthood;
3   providing employment;
4   entertaining customers;
5   dispensing drugs;
6   integrating a community;
7   producing customers for taxi firms;
8   scheduling work for the police; and so on.

Similarly, a research institute in a university may be seen in a variety of different ways, for example as a system for:

1   undertaking research;
2   gathering research funds;
3   training and educating research students;
4   developing the careers of researchers;
5   providing innovative ideas for industry;
6   producing patent applications;
7   attracting foreign workers and visitors;
8   raising the profile of the host university; and so on.

These views are relevant in so far as they cast light on the situation. Relevant systems can be task-based (for example, viewing a pub as a system for dispensing drinks) or issue-based (for example, a system for initiating adolescents into adulthood). This part of SSA is absolutely critical to its success. The analyst selects views (relevant systems) which s/he believes may be fruitful for uncovering aspects of the problem situation. The process of selection is informed by what makes most sense to the analyst and/or the participants, and by what promises to take their level of understanding further. This process is iterative as the formulation can always be modified later as understanding deepens. Thus the function of the relevant system is to provide 'an alternative way of viewing the problem situation which, when developed further in succeeding stages of the methodology, will provide the analyst with a sharp comparison between it and what is observed to go on in the real world situation' (Naughton, 1984: 36).

For each of these views, the analyst derives a root definition. Thus for every relevant system that is examined in detail, a root definition is developed. The root definition should follow logically from the choice of relevant system. The root definition is a precise verbal description of what is implied by the choice of relevant system. Normally speaking such a definition will include a statement of each of the following: the customers of the relevant system; the actors in the system; what the system transforms; the underlying *Weltanschauung* or world view; the owners of the system; and its environmental constraints. These can be remembered using the mnemonic CATWOE and they are more fully explicated in Table 11.2. Checkland stresses that CATWOE is intended as a useful way of thinking about the root definition, but not all definitions need all these components and other elements may be added to help provide a definition. The only mandatory element in a definition is a statement of what the system transforms.

A key point is that the root definition and its constituent parts will vary according to the chosen relevant system. For example, in the case of viewing the 'pub as an entertainment system', it is transforming people who are not

Table 11.2   *Elements in a root definition*

To illustrate what is meant, instances are given describing a pub, using the relevant system that it can be viewed as an 'entertainment system'.

Customers	These are the people who receive whatever it is that the system does, perhaps its beneficiaries or victims, e.g. the paying cutomers who visit the pub
Actors	These are the people who carry out the activities undertaken by the system, e.g. the people who work in, and for, the pub
Transformation	This is what the system changes, from one state into another, e.g. customers who are not entertained into people who are
Weltanschauung	This is equivalent to the underlying world view, e.g. that pubs are part of the entertainment industry and that the customers are seeking much more than drinks alone
Owners	This refers to the owners of the system, those who have power over the system to cause it to cease to exist, e.g. this might be the brewery which owns the pub
Environmental constraints	These are the constraints that the system has to take as given, e.g. these would include the location of the pub, and laws about hours of opening and ages of customers

Notes
1   Root definitions vary with the choice of relevant system.
2   Root definitions may (but do not have to) include all the above elements, and they may also include other elements (if that proves useful). However, a root definition must include a statement of what the relevant system transforms.

entertained into people who are, whereas the 'pub as a community integrator' is transforming a community that is not well integrated into one that is. The output of stage 3 is a selected relevant system and its associated root definition.

Our experience is that people enjoy this part of the method and do not have too much difficulty generating alternative views once they understand what is required of them. The analyst can provide a useful role in leading and facilitating these discussions.

Stage 4

This is also a conceptual stage. Here the analyst (perhaps with help from the participants) develops a model of what the system would logically have to do to meet the requirements of the chosen relevant system and its accompanying root definition. The model is derived using deductive logic and is abstract. At this stage it does not necessarily bear any relationship with the real world. This model is explicitly a systems model and is described using transitive (i.e. active) verbs. The verbs are arranged in a logically coherent order. Naughton (1984) advises that such models should contain around 6 to 12 main activities; they should be simple rather than complex. A key point is that the model is concerned solely with 'what is done'. The conceptual model has no interest in 'how something is done' or in 'who does it'.

For example, in the case of viewing 'the pub as an entertainment system', key activities in the conceptual model might include the following:

1   gathering information on what existing (and potential) customers want;
2   gathering information on what entertainment services and products are available;
3   booking/hiring various services and products;
4   advertising and marketing the services/products;
5   providing the services/products;
6   maintaining quality control of these services/products; and
7   evaluating customer reactions.

The core of SSA lies in stages 3 and 4 and these should be very tightly coupled one to another. Thus, if the relevant system is changed, then the root definition will need alteration, as will the conceptual model. There may be many iterations between these two stages in particular as the analyst and the participants try out different relevant systems to see whether or not they lead to definitions and models that seem useful. A great deal of the craft skill in using SSA lies in developing and trying out alternative ways of looking on the system and then following through the logic of that view. The output of stage 4 is a conceptual model of a chosen relevant system.

Our experience is that conceptual modelling is a difficult activity. Whereas most participants willingly and productively engage in stage 3 (generating new views), they can find it harder to develop the logically derived conceptual models. A key issue here may be the time, commitment and expertise that the participants can bring to this stage in the process. Certainly we have tried to develop conceptual models in group work with participants, or alone as analysts, only later showing the participants the models we have derived. Analysts may have some difficult choices to make here regarding the best way of undertaking this work in a particular situation.

Stage 5

This stage involves a comparison between the new conceptual model (from stage 4) and the rich picture (from stage 2). This comparison may identify things which are part of the conceptual model but which do not happen in the real world, and also activities in the real world which are not included in the conceptual model. Any such differences are noted and discussed in the next stage. This stage can be handled in a relatively unstructured way, by simply comparing the conceptual model and the real world. Or this can be undertaken in more structured ways, for example by examining each part of the conceptual model (perhaps each verb) and then asking: does this happen in the real world? Such comparisons lead to the identification of possible changes in the system under analysis. The output of this stage is an agenda of possible changes in the form of a series of topics for discussion. As before, the agenda is concerned with identifying what activities are present, absent, problematic or questionable. The focus remains on 'what' not 'how'.

Stage 6

In this stage the agenda is debated by the actors working in the system, along with the clients, problem-owners and problem-solvers (as identified in stage 1 of the method). The purpose of the debate is to identify those changes that are agreed as both systemically desirable and culturally feasible. Systemically desirable means that the change must make sense in system terms, i.e. that it should be consistent with how the system is intended to work. Culturally feasible focuses on whether or not a particular change is feasible to the actors concerned. Only if both criteria are met should a change be implemented. Where such agreement is not reached, it may be that the analyst needs to accept that 'no change' is the chosen solution, or alternatively that s/he needs to try to develop another relevant system to see if a way forward can be found, i.e. work through the method again seeking new ideas. The output of stage 6 is an agreed set of changes, or an agreement not to change.

Stage 7

This stage involves the implementation of changes that have been agreed as both feasible and desirable. For example, changes may involve new structures, procedures, policies or processes.

We now describe two examples of the application of soft systems analysis.

Implementation of a CADCAM system

In this instance, SSA was used in a research and development project examining the implementation of a computer aided design, computer aided manufacturing (CADCAM) system in an engineering company. The researchers worked with the company from 1988 until 1990, making two sets of recommendations (in 1989 and 1990). A follow-up visit was undertaken in 1996. (A fuller account of this study is given in Symon and Clegg, 1991a, b, c.) The researchers used SSA as a means of organizing and integrating some complex data, and as a vehicle for recommending how the implementation process could be better managed. For illustrative purposes, the project is described chronologically using the stages of SSA. As will become clear, the method was used iteratively and some of the stages were revisited as the project progressed.

Stage 1: the problem situation

The study was undertaken in an aerospace engineering company employing around 2,000 people. The company is part of a multinational corporation and has a good reputation for the design and manufacture of high precision, small batch, engineering products. The company has a complex organizational structure. Of particular relevance here are three major functions: design, manufacture and corporate engineering. The design function is split into different product groups. The manufacturing department has a traditional organization based on machining process. It manufactures for all the design product groups, and the products flow through the production process from one machine area to another. The corporate engineering function is a central head office group which provides specialist engineering support to the whole company. Historically the company has been good at innovative engineering. Typically the design engineers take pride in designing new products to meet the needs and specifications of their customers. They then hand over the design to the manufacturing department who are responsible for making the product. These two functions operate relatively autonomously and there has been little success at improving integration between the two functions.

Senior managers in corporate engineering decided to invest in an advanced CADCAM system. The main objectives for this investment included: reduced lead times for meeting customer demand; improved quality; reduced cost; increased integration between design and manufacture; and improved design for manufacturability. The initial direct cost of the new system was around £3 million and this included 55 CADCAM terminals.

To manage the purchase and implementation of the new system, the director of corporate engineering set up a project management team supervised by a project board. The project team was led by a full-time project manager from corporate engineering (whose title was project manager of computer aided design). He was assisted by a specialist in information technology (on part-time secondment from the management services department, also located in head office). The project board was chaired by a senior manager from corporate engineering and included representatives from engineering, management services, design and manufacture (all on a part-time basis).

The role of the researchers was to investigate the implementation process and to make recommendations for improvement from an organizational (as opposed to technical) perspective.

Stage 2: the rich picture

Symon and Clegg gathered data using a variety of research methods over 18 months, including:

1 interviews with 35 employees, including all the key actors in the change and a sample of people from different functions and levels who were directly or indirectly affected by the CADCAM;
2 participant observation over a period of 9 months after the first report, attending meetings of the CADCAM user group (set up as a result of the first set of recommendations);
3 a tracer study of approximately 100 parts, tracing their progress through the design and manufacturing process;
4 questionnaires, administered to 36 key actors (again after the first report).

Symon and Clegg found that the implementation of the CADCAM was led by headquarters staff in corporate engineering and that the main concern was with getting the technology implemented at the minimum cost. Very little attention was paid to the wider organizational impact of the CADCAM, or indeed to the opportunities that were open to reorganizing and restructuring the work to improve the levels of integration between design and manufacturing. The CADCAM was not seen as a catalyst for organizational change; rather it was seen as a change in 'medium'.

A simplified version of the researchers' rich picture of this problem situation is given in Figure 11.2 for illustrative purposes. (For information, Colin and Tim are the project manager and his associate.)

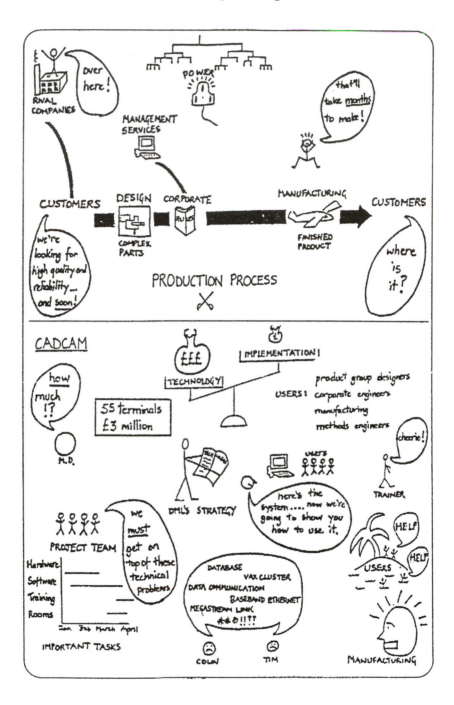

Figure 11.2   **Rich picture of the CADCAM implementation
(reprinted from Symon and Clegg, 1991c, NCC
Blackwell)**

Stage 3: relevant systems and root definitions

The researchers decided it would be useful to describe the existing relevant system that they believed (from the data collected) was guiding the implementation process. They also developed its associated root definition. This is equivalent to identifying the existing 'theory in use' (Argyris and Schon, 1978). This was then compared with an alternative relevant system and root definition.

Symon and Clegg argued that the project was seen and managed as a 'technology implementation project'. This was the underlying 'relevant system'. Accordingly, they described the existing root definition guiding the project in the following terms:

> The company are replacing an existing, largely manual system for design and manufacture with a CADCAM system (transformation); this represents a change in medium and this process is owned (owners), led and managed (actors) by corporate engineering, with some help from management services, product designers and manufacturing. The clients are primarily the corporate engineers and the designers in the different product groups (customers). The emphasis is heavily on technical issues and problems, and the view is that organizational issues can be addressed later (*Weltanschauung*). This process is being undertaken using the minimum of scarce company resources (constraints).

Symon and Clegg argued that a useful alternative relevant system in this case would be to regard this process as an organizational (rather than technical) change. As such they developed a new root definition to guide the implementation process. This is described below:

> The key task is to design a new organizational system integrating design and manufacturing (transformation), assisted by the use of CADCAM. This process is owned and managed by both design and manufacturing, with help from management services, and with a strong emphasis on end-user participation (owners, actors and customers). The project involves joint consideration of technical, strategic and organizational issues (*Weltanschauung*). The process should be undertaken cost effectively using appropriate resources (constraints).

Stage 4: conceptual model

Using this root definition, the researchers developed a conceptual model of what needed to be done to meet the needs of this definition. This model is shown in Figure 11.3. This was then used as a basis for making a first set of recommendations to the company.

Stage 5a: comparison and agenda

The researchers compared their new model with what was happening in the real world and identified some major gaps. These stemmed from use by the company of a rather limited relevant system. Consideration of a new relevant system and its associated root definition led the researchers to

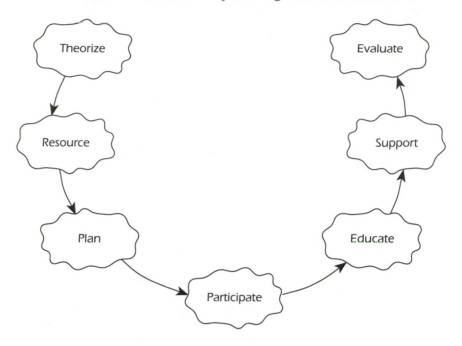

Figure 11.3   **Conceptual model of an organizational change**

generate an agenda for change. The key items were recommendations that the company should:

1   adopt a new view (or theory) of the implementation, placing more emphasis on organizational and end-user aspects of change;
2   invest more resources in the change programme;
3   formulate a plan which recognizes the strategic importance of CADCAM as a catalyst for change and examines the wider organizational opportunities it presents;
4   allow for and encourage more participation by end-users;
5   place more emphasis on wider education, awareness and communication for end-users and others;
6   develop an infrastructure to support end-users during the introduction and operation of the CADCAM system;
7   evaluate the introduction and operation of CADCAM, not just in financial and engineering terms, but also covering the human and organizational issues.

Stage 6a: debate

An open report describing the findings, relevant systems, root definitions, conceptual model and agenda for change was presented to all the interested parties. Two presentations were also given, one to the end-users and one to senior managers. Reactions were divided. The users were 'satisfied with the outcomes and acknowledged the perception of the implementation as technology-led, under-resourced and lacking an organisational strategy. They were keen to see the recommendations implemented, but suspected that senior managers would not agree with the conclusions reached' (Symon and Clegg, 1991a: 282). They were right: indeed the director of engineering called the feedback report 'a moaning minnies charter'. Further debate followed.

Stage 7a: implementation

Some of these recommendations were accepted and implemented. A CAD-CAM user group was set up to address some of these issues, in particular concerning resources, end-user participation, education and training, and infrastructural support (i.e. covering recommendations 2, 4, 5 and 6). Also the researchers were invited to continue their work, including further evaluation of the human and organizational impact of the CADCAM (i.e. covering recommendation 7 above).

Stage 5b: a new agenda

The changes were implemented from March 1989 onwards. The researchers continued working in the company until April 1990, gathering further data using participant observation, tracer and questionnaire techniques (as described earlier). These data were used to compare how the process of change was now being managed with the conceptual model offered by the researchers. Thus, the researchers maintained their proposed relevant system and root definition (stage 3) and their associated conceptual model (stage 4).

This work culminated (in April 1990) in the presentation of a second report including a further agenda for change. These recommendations included the following:

1 senior managers should develop a strategy for the organizational and technical integration of the design and manufacturing functions (some specific suggestions were made for how this could be achieved);
2 the project management infrastructure should become more integrative (of design and manufacture); for example by
3 changing the roles of the existing CAD manager and CAD trainer into those of manager and trainer of the complete CADCAM system; and
4 rotating the chairmanship of the CADCAM user group so that representatives from manufacturing act in that role.

Stage 6b: debate

Presentations based on the researchers' second report were made to two groups of people, the end-users and the board of directors. The end-users were in broad agreement with the second report, though some were concerned that it appeared critical of the manufacturing function. The board of directors also approved the report ('what I have been saying for the past eight years', according to the director of corporate engineering!). The managing director (new in the role) stressed that the benefits of integrative technologies can only be achieved with organizational changes: 'The brick walls between design and manufacturing have to come down.'

Stage 7b: implementation

Over the following months some of the recommendations in this second set were implemented, in particular regarding a more integrative approach to project management (recommendations 2, 3 and 4). But no progress was made with a more strategic plan to integrate design and manufacture organizationally as well as technically (recommendation 1). The researchers continued to visit the company regularly for nine months after the second report. They reported that the CADCAM user group 'continued to operate very successfully addressing "bottom-up" issues . . . [but that] little changed from a "top-down" perspective' (Symon and Clegg, 1991a: 285).

Postscript

One of the researchers was able to revisit the company six years later (in 1996). The CADCAM project has been a success in the sense that the technology is fully operational, is widely used and is well liked. The CADCAM user group continues to function, seven years after its inception in March 1989. It continues in its role of handling important 'bottom-up' issues. Just as interesting, however, there remain problems of integration between design and manufacture. 'Design for manufacturability' has not been achieved. The investment in CADCAM (total cost by now around £12 million) has not delivered the level of organizational integration that was sought. Design and manufacture still operate separately. The project failed to address some major strategic and political issues that would have enabled structural change and increased integration within the company. Unfortunately this is not an unusual scenario for technical change of this kind. In the language of soft systems analysis, the organizational integration of design and manufacture was not 'culturally feasible' to certain very powerful people in the company.

Performance in command and control systems

The aim of this study was to develop an approach which would identify critical performance criteria for a naval command and control system on board ship.[1] Two different kinds of command and control system were considered for comparative purposes, a naval system and an off-shore production system (e.g. for extracting oil). SSA was used to provide the basic approach. The analysis was undertaken in a workshop format involving a range of people (13 in all), most with extensive expertise and experience in these different kinds of environment.

In this case, the workshop focused solely upon stages 3 and 4 of SSA, that is on developing some relevant systems, their root definitions and associated conceptual models.

Stage 3: relevant systems and root definitions

Several relevant systems were explored in groups in the workshop. For example, command and control can be seen as a system for:

1   making decisions (applies to both naval and off-shore production);
2   processing information (both);
3   making unsafe situations safe (both);
4   developing the careers of staff (both);
5   protecting the environment (both);
6   deploying resources (naval);
7   protecting the country (naval);
8   generating revenue (off-shore); and
9   distributing dangerous liquids and gases (off-shore).

One of the most useful relevant systems proved to be the view that these can be seen as information processing systems. 'Proved to be' requires some clarification. In this instance, the participants felt this view helped further their understanding of the system, and also helped with the task of identifying critical performance criteria. Of course, this only became clear later in the workshop.

Adopting this task-based view led to the generation of the following root definition for naval command and control systems:

> This is a Government owned system (owner) for transforming multi-source, variable quality information into accurate, actionable information (transformation) for use by the Commander (customer) in decision-making. The system comprises a team of humans using a variety of systems and technology (actors) and operates in a constrained environment in particular concerning time and money (constraints). Furthermore, the environment is potentially hostile such that errors in information processing can prove very costly and dangerous (*Weltanschauung*).

Stage 4: conceptual model

This relevant system and root definition were used by members of the workshop to generate a conceptual model of the main constituent parts

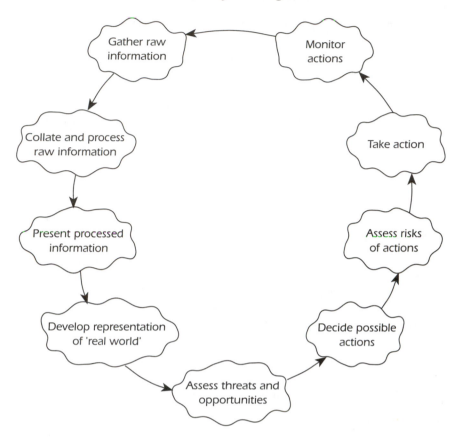

Figure 11.4   **Conceptual model of an information processing system**

of this information processing system. This model is summarized in Figure 11.4.

This model was then used to develop a set of performance criteria associated with each of these elements. In other words, SSA was used as a way of breaking down the main activities in a command and control system, each of which could then be assessed using specific performance criteria. How each one would be assessed and measured was not the concern of this particular exercise.

For example, under the activity in the conceptual model concerned with 'present processed information', sample performance criteria that were generated in the workshop included the following:

1   Is the information clear?
2   Is it understandable? Does it make sense?
3   Is it comprehensive?
4   Is the information relevant to its receiver?
5   Is the information sufficient to allow the next activities to be carried out?

6 Is the information presented in a timely manner?
7 Is it credible?
8 Is it vulnerable to error?
9 Is it valid?
10 Is it reliable?
11 Does it explain what is going on?
12 Can the information be audited?

In this instance, the conceptual parts of SSA, i.e. stages 3 and 4, were used to develop an approach which would allow its users to identify critical performance criteria for command and control systems.

Strengths and weaknesses of SSA

In this section we consider some of the apparent strengths and weaknesses of SSA, recognizing that these may vary with the situation in which usage is planned. We stress here that these views are inevitably idiosyncratic and based upon our own somewhat partial experiences.

Strengths

The 'usefulness' of a method like SSA can be assessed in a variety of ways. For example, users could regard SSA as useful if it achieved some, or indeed any, of the following:

1 helps add something new to a problem situation, e.g. a novel view of the problem, a new set of solutions;
2 helps legitimize the inclusion of a wider set of perspectives than might normally be addressed, e.g. by involving new stakeholders in the analysis and implementation of change;
3 gets users to the same place as they would with their normal methods of problem-solving, but more quickly;
4 helps carry more people along with the process of change (because of its participative emphasis perhaps);
5 'prevents' users from imposing fixed views of the nature of the problem from the outset – and thereby may help break down existing mindsets;
6 'encourages' users to consider explicitly different ways of looking on the problem situation – and thus can be a force for innovation and creativity;
7 helps users organize a complex process of change (by giving a structure to work through);
8 helps users organize complex data from multiple sources.

Of course, users' views of the strengths of SSA are likely to vary with their own particular experiences; it may well be that some users have achieved many of the above, whilst others may have achieved none. However, in our experience, the major strengths of SSA are fivefold, recognizing that these potential benefits in use can be interconnected.

First, the method is broadly participative, although different studies will vary in the extent and nature of participation. Furthermore, the method stresses the inevitability, and thereby the legitimacy, of the different views and perspectives held by the participants. As such these are not aberrant behaviours to be ignored, worked around or smoothed over. These differences become part of the process. The underlying assumption is one of pluralism, a refreshing antidote to many more managerially oriented approaches which stress more unitary outlooks (see Fox, 1974). Thus, in the earlier case of command and control systems, the participation of people from different backgrounds and with different expertise proved invaluable in generating the relevant systems, root definition and conceptual model.

Second, the method provides structure and organization to the process of investigating complex systems and managing change. Such structure can be helpful to all the actors in the process who can see what they are doing, where they are going and how they are getting there. SSA offers a 'grammar', a set of rules, but without being too restrictive for its users. Multiple iterations are allowed, indeed expected, as are uses of parts (rather than all) of the method. For example, the CADCAM case study ran for a two year period and incorporated the collection and collation of data from different stakeholders using a range of data gathering methods. SSA proved particularly useful in helping structure and organize the project without proving too prescriptive.

Third, a great strength of SSA lies in its explicit requirement that its users spend time looking for different views of the problem situation. It is all too frequent an experience that working groups behave in predictable and destructive patterns. To provide possible alternatives to these well worn paths can provide a sense of liberation. Our experience is that groups of people, with practice, enjoy this activity and can become skilled at it. Groups can, and do, become highly innovative in this situation.

Fourth, SSA seems to us a very powerful analytic tool. The emphasis on tracing the logical implications of adopting a particular view of the problem situation is potentially a very rigorous and useful discipline. Nevertheless, as we described earlier, conceptual modelling of this kind can prove a very difficult activity.

And finally, we have found that the thinking underlying SSA does become internalized with use. This applies especially to stages 3 and 4 which are the conceptual heart of the method. Thus we have found ourselves using the ideas of relevant systems, root definitions, CATWOE and conceptual models in our own professional work, especially when working in complex systems and with a range of people who hold quite different perspectives and views.

In this way, parts of SSA have become personal professional tools, providing a useful addition to our skill set.

Weaknesses

Inevitably SSA also has what one might choose to call weaknesses, and it is worth trying to articulate these. Again, however, these may well be idiosyncratic, reflecting particular experiences. Our own experience of SSA has revealed three potential weaknesses.

First, it is certainly the case that the 'language' and terminology of the method can get in the way. Central constructs such as rich pictures, relevant systems, root definitions and conceptual models are not easy to convey to others, or necessarily easy to use. The method is difficult to learn and there is some considerable craft skill in its use. This can make it very hard to 'sell' the technique to people in organizations who may be experiencing problems and difficulties. They may already be uncomfortable with accepting 'outsiders' to help analyse their problem situation, without the additional problem of learning what can appear to be some arcane jargon that does not have immediate face validity. It is ironic perhaps that these very elements may also be one of the strengths of the approach.

Second, the method can be conservative in the results it helps achieve. Thus, whilst it can be used to develop and enlarge upon quite radical perspectives and ideas, the method does stipulate that change is only made where agreement is reached, in particular that the changes are both systemically desirable and culturally feasible. However, powerful stakeholders can resist and veto change, and this was certainly evident in the first case study described above, where the senior managers responsible for the key functions effectively blocked further attempts at organizational integration.

And third, the method has little to say about the implementation of change. It is mainly focused on reaching some agreement about the nature of change, and offers little to help managers and others in handling more detailed aspects of making those changes happen. Of course, one could equally argue that reaching some agreement represents a major step forward in such circumstances. Furthermore, implementation processes may well vary with each organizational situation and with the nature of the actual changes, such that general advice and support in these areas may be of limited use.

For example, returning to the CADCAM case, it became clear that fundamental changes in organization structure are required before the full potential benefits of the CADCAM system can be realized. SSA as a method can help identify the issues, analyse the particular problems, and point to new ways of working. But the method does not provide for a way of addressing and managing the politics of change. Whilst it may be unrealistic to expect detailed support of this kind from any method, SSA does not offer any suggestions for how to handle situations where groups of people disagree regarding the nature of the problem and the ways forward. Given the pluralistic emphasis of SSA, this seems ironic.

Conclusions

SSA is primarily a method for discussing and planning change in complex systems involving human activity. It is highly pragmatic and organized in a series of iterative stages. The method is broadly participative, provides a structure for managing and coping with complexity and change, encourages the use of imagination and innovation, and requires logical analysis. It is also a useful research tool, especially for those working in an action research mode. Thus, it helps organize complex research projects, especially when incorporating different forms of data from different sources. In addition, it provides a means for analysing and understanding problems in complex systems, as well as for identifying alternatives and options for improvement and change. Particular theoretical ideas and propositions can be introduced to help illuminate such analyses; in that sense, SSA is not theory specific. Overall, it can be a very powerful method and a useful addition to the skill set of people involved in research and development.

Notes

1   The authors acknowledge the work of Sally Maitlis and Roy Payne in this study.

References

Argyris, C. and Schon, D.A. (1978) *Organizational Learning: A Theory of Action.* Reading, MA: Addison-Wesley.

Burrell, G. and Morgan, G. (1979) *Sociological Paradigms and Organisational Analysis.* London: Heinemann Educational.

Checkland, P. (1981) *Systems Thinking, Systems Practice.* Chichester: Wiley.

Checkland, P. and Scholes, J. (1990) *Soft Systems Methodology in Action.* Chichester: Wiley.

Cummings, T.G. (1995) 'Systems theory', in N. Nicholson (ed.), *Encyclopaedic Dictionary of Organizational Behaviour.* Oxford: Blackwell.

Foster, M. (1972) 'An introduction to the theory and practice of action research in work organisations', *Human Relations,* 25: 529–56.

Fox, A. (1974) *Beyond Contract: Work, Power and Trust Relations.* London: Faber & Faber.

Morgan, G. (1986) *Images of Organization.* London: Sage.

Naughton, J. (1984) *Soft Systems Analysis: An Introductory Guide.* Milton Keynes: Open University Press.

Symon, G.J. and Clegg, C.W. (1991a) 'Technology-led change: a study of the implementation of CADCAM', *Journal of Occupational Psychology*, 64: 273–90.

Symon, G.J. and Clegg, C.W. (1991b) 'Implementation of a CADCAM system: the management of change at EML', in K. Legge, C.W. Clegg and N.J. Kemp (eds), *Case Studies in Information Technology, People and Organizations*. Oxford: NCC Blackwell.

Symon, G.J. and Clegg, C.W. (1991c) 'Implementation of a CADCAM system: the management of change at EML', in K. Legge, C.W. Clegg and N.J. Kemp (eds), *Teachers' Guide: Case Studies in Information Technology, People and Organizations*. Oxford: NCC Blackwell.

12 Approaching Observation

Joe Nason and David Golding

Many new students and new researchers are introduced to the idea of using observation in research during an initial research methods and/or methodology course. Such introductions typically pose observation as an alternative method to other approaches, such as interviews or questionnaires, and generally point to three main advantages of observation methods:

1 They are said to be less obtrusive, and therefore researchers are less likely to influence the data being collected – although against this is said to be the disadvantage that the maintaining of that unobtrusiveness may require a sacrifice of the ability to focus questions as would be done in certain kinds of interviews.
2 They can lead to greater depth of data collection from client systems, and are therefore said to be more sensitive to variations and nuances of meaning – the disadvantage being that the researchers may be taken down a path which is not close to the aims of the programme (and which the funding bodies may not have agreed to fund!).
3 They are suitable for longitudinal studies which can examine changes taking place in the host culture or subculture – although against this might be the costs of such time consuming work.

These kinds of introductions to observations, although strongly grounded in traditional conceptions of research processes and understandings, involve a separation between different methods which is sometimes difficult to sustain. Indeed, the curious chronology in which consideration of observation often follows a prior consideration of other methods such as interviews and questionnaires reflects an unfortunate, often unspoken (and occasionally even unintended) hierarchy of legitimacy, which is at odds with the practical execution of any of the methods concerned.

Such an introduction to the idea of using observation in research implies, too, that there exists a discrete series of processes which can be isolated, studied, and learned. Indeed, an underlying assumption seems to be that the processes of observation are independent of other methods, and can therefore be harnessed and put to the service of more general processes of knowledge acquisition.

Problems with traditional conceptions of observation

In this chapter we propose to challenge some of the assumptions underlying such typical approaches to observation, and suggest that a contrary view might be to consider observation as a more pervasive, natural and familiar social process (albeit often unconceptualized and therefore unrecognized as such).

In pursuing this approach, we shall suggest that the notion of observation, rather than being seen as a discrete series of processes (reflecting a common tendency to treat the notion of method as though it were unproblematic), might alternatively be regarded as comprising processes which pervade a whole series of situations in human action. Thus rather than observation being seen as a separate category amongst a list of alternative research approaches, it might be conceived as consisting of processes which form part of other 'methods' too – from those as disparate as experimentation, and modelling, to the administering of postal questionnaires.

Given this potential for overlap in research processes, in this chapter we shall attempt to reconfigure the problems of what constitutes observation in research, through an exploration of alternative conceptions of the processes involved. Thereby, we aim to set out some alternative entry points and means of procedure, which will form a contrast to some of the more general approaches to observation found in typical methods/methodology courses.

Of course those more general introductions to research are often governed by the needs of course designers to provide quickly accessible overviews of a number of approaches to data collection, in severely limited timescales. This situation has been fuelled by the emphasis placed upon overviews in initial research training by the requirements of research councils. Indeed it takes a particularly creative and enterprising course design team to avoid being drawn into the provision of a Cook's tour in some form or other, no matter how determined they are to avoid that.

It is not surprising, therefore, to find so many situations where observation is introduced as one item in a list of alternatives, generally with two or three other approaches preceding it. But what do such approaches tell us about some of the more prevalent assumptions concerning observation in research? For one thing, perhaps it should strike us as a curious situation that observation should need an introduction! For a species in which the use of observation of the world begins very early in life (perhaps as soon as we open our eyes – or maybe even before that!), isn't it a bit late to provide an introduction? For the whole approach of an infant to learning is based upon developing awareness through observation, and is severely handicapped in those situations where observation is prevented or limited owing to lack of development or malfunction.

One response to such a proposition is to suggest that whilst those attending introductory research methods/methodology courses may be familiar with observation in an everyday sense, the processes of observation in research are of a different order, requiring more advanced techniques or skills. Thus students are sometimes drawn into devaluing the very processes they have been using for survival, for at least as long as they can remember. Such extra-dimensional conceptions of what are everyday familiar processes involved in observation are often explicated in the social science literature too (see for example the discussion of theoretical metalanguages and the idea of second order conceptions in Giddens, 1976).

In this chapter we want to question the extent to which such special status of observation research processes is justified, and whether the real difficulty might not rather be in the very elevation of research versions of such processes to a level of proposed superiority. This is not to deny the immense complexities involved in research processes, nor indeed to deny that learning about observation may be a lifelong process in itself, but rather to question whether the differentiation of these complexities might be more realistically approached through stronger epistemological programmes (involving questions of what is to count as knowledge) and more rigorous examinations of ontological roots (involving questions of how we define who and what we are, and therefore how we define our relationships with what we come to call data).

It seems to us that these questions are fundamental to the problems faced by any researcher, given the daunting task of establishing legitimacy in research outputs, bearing in mind the nature of research evaluation processes. We shall return in particular to O'Neill's (1972) oft-neglected call for a less egotistical, but more grounded, conception of research processes in this context.

The centrality of participation in observational processes

The issue of participation has been an important focus for many theorists. Hammersley and Atkinson, for example, have suggested that not only observational processes but all social research can be seen to have participation at its heart: '. . . all social research takes the form of participant observation; it involves participating in the social world, in whatever role, and reflecting on the products of that participation . . .'(1983: 16).

In this context, one of the more widely used frameworks for assessing degrees of participation was developed by Gold (1958) who suggested that observational approaches could be distinguished according to the degree of participation in the context or setting concerned. From this notion he developed a framework, based upon a particular identification of the roles of the people involved. Thus Gold distinguished between:

1   the complete participant – in which the 'true' identity and purpose of the observer are not known to those being observed;
2   the participant as observer – in which the observer and the subjects are

aware that their relationship is overtly one of observer as against observed;

3 the observer as participant – which might represent a situation used in one-off formal observations.

4 the complete observer – in which no social interaction takes place.

The attempt to analytically separate categories with a view to identifying different levels of participation is an attractive one. In practice, however, research interactions frequently turn out to have aspects which cut across those categories. As an example of this, the fourth category may be thought to reflect an apparently straightforward and desirable state of non-involvement for a researcher, in which data can be collected with minimum engagement with the client system. Indeed this kind of categorization has been of great influence upon the ways in which the processes of observation have been conceived. The idea of a completely unobtrusive observer, with no interaction, and therefore no participation taking place, has obvious attractions (in terms of the 'purity' of data for example).

A typical illustration of this kind of formulation would be in the kind of educational research in which children at work and play have been observed without their knowledge (see for example King, 1978). Ways of hiding researchers have been inventive, from Wendy houses (in King, 1978) to two-way mirrors.

There are obvious ethical problems with the idea of secretly observing others without their knowledge, but this kind of approach has been widely used in educational research (both in data collection and in the training of teachers), as is evidenced by the fact that in one of our own universities, until very recently, there were two classrooms with two-way mirror facilities (inherited from previous teacher training college days). So far as we know (which it might be argued could never be far enough!) these facilities have not been used for concealed observational studies of adults, and indeed have fairly recently been demolished in order to use the space occupied by the observers' chambers to extend the actual teaching spaces. In fact, this kind of concealed observational approach has been used less widely in other fields beyond the observation of children, presumably reflecting an assumption that it is permissible to observe children without their knowledge, but not adults, which raises its own ethical questions.

To return to the question of the degree of participation with respect to the above examples of observing children at work and play, the question of who had knowledge about the existence of concealed observers would seem to be an important one. If the teacher involved in the research settings concerned was aware of the presence of observers, then the possibility of influence (intentional or not) upon the action cannot be ruled out. Equally, in that situation, the observers could hardly claim that their presence was non-participative – with respect to the school social system. In situations where the teacher engaged in the setting had no knowledge of the presence of the observer, then the question of who in the school did have knowledge of their presence is relevant (in these days of increased security, they could hardly have walked in off the street). This is important, in that whoever in the school did know of their presence (e.g. head of department or head of school) may have influenced the teacher (intentionally or not).

Furthermore, when the practical difficulties of setting up research conceal-ments are considered, a certain amount of interaction is likely to have taken place beforehand. It is, in short, difficult to imagine a situation in which no participation whatsoever takes place. Recalling Hammersley and Atkinson's argument that all research involves participating in the social world (in some way), then the metaphor of a fly on the wall may be no more than that – i.e. a metaphor (and therefore not realizable).

For these reasons, researchers who have initially set out to see themselves entering into a research situation as complete observers (as in category 4 of Gold's typology) have often found themselves participating beyond their wildest imaginings (or fears!) One of the most potent examples of this kind of change in position can be found in what have become known as the 'Hawthorne studies' (see Roethlisberger and Dickson, 1939). Observers here began by observing a number of different industrial situations at the Hawthorne works of Western Electric, and not only became involved as participants, but had such an interventionist effect upon the outcomes that the effects of the researchers upon the situation (e.g. the 'halo effect', referring to the impact on the subject of the knowledge that they were being observed) have become more significant, and more commented upon, than their originally intended work.

Moreover, the ethical problems discussed above also arise in studies in which researchers become stronger participants. In the Hawthorne studies, for example, problems of the rights of those being studied were presumably relegated to second level of importance in the interests of knowledge acquisition. Given the fame/notoriety that was to follow (no matter how much confidentiality was assured?) that seems questionable.

To deal with these kinds of complexities, ethical issues are sometimes differentiated according to whether those being observed are being 'used' with or without their knowledge. Unfortunately this complicates the issue of participation even further, since the categories are seldom clear enough to make those kinds of lasting decisions. Situations change over time, and to argue that in the two-way mirror example those being observed were not told that they were being observed, whereas in the Hawthorne studies the workers knew that they were being observed because everything was done visibly, is unsustainable, if only because in the latter the workers did not know for what purpose they were being observed, and could not, because the reasons had changed!

The same sorts of problems occur in categories 1 and 2 of Gold's model, where for example the complications of participants emerging from natural settings to become observers make it quite normal in those situations for respondents not to be told that they were being observed. On the other hand there have been studies, too, in which those being observed have deliberately been told lies about what was being observed (see Milgram, 1963 for an especially notorious example). The ethical problems with such approaches are immense, and coupled with the issue of participation, cannot be resolved outside of the continually changing questions of who is observing whom, and for what purposes.

Observation as an emergent social process

Our own experiences of research observation in fact began in settings in which we emerged as observers. In both our cases, we were involved in situations in which it began to occur to us that we were both deemed to be participants of something, and also trying to distance ourselves from that in order to contextualize what we were observing. It began to occur to us, in other words, that what we were participating in might be rather different from what we had initially envisaged. (As it turned out, we produced research theses which had not been planned when we first became participants, but equally this kind of situation may be encountered by full-time researchers finding themselves engaged in developments of which funding bodies have not yet been made aware.)

The framework of Gold (and of others taking that kind of apparently 'systematic approach') frequently left us wondering where to place ourselves on that framework, since the situations we were in were changing, in the sense of both sometimes developing new understandings and sometimes reverting to previous understandings.

We began to think that perhaps we were incompetent, and it was only the realization of the primacy of emergent analysis in every situation that rescued us from giving up because we could not 'make things fit'. The categories seemed to be continually breaking down, as we tried to make the multiple roles and meanings and changing definitions of situations conform to predetermined frameworks.

We began to explore the notion of covertness and degrees of disclosure and discussion of what we were doing. But not only did we find that, as might be expected, this would vary depending upon the position and role of 'the other', but we also found that this varied with the same 'other' according to degrees of belief, forgetfulness, interest etc.

Accepting that our difficulties were grounded in our situated experiences, we began to question whether the distinct categories expounded in textbooks had been derived from entirely different settings and cultures which we ought to be able to adapt, or whether they were quite simply over-generalized. The boundaries we were being encouraged to adopt in our tentative analyses seemed to be continually shifting, especially those relating to the extent to which we felt able to disclose our changing purposes. The fixing of such boundaries seemed to be in tension with changing perspectives upon whatever we decided were appropriate data, and upon the desire or need to protect the identities and confidentialities of ourselves and others.

An example from the field notes (of Nason) will serve to illustrate the tension inherent in those processes:

> Joe at this point I would like to say that I'm giving you all this information of my own free will and I trust that it is anonymous in terms of not being actually replayed by the tape to anyone else and that my name will not appear on any documentation where the transcript is used as I said earlier there is a fear of speaking out and going beyond a certain limit and I think some of the statements made today have gone beyond that limit and would certainly be used against me.

This respondent had provided some very valuable data, over a period of time, and as the relationship (between Nason and respondent) developed, levels of mutual disclosure increased to a point whereby the research theme had become overt and responses much less guarded. The boundaries had shifted within a defined context of the mutual trust that had developed, such that what often starts off as covert research ends up as a complex, interactive, interwoven process that necessitates such shifting boundaries in order for the work to continue. Such levels of shift depend upon the judgement of the ethnographer in relation to the risk being taken by disclosure. Indeed this kind of changing situation reflects the reality that it is often not in the interests of senior powerholders within social systems to have their actions publicly discussed.

It is also sometimes not in the interests of researchers to disclose to others more senior in their own organization the real nature of their research. This applies equally to full-time researchers in university departments as to students on masters' programmes who are practising managers in a variety of organizations, and who decide to explore contentious organizational issues for their dissertations.

It is also acknowledged here that covert research is sometimes employed to maintain naturalism or ecological validity in certain circumstances, just as it is possible to see in the above example that the boundaries between observation and interviewing were being stretched in that situation. The language of the respondent certainly conveys an impression that would not be out of place in an interview transcription, and the existence of a tape recorder, too, suggests that. However, an attempt to cast the scenario as an interview which took place within an overall observational study, although not contradicting the view of the observer at the time, would do little to resolve the boundary question, but would merely displace it.

Observation as ethnography

Our difficulties in research have led us to see the importance of individual researcher experiences, and through our own experiences and struggles we now present an introduction to observation which comprises an analysis of what observation is for us. Through that analysis, we aim to develop an alternative, more dynamic framework for conceptualizing (and continually reassessing) the process involved.

We propose to do this, then, through an interrogation of our introductions to research and subsequent attempts to re-examine how we conceived what we were doing at the time, and why we located our efforts in particular analytical frameworks. In both our cases, we began by carrying out what we came to see as covert research (although the degrees of covertness were always changing) and we shall therefore approach the task of exploring the nature of observational approaches through the difficulties and resistances we encountered, both in the field (for instance ethical dilemmas) and in the seminar room (for example paradigm prejudices) as we tried to make sense of our activities. We have chosen to cast this in an ethnographic framework since this reflects the kinds of observational experiences we were engaged in.

Ethnography, which has its roots in anthropology, is largely an act of sense making by the researcher as they focus upon the manner in which people interact and collaborate through the observable phenomena of daily life. Organizational ethnography, as the name suggests, concerns itself with attempting to uncover and explicate the ways in which people in particular work settings come to understand, account for and take action within their day to day work situation (van Maanen, 1979: 540). As Rosen further explains:

> The goal of ethnography in general is to decode, translate, and interpret the behaviours and attached meaning systems of those occupying and creating the social system being studied. Ethnography therefore is largely an act of sensemaking, the translation from one context to another of action in relation to meaning and meaning in relation to action. Ethnographic description, however, is not to be confused with recounting that would be provided by the actors in the social setting. It is, instead, a construction cast in the theory and language of the describer and his or her audience (1991: 12).

Central to good ethnographic accounts is a recognition of the reflexivity of the researcher (Watson, 1993: 3–4). The researcher in such settings cannot be a 'fly on the wall' (Hammersley and Atkinson, 1983: 18) as they themselves become part of the research process itself. As such, we would argue that an ethnographer must be reflexive, i.e. they must attempt to understand how their own 'philosophical bias' underpins the 'theory laden' nature of how they make sense of what they observe (Gill and Johnson, 1991). That is to say they must attempt to understand how their prior values and knowledge influence what they see whilst observing. An exploration of the researcher's ontological and epistemological beliefs can often provide a good framework to develop and make explicit such reflexivity.

Difficulties of entry and conception

What follows is a reconstruction of exchanges which took place between the two authors of this chapter. The exchanges focus upon a particular experience of observation in research carried out by one of the authors (Joe, whose research was operationalized as an emergent process whilst he worked as a practising manager for a large bureaucratic organization operating within the private sector). The aim has been to reflect the contributions of each author, and to give the reader access to some of the nuances of perspective (e.g. particular emphases) in the make-up of the chapter. The reconstruction has been presented in the form of a conversation, so as to aid the identification of each author's contribution. There has been no attempt to capture particular conversations word for word (and pause for pause etc.) as might be done in some forms of conversation analysis. Rather, the aim has been to reflect the way in which the chapter has come about, as distinct from providing a verbatim account of meetings and/or conversations etc. which occurred. The aim throughout has been to make the process of writing about the experience of the two authors a little more accessible in the context of their different (albeit historically similar) approaches to observation in research.

> *David*: What was the first difficulty you encountered in embarking upon observational research?
>
> *Joe*: On reflection that is not an easy question to answer. The reason why is worthy of exploration within the context of this work. Initially, after I cast my mind back several years, and thought for a while, I found myself about to rattle off 'an answer', to share with you an experience from my 'life history' (Denzin, 1970). As I mentally recalled and reconstructed this experience, which amounted to analysis from my individual biography (Bertaux, 1981), I found myself immediately beset by a problem facing all researchers as they recall and use data. The gravity of this problem makes answering such a question very difficult, if not, impossible.
>
> *David*: It's interesting that you felt the need to stop yourself from 'rattling off an answer' to the question of what was the first difficulty you encountered. I found myself pretty soon regretting that I'd asked the question – damned silly question etc. – almost as though I'd asked the question without thinking about it, which is probably near to what happened! This poses the possibility that we may quite often raise questions without thinking particularly about the impact or relevance of such questions. Perhaps we do that especially at the beginning of encounters and conversations, as though the need to get things under way is paramount. But in doing this we run the risk of suggesting that the matter of where we begin might be of less importance than that we do at least begin somewhere.
>
> Perhaps, too, the example is more than incidentally related to the ways in which we make sense of our observations in research settings, the need to begin to say something meaningful becoming more important than what we actually say. Now that could have a potentially devastating effect upon anyone's efforts.
>
> *Joe*: Yes, a problem which my experience suggests is either unrecognized or unacknowledged in the majority of research accounts, for perhaps the 'real' problem is that of the selective memory of the researcher.
>
> Like Hammersley and Atkinson (1983) I would argue that all social research takes the form of observation. Whatever the individual 'philosophical bias'

(Gill and Johnson, 1991) of the researcher (based upon their implicit epistemo-logical and ontological beliefs) and whatever role they find themselves in, their task entails participating in the social world they are researching, prior to reflecting upon how they make sense of the experience of that participation. Once we attempt to record, make sense of and interpret our experiences we become reliant upon memory. Thus our memory is the creator of meaning. It is the catalyst for creating an account or, within the specific context being addressed here, 'an answer' to the question concerning the first difficulty I encountered. Everything I experience is immediately embedded in the personal biography that constitutes my 'life history'. As it is in the past, I am reliant upon memory to recall the event.

David: And this raises a question, in effect, of whether you would be able to remember what the first difficulty was, and whether or not it would matter if you couldn't, because in any case, the account you would give of that first difficulty (whether or not attaching the status of 'first' to it) would be different to what you would have said if asked at that time, or one year later, or at any other time than the one we are concerned with now (which has by now in any case changed . . . again . . . and again . . .).

Joe: Indeed, although I'm also left with a feeling that my recollections, when described to others, appear to lose some of their original richness and meaning, owing in part to the experience itself being embedded and contained within myself and structured through my memory and perceptual set (Laing, 1967). The dilution of this 'original richness' is further exacerbated by the limitations of language as a medium to express to others how we feel or felt during our lived experiences

As we recall these lived experiences we cannot escape from memory or language; thus our recollections of events, which we label data, are really forms of our own fiction. They are stories rich in rhetoric, structured by our memory as we attempt to produce an account open to interpretation by others that serves the interests and agendas at hand (Morgan, 1993).

David: And so the impact of memory, as you have suggested, is fundamental to the process of relating our experiences in any situation. Indeed Raffel (1979) suggests that this is so for all research, whether concerned with social or physical worlds (!), in that the attempt to relate something about an event or a phenomenon cannot avoid relying upon the researcher's selection of what relative perspective and importance to attach to create a readable 'story' in the form of a meaningful account of 'what happened'. Thus in the social world, even if we videotape an event, in addition to those dimensions which cannot be captured (smell comes to mind?) we also rely upon our memory from our privileged position of observer through which we make selections of which bits to use!

Thus memory is central to the process of producing a privileged account of any research setting (privileged that is by virtue of the researcher's presence and the reader's absence at the event about which something is being conveyed: see Silverman, 1975).

Joe: That's right. I think what we have achieved so far is to begin to expose a difficulty facing all social researchers. A difficulty especially prevalent to those engaged in organizational research through an ethnographic approach. The problem is one of their own selective memory in making sense of, interpreting and deciding what data to incorporate into their account. It also highlights the complexity, if not impossibility, of attempting to answer your original question without operating at high levels of superficiality, as we are constrained by the number of words available for published articles or thesis production. I suppose it also highlights that most of our engagement with others is not as sophisticated as some of us would like to think it is.

David: And in a sense, what we are doing now in this reconstruction is to undertake a 'repair' (as though our account was damaged?) – the essence being that we have not allowed the status of each exchange that we had whilst preparing this chapter to direct the overall integrity of what we are trying to convey. The superordinate goal, if you like, is to construct a meaningful account of our reflections upon our experiences of observation in organizations. Such reflections are always subject to refinement and never complete, but neither do they warrant being placed in tablets of stone, simply because one idea preceded another (at the time).

Joe: Of course within the context of management research this recognition is central to ethnographic approaches to organizational analysis. Talking of which, in such research perhaps there would be more value *in incorporating data that we cannot make sense of.*

By incorporating data that we cannot make sense of through a post-rationalization of the 'theory laden' nature of our observation (Gill and Johnson, 1991) we would identify weaknesses in the social theory, guiding our sense making activities. This would indeed be an area worthy of intellectual pursuit, offering vast potential to contribute to the sociology of knowledge.

Anyway, moving forward, or back because I'm not sure which I'm doing any longer (which I take to be quite a healthy situation), let me return to the original question concerning the first difficulty I encountered as a researcher. In providing an 'answer', whilst acknowledging the difficulty of a selective memory, I no longer know whether the question has value or not. Perhaps that is for others to decide. For me, the question has already served its purpose: it has provided the focus for more questions, and to me that is the purpose of a question.

David: Now that's really interesting – the suggestion that the purpose of a question is to give rise to other questions. In saying that, I think you not only put your finger on a fundamental point about research, but more than that, implicitly fire a cannon across the bows of the very basis of most Western approaches to education. And if an explication of the nature and processes of observation in research results in such a sideswipe, then perhaps we have our own response (answer?) as to why observation is not more central in research methods/methodology courses. The implications are immense. Moreover, questions about research courses are merely the beginning – of a reformulation requiring an examination of societal structures and processes that would take us way beyond the boundaries of this chapter. Suffice to say, for the time being, that stopping themselves from answering questions might be a good starting point for any would-be participant observer. Followed by a moratorium upon asking questions at all (as a means of limiting the imposition of pre-existing perspectives). Leaving us to . . . what? Listen, perhaps? Thereby, as Whyte (1955) puts it, getting answers to questions that we didn't even know we wanted to ask?

Joe: Forcibly stopping myself from taking that one further, but being unable to escape convention, however much I would like to, I am now going to 'answer' that first question! Why am I doing this? I don't know, but here goes.

Perhaps the first difficulty I encountered was one of perceived paradigm prejudices during the initial stages of the preparation for my MBA dissertation. This dissertation concerned itself with the concept of alienation within the context of the managerial role. Alienation had fast become of interest to me during my studies as I began to recognize the alienating forces that were impacting on me at that time owing to my role as a practising manager within industry. My initial reading on methods and methodology (the latter being a consideration of the implicit assumptions underpinning my favoured methods) led me to believe the most suitable approach for what I wanted to explore would be an ethnographic type of study, with my primary research role being that of participant-as-observer (Junker, 1960). For political expediency and self-protection I had decided to keep the focus of my research to myself whilst at work and therefore employed a considerable amount of covert research. Such an approach is not uncommon for those in that position (Golding, 1979; Dalton, 1959).

As part of the MBA academic process a dissertation proposal had to be produced which had to be approved by a board of studies prior to being allowed to proceed. The proposal was intended to focus the student's thoughts and contained the usual type of headings, i.e. aims, objectives, relationship to previous work, methodology etc. etc.

At the time, I discussed the approach I wished to take with my research methodology lecturer who was very supportive of my chosen 'mode of engagement' (Morgan, 1983). However, at the same time he warned me that he did not think the panel responsible for validating my proposal, such that I may proceed, would be very supportive of either the subject topic or my methodology. I was quietly advised that the panel had a history of rejecting inductive, ethnographic based proposals. This took me, at the time, by surprise. Here was this vast body of knowledge that the validating board had a tendency to ignore if they did not like it. This was a reflection of power and paradigm prejudice. Or at least that is how I made sense of it.

Forewarned and forearmed, I decided to employ my own political strategy. I wrote my proposal carefully, selecting my words to avoid a conflictive situation. I attempted to manage meaning, and it worked. My proposal was accepted and I was allowed to proceed. I find that in itself quite funny when I reflect back upon what I wrote in the methodology section of the proposal. I advised the committee that through ethnographic study I would test my hypothesis, which is a complete epistemological contradiction. Ethnography may be concerned with creating a hypothesis, but it is difficult to see ethnography as being concerned with testing one. Whether the panel read or understood my proposal I do not really know. What I do know is that if someone presented me with such a proposal I would take the opportunity to discuss it further with them. I believe that the panel saw that I was going to 'test a hypothesis' and as such believed I was engaged in traditional deductive research. Once approved, I renegotiated my methodology with my supervisor who, as previously suggested, was more sympathetic to the approach I wished to adopt. As he reminded me, a proposal is a licence to proceed; what is actually delivered, emerges and changes along the way

Legitimacy and validity in observational approaches

David: In proceeding, however, if we accept that observation is a natural human process, and that observation in research is not of a different order but merely of a different intensity, or at least comprising a more specifically and consciously focused manner, then the question of extent of participation is crucial. Clearly our own previous situations have concentrated upon occasions where we emerged in locations in which we were already participating heavily, by nature of what we were paid to do (albeit not to carry out covert research!) Equally, however, a researcher may enter an organization as a stranger (whether a complete or a relative stranger) and we ought to consider now the kinds of different problems encountered in such situations.

As we have previously noted, there have been a number of attempts to distinguish degrees of participation in a situation involving observation for research purposes, Gold (1958) being a particular example. The situation in which a participant gradually becomes an observer for the purposes of collecting information/data for use in a specific research context, but does not immediately disclose that activity or purpose, is likely to result in a continuing series of dilemmas involving decisions on whether to disclose or not, and if so, how much, and when.

In a situation of a researcher (e.g. those who develop careers in 'contract research') newly entering an organization, the problem is not so much one of how to distance themselves, but one of how to enter as a stranger, and indeed the extent to which participation may be unavailable or inadvisable, as against recommended or unavoidable.

Joe: Recognizing the importance of what you're saying here, but also wishing to ground this in personal experience and how I make sense of the research process, perhaps we ought to return to some of the practical limitations we've highlighted with respect to Gold's taxonomy of field roles.

If you reflect on your own entry into research, which was based upon your employment at that time, as was my own, you tended to label it covert. Perhaps however it was really covert and overt at the same time, depending upon who you were talking to. Certainly within my own organization some people knew what I was researching, as I'm sure they did in yours. They also recognized their own position of operating within a political framework at times. My covertness was perceived by some as an indication that I could be trusted to 'hear it as it was'. Therefore to such people (who I knew well and trusted) my work was overt. In fact my covertness was almost a security blanket for some of the respondents who provided data through my overt fieldwork. If I had revealed what they had said to me, they would have revealed what I was really up to. Such an exposure would not have stopped my work, but it would have made it more difficult.

The point I'm making here is that if we consider Gold's taxonomy, perhaps the reality is that there is the high possibility that elements of both overt and covert research exist no matter where a researcher is at any one moment.

If we place this within the context of a relative stranger entering an organization, then some possibility of covertness and overtness still exists. If they are invited in, they will be working to some form of client brief and may not be able to disclose to all what they are doing. This in itself is interesting, as such a belief will influence what observations the researcher decides are of relevance and what are not.

To attempt to explain what I mean here, I will recall an event that happened to me recently. Over a bank holiday I drove with a friend to Yorkshire. During the journey she passed the comment that in recent weeks she had never seen so many cows in the fields beside the roads. She then said she felt this was due to the CJD scare and felt farmers were putting cows out to graze rather than feeding them cereals etc. Perhaps this was so; perhaps there was another reason. What is important here is that she would accept no other explanation. Within the context of this work what is important is that the impact of what she had recently heard about CJD was the framework implicitly used to make sense of the number of cows she had been observing. In a similar way, the researcher's brief provides a framework from which they will make sense of what they observe.

David: Then following this through, perhaps a framework drawn from social interaction theories would be of more value to a researcher than an understanding of Gold's framework. McCall and Simmons (1966), for example, have provided a useful framework for conceptualizing some of the complexities involved in even the simplest of two-person interactions. Noting the essentially dynamic nature of exchanges, they have suggested that attention should be paid to both presenting positions and imputed positions (i.e. the transmission of assumed responses to any presenting positions).

In research situations the degree of covertness or otherwise is clearly an aspect of how much is revealed, by whom and to whom, which will inevitably involve presenting positions towards different individuals, depending upon aims, perceived trusts etc. by both parties (i.e. this applies to both 'researchers' and 'respondents').

In McCall and Simmons's view, any presentation of self includes a whole series of 'clues' as to the assumed (and therefore expected) responses which have led to (and perhaps enabled) any particular aspect of presentation of self. That kind of process is of course two-way, any sending of expected responses/meanings etc. by the 'researcher' being matched by other (and different) sendings by the 'respondent'. McCall and Simmons refer to such processes as altercasting, which they suggest we are all engaged in each time we interact and which may be useful interpretive devices for examining aspects of exchanges in researcher/respondent relations.

Building upon this kind of dynamic framework, Denzin (1989) for instance has pointed to the importance of particular biographies and historical foundations in interactions. The part played by attempts to establish particular agendas is paramount in this, and Denzin has suggested that the idea of epiphanies (defining moments in anyone's development) are central to the way in which we present ourselves (and therefore altercast too).

Perhaps the most significant element in this, for any researcher, is the importance of questions about 'who we are' – or at least how we respond to questions about who we are (as researchers). This suggests that explorative interactive sessions (e.g. through the examination of alternative epistemological frameworks) might be seen as an important part of a researcher's training in research methodology – at least as valuable as typical Cook's tour approaches.

Concluding note

In this chapter, we have argued for the treatment of observation as a more familiar kind of process. We believe that this can only aid the development of more observational studies in research. However, that familiarity needs to be tempered by the provision of a practical means (e.g. through seminar and workshop foci) of engaging in reflexive practice through reflection upon the nature of observational processes, both in the context of specific studies and in a more general applicational sense as researchers gain in experience of field research.

Furthermore, observational approaches need to provide for the periodic examination, and indeed interrogation, of the assumptions being made. The development of abilities required and gained through such examinations (not least in ontological and epistemological groundings) ought to form an important part of initial research training, and ought too (e.g. through workshop and conference agendas) to provide means for continuing such processes in the execution of future research investigations.

References

Bertaux, D. (1981) *Biography and Society: The Life History Approach in the Social Sciences.* London: Sage.

Dalton, M. (1959) *Men Who Manage.* New York: Wiley.

Denzin, N. (1970) *Sociological Methods: A Sourcebook.* London: Butterworth.

Denzin, N. (1989) *Interpretive Interactionism.* London: Sage.

Giddens, A. (1976) *New Rules of Sociological Method.* London: Hutchinson.

Gill, J. and Johnson, P. (1991) *Research Methods for Managers.* London: Paul Chapman.

Gold, R. L. (1958) 'Roles in sociological field observations', *Social Forces*, 36: 217–23.

Golding, D. (1979) 'Symbolism, sovereignty and domination in an industrial hierarchical organisation', *The Sociological Review*, 27 (1): 169–77.

Hammersley, M. and Atkinson, P. (1983) *Ethnography Principles in Practice.* London: Tavistock.

Junker, B. H. (1960) *Fieldwork.* Chicago: University of Chicago Press.

King, R. (1978) *All Things Bright and Beautiful? A Sociological Study of Infants' Classrooms.* London: Wiley.

Laing, R.D. (1967) *Politics of Experience and the Bird of Paradise.* Harmondsworth: Penguin.

McCall, G.J. and Simmons, J.L. (1966) *Identities and Interactions.* London: Collier Macmillan.

Milgram, S. (1963) 'Behavioural study of obedience', *Journal of Abnormal Social Psychology*, 67: 371–8.

Morgan, G. (1983) *Beyond Method.* London: Sage.

Morgan, G. (1993) *Imaginization.* London: Sage.

O'Neill, J. (1972) *Sociology as a Skin Trade.* London: Heinemann.

Raffel, S. (1979) *Matters of Fact*. London: Routledge and Kegan Paul.

Roethlisberger, F. J. and Dickson, W.J. (1939) *Management and the Worker*. Cambridge, MA: Harvard University Press.

Rosen, M. (1991) 'Coming to terms with the field: understanding and doing organisational ethnography', *Journal of Management Studies*, 28 (1): 1–24.

Silverman, D. (1975) *Reading Castaneda*. London: Routledge and Kegan Paul.

Van Maanen, J. (1979) 'The fact of fiction in organisational ethnography', *Administrative Science Quarterly*, 24: 539–50.

Watson, T. (1993) *In Search of Management*. London: Routledge.

Whyte, W. F. (1955) *Street Corner Society*. Chicago: University of Chicago Press.

Index